I0883452

Sam Dellinger

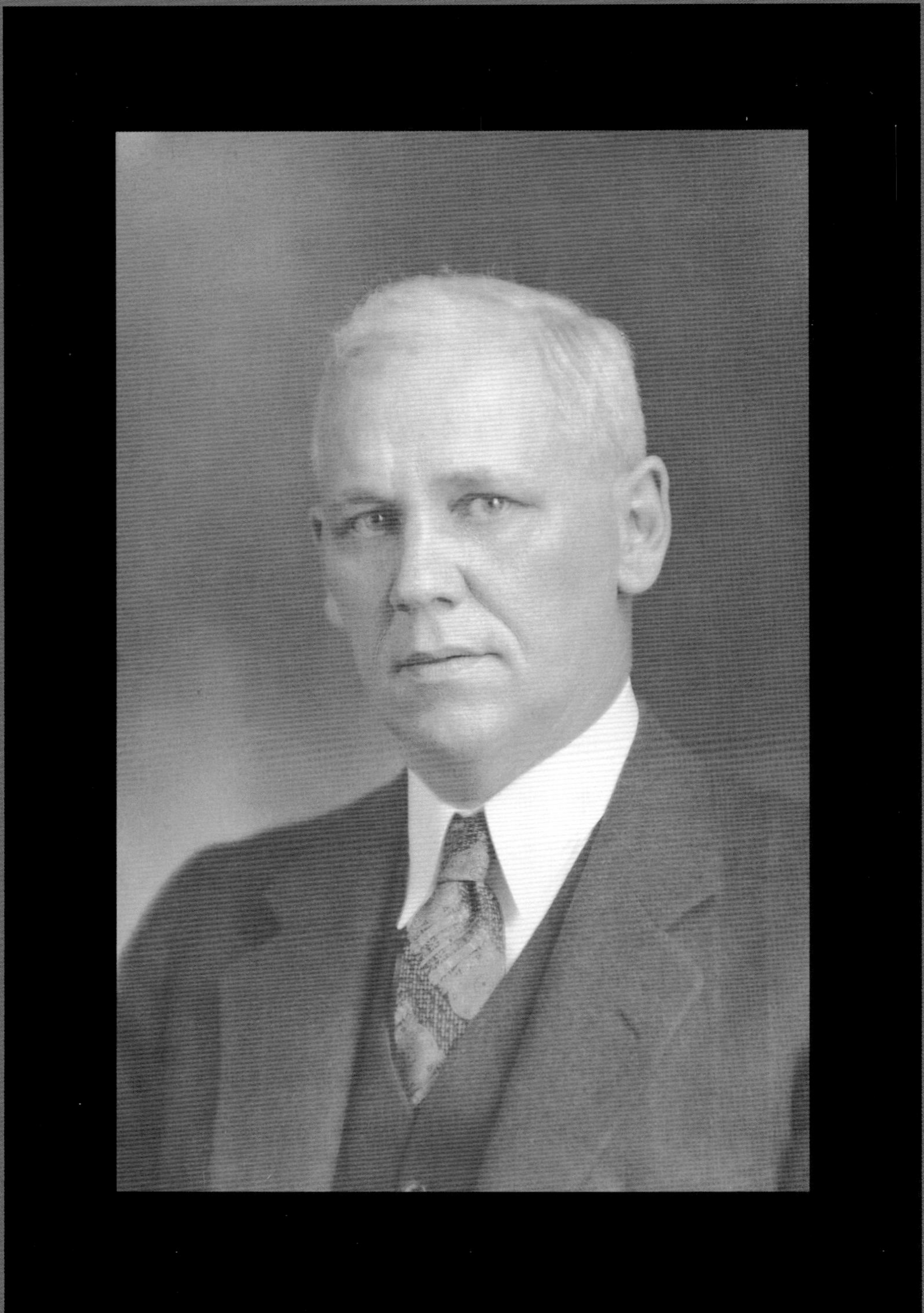

Sam Dellinger

Raiders of the Lost Arkansas

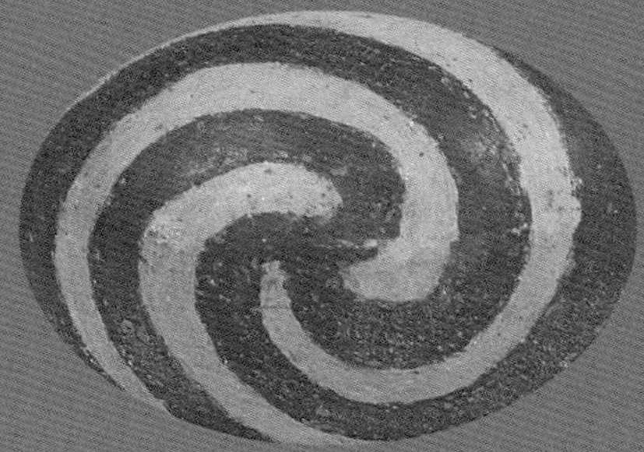

ROBERT C. MAINFORT JR.

THE UNIVERSITY OF ARKANSAS PRESS

FAYETTEVILLE

2008

Copyright © 2008 by The University of Arkansas Press

All rights reserved
Manufactured in the United States of America

ISBN-13: 978-1-55728-886-8

12 11 10 09 08 5 4 3 2 1

Text design by Ellen Beeler

⊗ The paper used in this publication meets the minimum requirements of the American National Standard for Permanence of Paper for Printed Library Materials Z39.48-1984.

Library of Congress Cataloging-in-Publication Data

Mainfort, Robert C., 1948–

Sam Dellinger : raiders of the lost Arkansas / Robert C. Mainfort Jr.

p. cm.

Includes bibliographical references and index.

ISBN 978-1-55728-886-8 (cloth : alk. paper)

1. Dellinger, Samuel C. (Samuel Claudius), b. 1892. 2. Indianists—Arkansas—Biography. 3. Archaeologists—Arkansas—Biography. 4. Indians of North America—Arkansas—Antiquities. 5. Arkansas—Antiquities. I. Title.

E76.45.D45A3 2008

976.7'01092—dc22

[B]

2008026297

Publication of this book was supported by the Old State House Museum in Little Rock, Arkansas, whose exhibit on Sam Dellinger's life and work was curated by the author.

For Mary Suter—friend, colleague, and unsung hero

CONTENTS

FIGURES

This catalog is published in conjunction with the exhibition "Sam Dellinger: Raiders of the Lost Arkansas," at the Old State House Museum, Little Rock, Arkansas. The exhibit was funded in part by grants from the Arkansas Humanities Council and the Arkansas Natural and Cultural Resources Council.

LENDERS TO THE EXHIBITION

American Museum of Natural History
Dr. Kent Westbrook
Museum of Anthropology, University of Michigan
National Museum of the American Indian, Smithsonian Institution
Peabody Museum of Archaeology and Ethnology, Harvard University
The Field Museum
University of Alabama Museums
University of Arkansas Museum Collections Facility

PREFACE

In September 1994 I came to Fayetteville, Arkansas, to interview for a position with the Arkansas Archeological Survey. A highlight of those two hectic days was a visit to the University of Arkansas Museum's collections in Vol Walker Hall. I already had a research interest in the late prehistoric societies of northeast Arkansas, and I was aware that the museum had conducted excavations there in the 1930s, but I was quite unprepared for the sheer quantity and quality of the collections themselves. My schedule allowed only a short stay amidst the collections, but as we were leaving, I asked Tom Green, director of the Survey, if (should I be hired) I would have an opportunity to explore the research potential of the collections. When he answered strongly in the affirmative, I knew that if the Survey offered me a position, I would accept. Evidently my enthusiasm about the collections made a favorable impression because a few days later I was offered the job.

Since my arrival in Fayetteville, the collections and field records generated during Sam Dellinger's tenure as curator of the University of Arkansas Museum (1925–1960) have been central to my research and that of most of my graduate students. The substantive results are noted in a subsequent chapter, but there remains much to be done. As we will see, Dellinger's archaeological efforts were by no means limited to northeast Arkansas, but also included the Arkansas River valley, the Ozark Mountains, and southern Arkansas, all of which are represented here and in the exhibit.

"Sam Dellinger: Raiders of the Lost Arkansas" was conceived by Bill Gatewood (director, Old State House Museum), who became familiar with the museum's collections while earning a bachelor's degree in anthropology at the University of Arkansas. When Bill asked me to serve as guest curator for an exhibit on the legacy of Sam Dellinger, I accepted immediately. I already knew a fair amount about Dellinger, and I welcomed the opportunity to conduct biographical research on him, as well as the history of the University of Arkansas Museum.

Incorporating "Raiders" into an exhibition on archaeology in *Ark*ansas simply could not be resisted, and in fact speaks to Sam Dellinger's efforts to save Arkansas antiquities for Arkansans. As detailed in a subsequent chapter, the material culture of the late-prehistoric societies that lived in Arkansas—ancestors of the Caddo, Osage, Tunica, and Quapaw tribes—attracted the interest of various museums and private collectors as early as 1879, and an enormous quantity of artifacts has been taken out of the state over the years.

While appreciating the artistry of the objects shown in this volume, it is important to bear in mind that most had been placed in the graves of prehistoric Native Americans. The names of the deceased individuals may be lost, but collectively these people are very much remembered by their descendants.

The exhibit and this catalog bring to culmination one of my long-term goals—namely, to make accessible to the public and the archaeological community a sample of the pre-Columbian artistry curated by the University of Arkansas Museum. The accompanying text focuses on Sam Dellinger, the University of Arkansas Museum, and the historical context of the collections; matters of style and iconography are not treated here.

My hope, and that of all who have worked on the exhibit, is that readers will be inspired by the illustrated objects and will help the Department of Arkansas Heritage, the Arkansas Department of Parks and Tourism, and the Arkansas Archeological Survey to preserve and interpret the heritage of Arkansas.

—Robert C. Mainfort Jr., Guest Curator

ACKNOWLEDGMENTS

The exhibit would not have been possible without the cooperation and support of many individuals and institutions: Old State House Museum (Bill Gatewood, director; Jo Ellen Maack, curator; Gail Moore, exhibit director; Kristen Thompson, registrar); Arkansas Archeological Survey (Thomas Green, director; Hester Davis, state archeologist emeritus; Jerry Hilliard, research associate; Mary Kwas, educational specialist; Charles R. McGimsey, director emeritus); University of Arkansas Museum Collections Facility (Mary Suter, curator of collections); Department of Arkansas Heritage (Cathie Matthews, director; Barbara Heffington, assistant director); The Butler Center for Arkansas Studies, Central Arkansas Library System; National Museum of the American Indian, Smithsonian Institution (Erik Satrum, registrar; Patricia Nietfield, Collections Manager; Lou Stancari, photo archivist); University of Michigan Museum of Anthropology (Karen O'Brien, collection manager); Office of Archaeological Services, University of Alabama Museums (Mary Bade, collections manager; Eugene Futato, curator); American Museum of Natural History (Stephanie Carson, registrar); The Field Museum (Angela Steinmetz, registrar; John Weinstein, photographer); Peabody Museum of Archaeology and Ethnology, Harvard University (Genevieve Fisher, registrar; Diana Loren, curator; Patricia Kervixk, associate archivist; Julie Brown, imaging services coordinator); Special Collections, Mullins Library, University of Arkansas (Thomas Dillard, director; Anne Prichard, reading room supervisor); Dr. Kent Westbrook (University of Arkansas Medical School); the family of Harvey C. Couch.

Members of the advisory committee for the exhibit were Glen Akridge, Paul Austin, Marynell Branch, Ann Early, Michael Hoffman, Mary Kwas, Juliette Morrow, Nan Selz, Mary Suter, Joyce Wroten, and Donna Kay Yeargan.

Others who helped specifically with this volume include John Miller (Section Head—Archeology, Arkansas Department of Highways and Transportation); Judy Robinson (periodicals assistant and archivist, Bailey Library, Hendrix College) Eunice Schlichting (chief curator) and Kristina Kastell (curator of history), Putnam Museum of History and Natural Science, Davenport, Iowa; Milissa Burkhart (special collections paraprofessional, Department of Special Collections and University Archives, McFarlin Library, University of Tulsa); Interlibrary Loan office, Mullins Library, University of Arkansas; Old State House Museum (Kristen Thompson, registrar); Katie Simon (Center for Advanced Spatial Technologies, University of Arkansas); Mary Suter (curator of collections, University of Arkansas Museum Collections Facility); Thomas Green (director, Arkansas Archeological Survey); Jerry Hilliard (research associate, Arkansas Archeological Survey); Mary Kwas (educational specialist, Arkansas Archeological Survey); Ann Early (state archeologist, Arkansas Archeological Survey; Lindi Holmes (editorial assistant, Arkansas Archeological Survey); Elizabeth Leith (collection manager, Archaeology, Sam Noble Oklahoma Museum of Natural History); Julie Brown (imaging services coordinator, Peabody Museum of Archaeology and Ethnology, Harvard University); Marvin Jeter (UA-Monticello station archeologist, Arkansas Archeological Survey); Dan and Phyllis Morse.

Special thanks to the Caddo Nation (Larue Parker, chairwoman; Bobby Gonzales, NAGPRA coordinator), the Osage Nation (Chief Jim Gray; Carrie Wilson, NAGPRA coordinator), and the Quapaw Tribe of Oklahoma (John Berry, Chairman; Carrie Wilson, NAGPRA coordinator).

Finally, the members of the exhibit team and I are indebted to Jon Kennedy, who photographed the vast majority of the objects included in the catalog.

Samuel Claudius Dellinger

SAMUEL CLAUDIUS DELLINGER, the first child of Robert H. and Laura Loftin Dellinger, was born on January 14, 1892, in Iron Station (now part of Lincolnton), North Carolina.[1] After graduating from high school in the town of his birth, Dellinger attended Trinity College (later Duke University), where he was a "very good varsity wrestler and swimmer."[2] During the summers of 1913 and 1914, Dellinger served as assistant to Dr. Lewis Radcliffe, learning oceanography aboard the USSS *Fish Hawk* during a survey of the Gulf Stream and the fishing grounds off the Carolina coast. Dellinger earned his BA degree with honors in 1915 and later was elected to Phi Beta Kappa at Duke.[3] Two years after graduating from Duke, he received a master's degree in zoology from Columbia University in New York City.[4]

Dellinger served as assistant professor of science at Hendrix College in Conway, Arkansas, in 1915 and 1916, and as professor of science there in 1917 and 1918.[5] He spent the intervening year conducting graduate study at Columbia. On June 20, 1916, Dellinger married Elsie Adkisson, daughter of G. W. Adkisson, a "well known businessman of Conway."[6] The Adkissons's social connections would serve Dellinger well in his later fundraising efforts at the University of Arkansas. In 1918, Dellinger returned to Columbia for additional study. His return to New York coincided with the devastating Spanish flu epidemic that swept the country. Dellinger was one of the fortunate survivors, but the disease left him weakened, and he spent a year recuperating in Florida. Dellinger's training in biology allowed him to secure a job with the Florida Citrus Exchange in the orange groves, and he also taught high school in the town of Winter Haven.[7]

Dellinger's research specialty was fish, and after spending the summer conducting research at the renowned Marine Biological Laboratory at Woods Hole, Massachusetts, he began his long career with the University of Arkansas in the fall of 1921 as an

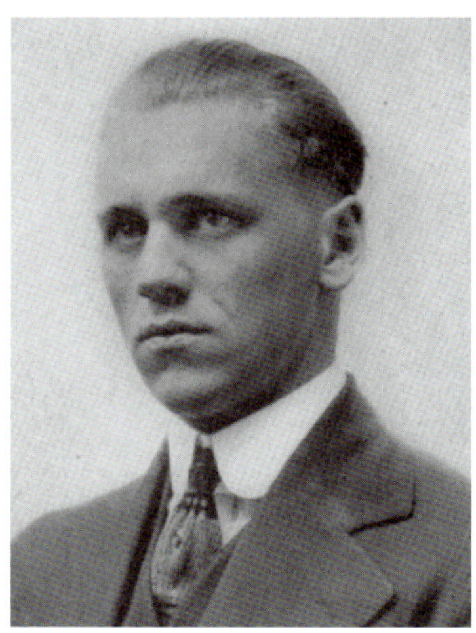

Figure 1. Formal photograph of Samuel Dellinger, 1916.

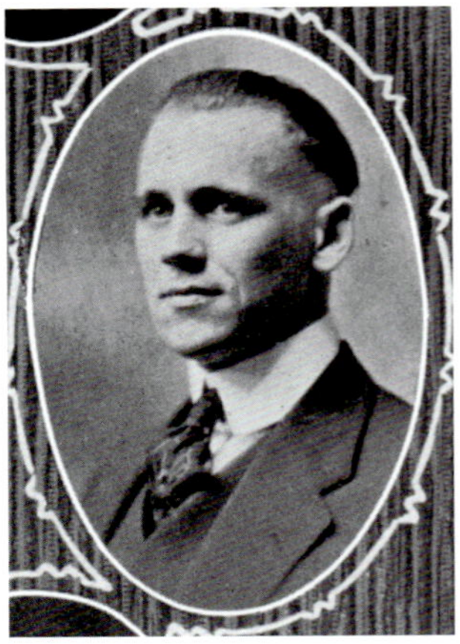

Figure 2. Formal photograph of Samuel Dellinger, 1918.

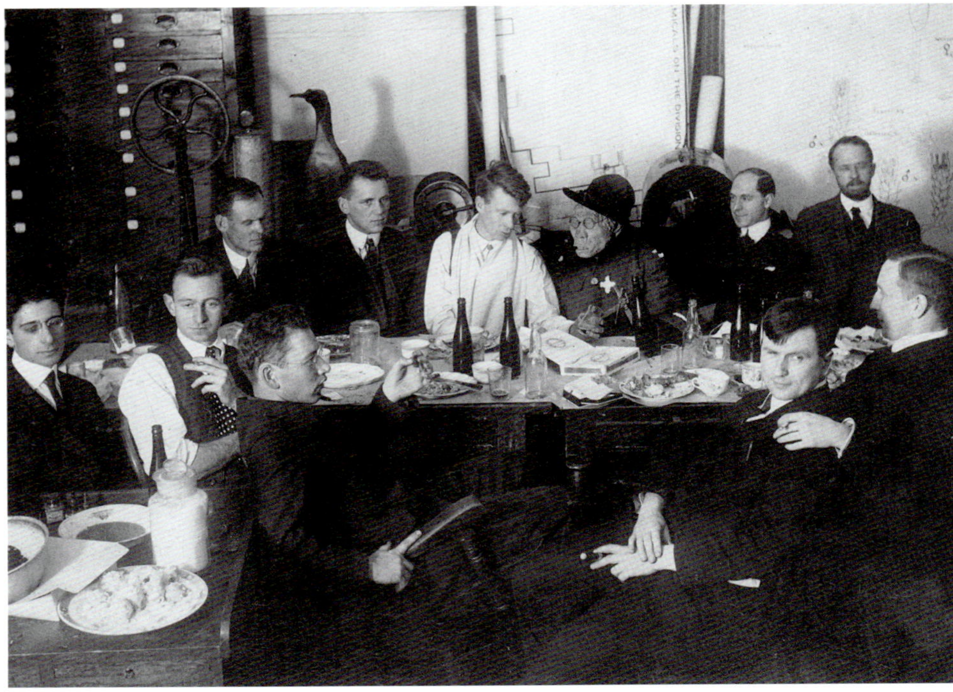

Figure 3. Party for A. H. Sturtevant (*front, center, leaning back in chair*) at Columbia University, 1919. Dellinger in back row, second from left.

assistant professor of zoology.[8] In 1924, Dellinger was granted a one-year leave of absence "to take graduate work leading to his PhD at Columbia University."[9] He completed coursework for doctoral degree in 1925, with the PhD "to be conferred at subsequent convocation when thesis is published,"[10] but for unknown reasons Dellinger never finished his degree. Perhaps this was partly because "Talking, not writing, was his forte."[11] Shortly after completing his studies at Columbia and conducting additional doctoral research at Woods Hole, in 1925 Dellinger returned to the University of Arkansas and was appointed curator of the museum and professor of zoology.[12] Around the same time, he was named chairman of the Department of Zoology, and he held both titles for over 30 years.[13]

Dellinger recollected to Dr. Charles R. McGimsey (hired as Dellinger's successor in 1957) that one afternoon while he was walking across campus, President John C. Futrall stopped him and asked Dellinger if he would be willing to assume responsibility for the museum, with no additional pay or reduction in his other responsibilities.[14] Dellinger had some interest in museums and agreed on the spot to Futrall's proposition.

Although he had no experience, much less formal training, in museum work, Dellinger's long-term vision of what the University of Arkansas Museum should be was well formulated by 1926—only a year after he was appointed curator:

> To a state, a museum is not merely a place for study. Here in the University we have specialists who can make a study of the natural history specimens of the state and at the same time instill in our own boys and girls not only a love for their state and its worth, but also give them some idea of her wonderful possibilities. We are training future teachers of Arkansas, who in turn will instill into their students the state's opportunities.[15]

In a 1933 article about the museum's ongoing archaeological fieldwork, Dellinger reiterated his strong sentiments:

> Exhibition is only one phase, and only a small side, of a museum according to Prof. Dellinger. Most states are issuing books on their cultures and natural resources that have been derived from the study of the historical and scientific sides of their states that have been in their museums. The University of Arkansas wants to publish such material for this state, and the information would be available to schools and residents of the state.
>
> The value of the objects from the standpoint of the teaching of history, anthropology and art is important. With her wonderful supplies of clays suitable for making pottery, Arkansas will someday have a school of ceramic engineering, and at that time the specimens in the museum will be invaluable for the study of clays, tempering materials and designs.[16]

What stands out clearly is that Dellinger was not concerned with collecting specimens simply for the sake of collecting them and placing them on shelves. First and foremost, Dellinger viewed the University of Arkansas Museum as an educational resource for the people of Arkansas, and especially students. Nor did he consider research and publications to be ends in themselves, but rather means to further education.

During his second year at the university (1922–23), Dellinger organized "Introduction to Anthropology," which focused on physical anthropology and evolution, in 1922–23. Due to his other commitments (a heavy teaching load, plus his leave of absence to finish his dissertation), however, the first anthropology course at the University of Arkansas actually was taught in the geology department (Geology 231) by Carey Croneis (later chancellor of Rice University), using Dellinger's notes, in the 1923 and 1924 academic years. Dellinger himself first taught Zoology 333 (Anthropology) during the 1925–1926 academic year and continued to do so for many years.[17]

Dellinger was an excellent public speaker, which undoubtedly contributed to his popularity among University of Arkansas students.[18] During his first semester on campus, 30 students were enrolled in general zoology, but by 1926 the enrollment had reached 150. It is likely that his anthropology course contributed to the popularity of zoology courses in general.

Shortly after the infamous Scopes trial in Tennessee, in 1928 Arkansas voters passed an act that prohibited teaching evolution in state schools. Dellinger stood by his convictions and was one of five University of Arkansas faculty members who signed an American Association of University Professors resolution calling the anti-evolution bill unconstitutional, and saying that it interfered with free speech.[19] Dellinger did not stop teaching his anthropology class, which focused on human evolution, nor his zoology classes, and in 1968, the U.S. Supreme Court declared the law unconstitutional.[20]

It is not entirely clear how Dellinger developed his passion for archaeology, so evident in the objects selected for the exhibit. In 1968, he told a reporter with the *Arkansas Gazette* that he became interested in the "Ozark Bluff Dwellers" while pursuing his graduate studies at Columbia University in New York City.[21] As a biologist interested in human evolution, it was natural that Dellinger would be interested in the Ozark bluff shelters because they resemble some of the famous fossil hominid sites of France. His early University of Arkansas colleague, geologist Carey Croneis, however, correctly realized that "man is younger in North America than he is in Europe."[22] Indeed, the archaeological remains in the Ozark bluff shelters date to the relatively recent past (i.e., the last 10,000 years), while some of those in France are tens of thousands of years older.

Dellinger's first excavations, however, were not in the bluff shelters, but in the Arkansas River valley and along the Ouachita River.[23] Unlike today, in the 1920s there was little or no concern about the effects of major construction projects on archaeological sites. Yet, in 1929 Dellinger was able to persuade Harvey Couch,[24] president of Arkansas Power and Light, to donate a substantial sum of money to fund excavation of several important archaeological sites along the Ouachita River in Garland County that would be inundated upon completion of the Carpenter Dam.[25] This work represents one of the earliest examples of "salvage archaeology" in the eastern United States.[26] Also unlike today, Dellinger gave some of the excavated pottery vessels to Couch and Couch's friend, Senator Thaddeus Caraway for display in their homes.[27]

Beginning in the 1920s and continuing throughout his career, Dellinger maintained an active schedule of public lectures, as well documented in the *Arkansas Traveler,* the *Arkansas Alumnus,* and the *Fayetteville Daily Democrat.* S. D. Dickinson recalled that Dellinger "could hold the attention of large audiences as well as single persons with accounts of his experiences." It is not surprising that so gifted a raconteur got the notice of state newspapers and attracted much publicity for his museum, much to the chagrin of other faculty members whose activities were ignored by the press."[28] Nor were public lectures Dellinger's only public service. He was one of the original appointees to the state Basic Science Board in 1931, and continued to serve in the capacity until his retirement.[29] Dellinger also remained active in zoology and in 1937 was named an *ex-officio* member of the Arkansas Game and Fish Commission, another position he held until he retired.[30]

Dellinger was responsible for obtaining a large portion of the museum's extraordinary archaeological collections. Dellinger's archaeological field crews collected many of the complete pottery vessels, as well as material from the Ozark bluff shelters, during the period 1931–1934. Funding for this work was provided by grants Dellinger received from the Carnegie Corporation, whose foundation supported a number of archaeology programs in the late 1920s and early 1930s. The first Carnegie grant, for $15,000 payable over three years, was awarded in 1931 "for the furtherance of the University's educational program in connection with the museum."[31] This money was used primarily to conduct excavations in the bluff shelters and in northeast Arkansas. A $5,000 grant in 1934 was used to study "camp sites on the Ouachita and Arkansas rivers."[32] While the sums seem relatively small today, the total value of the Carnegie grants in today's

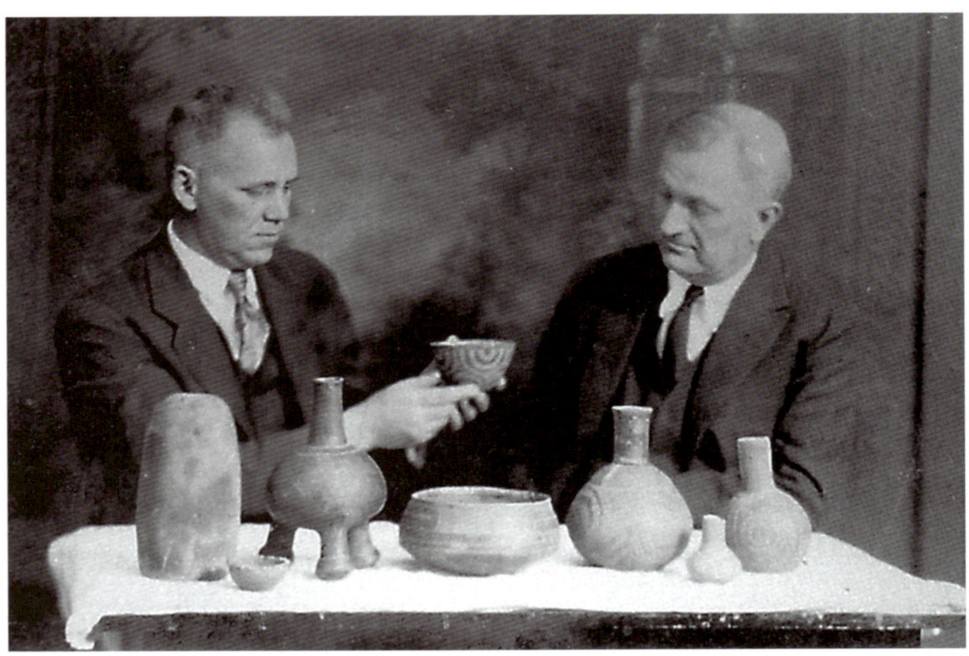

Figure 4. Dellinger and Harvey Couch examining pottery vessels from excavations along the Ouachita River prior to the impoundment of Lake Hamilton.

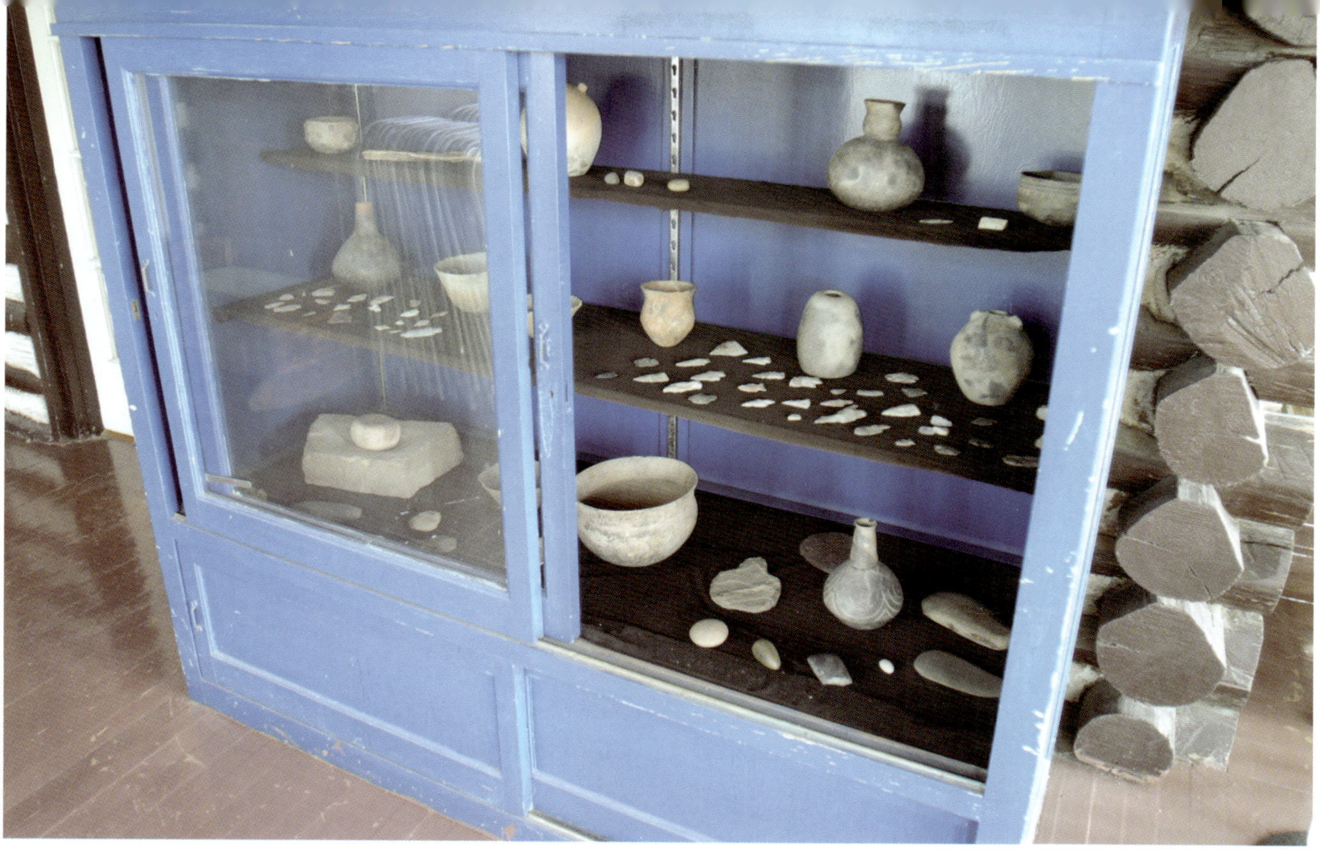

Figure 5. Artifacts from Dellinger's excavations exhibited at Harvey Couch's home ("Couchwood").

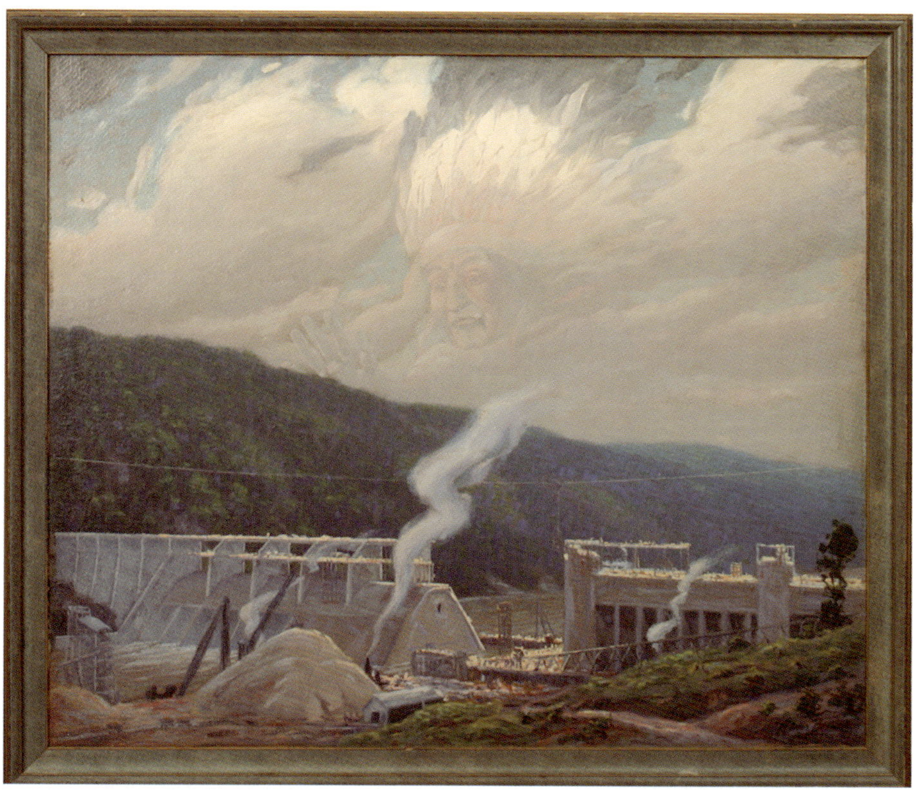

Figure 6. Remmel Dam, by Adrian Brewer. The myth of the "vanished" Indian is the theme of this painting, which was commissioned by Harvey C. Couch to accompany his collection of artifacts gathered by Dellinger from what would become Lake Catherine. Note that the historic Native Americans of Arkansas did not wear large headdresses.

dollars would be roughly $250,000. Dellinger's busy schedule did not permit him to spend much time "in the field," and the work was supervised by a cadre of his students, who hired local laborers for assistance.

Dellinger also was very successful in obtaining financial contributions for the museum from private individuals. Perhaps most noteworthy among these was Colonel T. H. Barton of El Dorado, Arkansas. During the mid-1930s, archaeological excavations by the museum were curtailed, but it was during this period that Dellinger obtained and cataloged a number of important artifacts that had been looted from the Craig Mound at Spiro, Oklahoma. Some of these objects must be numbered among the most important in the museum collections. Colonel Barton, president of the Lion Oil Refinery Company, donated much of the funding for this.[33] During the 1937–38 academic year, Barton provided $1,200 to the university to pay Dellinger's salary (the university used Dellinger's salary money to hire a temporary instructor), as well as over $500 for a graphic artist and a photographer to record the Spiro collections.[34] Over time, Colonel and Mrs. Barton donated over $2,000,000 to the university, including additional funds for the museum.[35]

Certainly from a modern museum ethics perspective, but even within accepted ethical principles of museums in the 1930s, Dellinger's decision to accept objects that originally had been purchased from individuals involved in looting the Spiro site was questionable. Dr. Carl Guthe, from whom Dellinger had long obtained help for his fledgling archaeology program, was sharply critical: "I fail to understand how individuals really interested in developing a university museum [presumably Colonel Barton] can justify their requirement that you undertake a project which is unethical and outside of your state in order to obtain their aid."[36] At the very least, it is ironic that Dellinger, who decried the activities of out-of-state archaeologists in Arkansas, accepted and studied important collections from Oklahoma. Nonetheless, Dellinger's acquisition of the Spiro material ensured that it would be available to later researchers.

Other important financial donors to the museum included Mrs. Rufus Garrett of El Dorado, Raymond Rebsamen of Little Rock, Winthrop Rockefeller, and ex-governor George Donaghey of Little Rock.[37]

During the 1930s, in addition to teaching, managing the museum, and supervising archaeological projects, Dellinger also was active in the archaeological profession, presenting papers at conferences and, in 1934, serving as chairman of the Conference on Southern Prehistory. The same year, Dellinger was appointed to a Department of Interior committee to create parks to preserve archaeological sites in Arkansas, Missouri, and Tennessee.[38] It would take several decades, but today there are archaeological parks in all three states, though none are managed by the National Park Service.

Despite his many responsibilities, Dellinger found time to pursue his other numerous and varied interests. In 1928 Dellinger, with Sam Leath and Vance Randolph, organized the first folklore meeting in Arkansas at Eureka Springs. In 1940 he was responsible for the first azaleas and rhododendrons grown in Fayetteville, to the surprise of local nursery owners.[39] Dellinger also worked hard on behalf of conservation efforts in Arkansas, and it was on his dining room table that the first map for what would become the Buffalo National Scenic River was drawn.[40]

The Depression era was economically disastrous to many institutions and individuals. In an effort to offset massive unemployment, the federal government initiated a number of public works projects that provided employment opportunities. During the 1930s, the government funded a considerable amount of archaeological fieldwork and other archaeology-related projects.[41] Dellinger made certain that the museum would receive some of the available federal funds and was awarded at least three federally funded projects. Two of these (including one involving $15,150, the other an

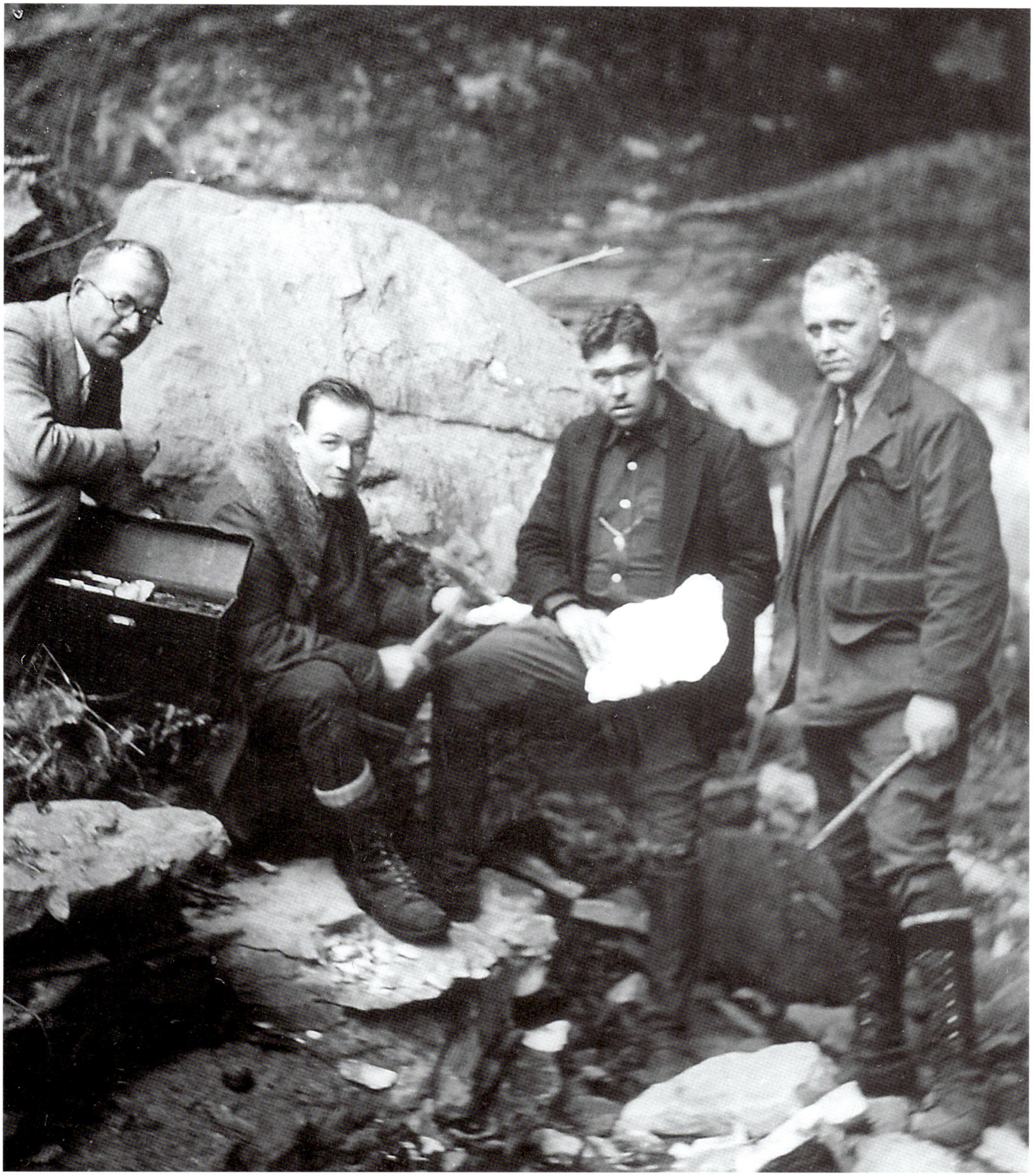

Figure 7. Outside Cob Cave, 1931. *Left to right:* Walter J. Lemke (for whom the University of Arkansas Department of Journalism is named), Mr. Slate, Thomas Millard (field assistant), Dellinger.

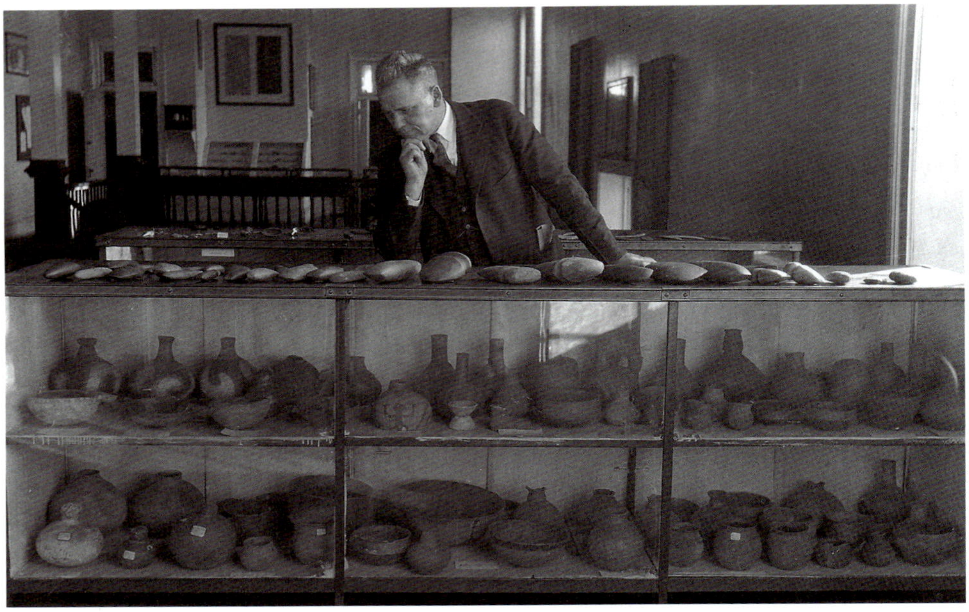

Figure 8. Dellinger in the museum with a case of pottery vessels (most from the Arkansas River Valley) and ground stone artifacts, circa 1930.

Figure 9. *Official Highway Service Map* [1939]. State Highway Commission, Little Rock. This graphic reflects Dellinger's success in making the public aware of the importance of Arkansas archaeology.

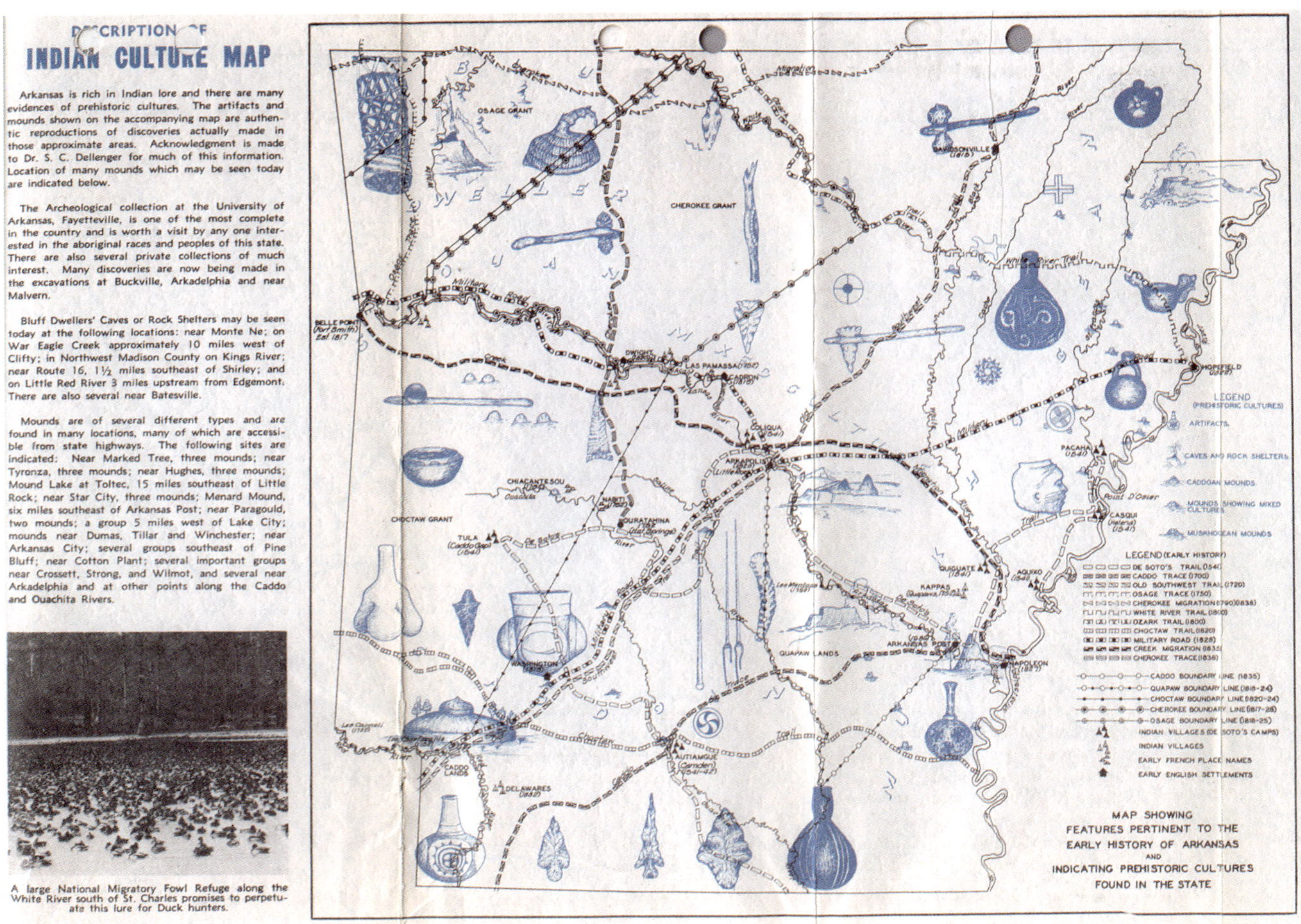

unknown amount) focused specifically on the museum as an institution. The project that started on Christmas Day in 1935 included "preparing charts for teaching and diagrams for display cases," as well as construction of "storage cases, work tables, cases for fumigating, tanks for frogs, etc."[42] The second (Project No. 5209–4), which started on June 16, 1936, was for "rendering additional services and enlarging activities of the University of Arkansas Museum."[43]

Dellinger also directed a roughly $115,000 (including both federal and university matching funds) archaeological excavation project from mid-1939 into 1940 involving several prehistoric village and mound sites along the Ouachita River.[44] Due to various administrative and personnel problems, as well as the onset of World War II, his more ambitious goal of a statewide archaeological survey was not realized, but the excavations produced information of lasting importance.[45]

Although Dellinger was very interested in archaeology, as attested to by the exhibit and this catalog, by no means did he neglect building the museum's collections in other areas. A biologist by training, it was only natural that he should continue to acquire plant and animal specimens, but Dellinger also increased the mineral and fossil collection and broadened the collections to include such areas as Greek and Roman antiquities, American glassware, bird eggs, and Arkansas folk pottery.

Dellinger was a large, powerful man and a tireless worker, but the stress of his many activities and responsibilities may have contributed to his 1935 diagnosis of high blood pressure.[46] Shortly after World War II, Dellinger suffered a heart attack, which undoubtedly slowed his activities to some extent.[47]

In June 1957, Dellinger formally retired from the University of Arkansas, though he continued to work part-time until June 1960 in a half-time capacity.[48] He remained active in retirement. Dellinger did not sever his ties to the museum, and always was available to answer questions about objects in the collections. Continuing his interest in biology, Dellinger began growing ornamental gourds and corresponded with gourd growers around the world.[49] As chairman of Fayetteville's City Beautification Committee, Dellinger had more than 1,000 red and white dogwoods brought in and planted around town.[50] He served as the first president of the Arkansas Chapter of the Nature Conservancy and during 1960 and 1961 Dellinger became the first president of the newly formed Arkansas Archeological Society.[51]

Dellinger's wife passed away in 1969, and during his final years, his own health was poor. He suffered from glaucoma and Parkinson's disease, but his mind retained a keen edge.[52] Samuel Dellinger died August 12, 1973, in Fayetteville. He was survived by his daughter Martha Ellen (a professor of architecture at the University of Arkansas) and a brother and four sisters. Dellinger and his wife are buried in Fairview Memorial Gardens in Fayetteville; their graves are marked with modest stones.[53]

Sam Dellinger was remembered fondly and respectfully by those who were privileged to work with him. James Durham, who moved to Fayetteville in June 1931 to work on archaeological projects for Dellinger and continued to do so into 1935, stated simply, "Professor Dellinger was a man who got things done."[54] Another of Dellinger's archaeological "field foremen" during the early 1930s, Charles Finger Jr., observed that Dellinger was "a large man, physically and in perspective" and that "he commanded respect by his intelligence and actions."[55]

S. D. Dickinson assisted Dellinger with archaeological investigations during the WPA era and remained in contact with Dellinger for many years thereafter. Dickinson (1973) revealed yet another aspect of Dellinger's personality: "In the late 1920's and early 1930's there was some anti-Semitic feeling at the University of Arkansas. Mr. Dellinger took a firm stand against it and was not afraid to express himself; as a matter of fact, he became sponsor of a Jewish fraternity."

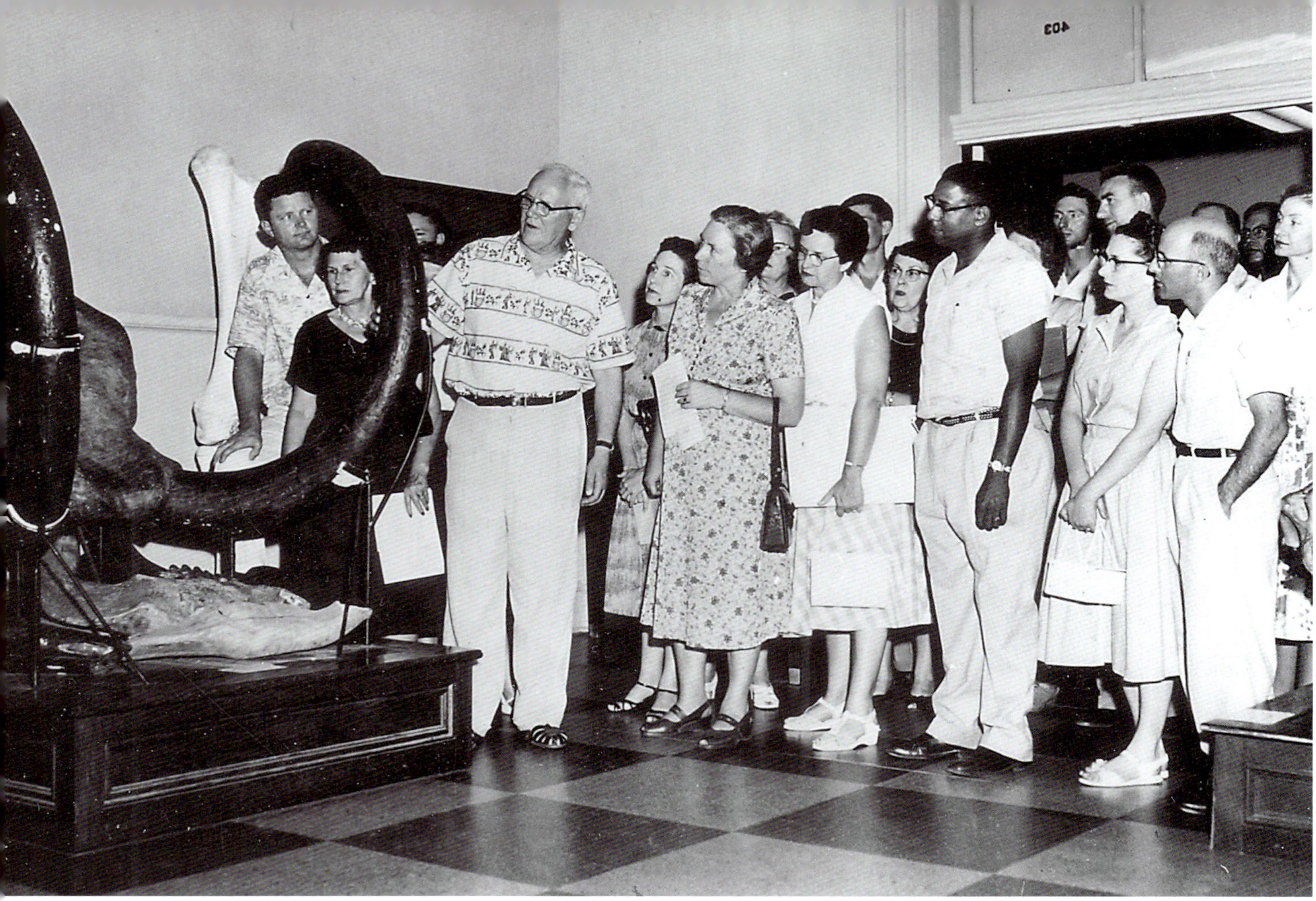

Figure 10. Dellinger giving a museum tour, circa 1960.

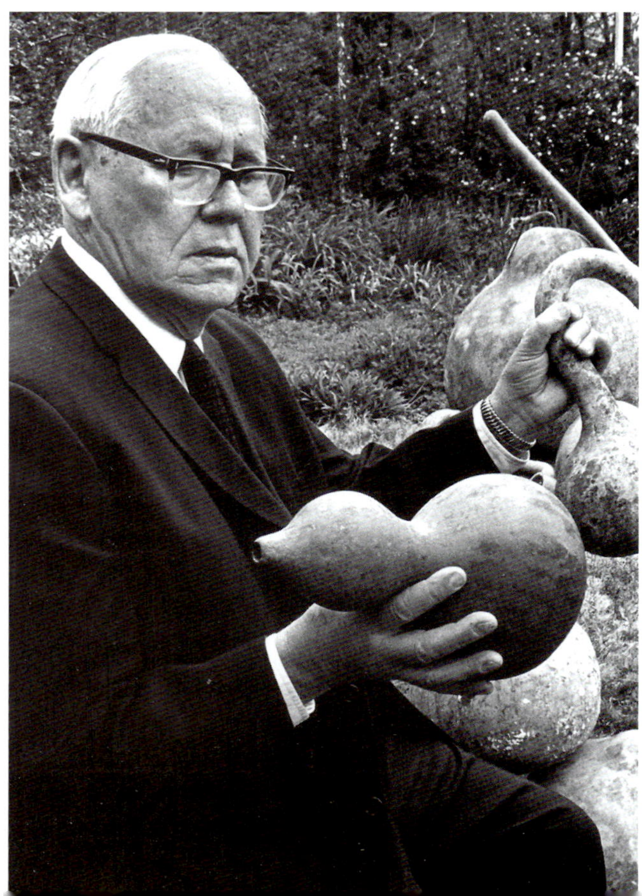

Figure 11. Dellinger with some of his ornamental gourds in the backyard of his home, May 1968.

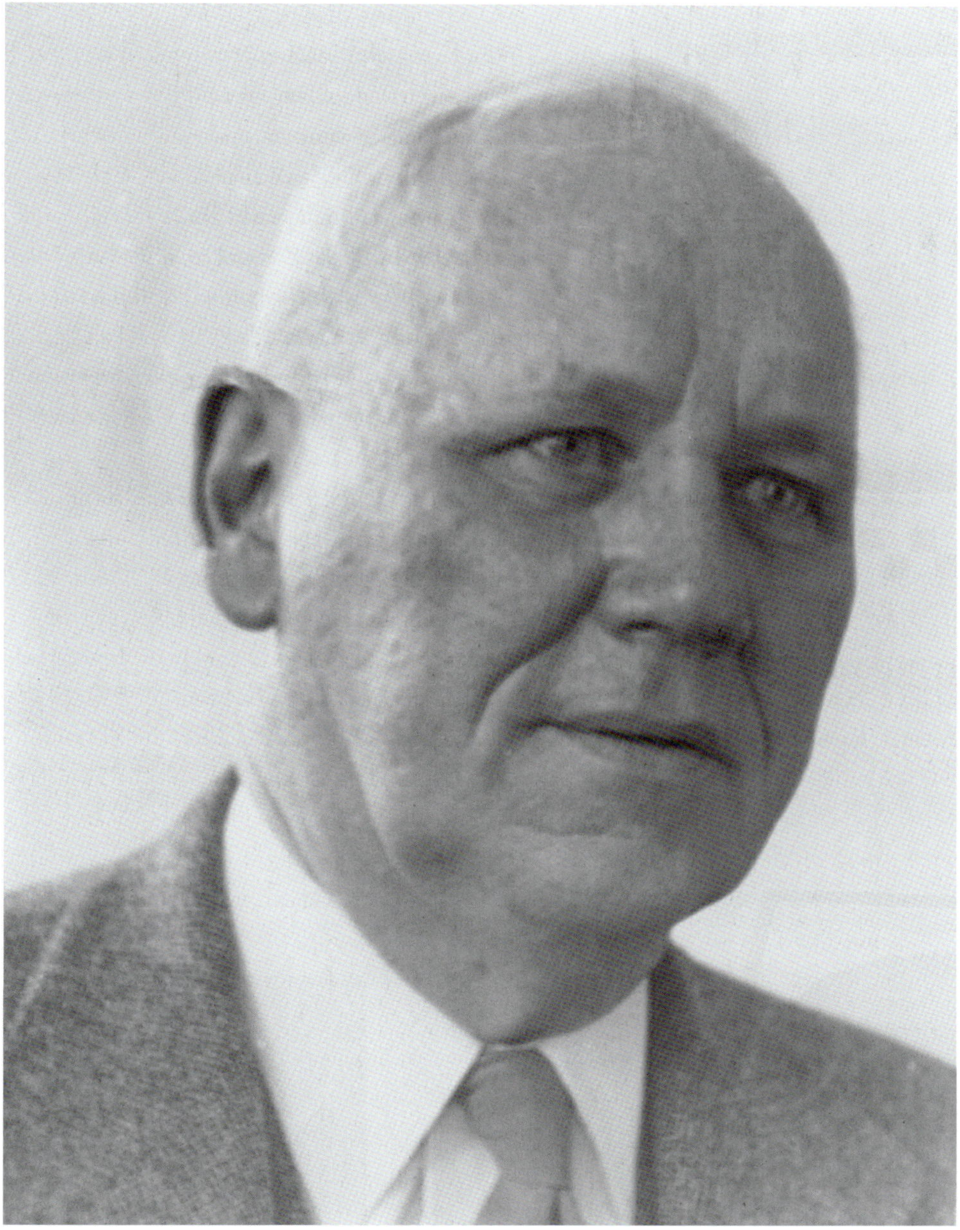

Figure 12. Formal photograph of Samuel Dellinger, circa 1970.

Dickinson went on to say: "During Mr. Dellinger's time, the University of Arkansas did not have the strong statewide support it enjoys today. Actually, the school had unfortunate public relations too often, and not many of the faculty were known to Arkansas outside the northwestern counties. Everywhere Mr. Dellinger went he endeavored to generate interest in the school. He was one of the best known and best liked members of the faculty outside Washington County." "It is unfortunate, indeed, that the University of Arkansas failed to grant Mr. Dellinger an honorary degree. He certainly was deserving of it."[56] I could not agree more.

Perhaps Dellinger's greatest professional disappointment was that he never completed a detailed monograph on the bluff shelter excavations in northwest Arkansas.[57] Indeed, if there were one major criticism that could be leveled against Professor Dellinger, it would be that he wrote very little about the wealth of archaeological material that was excavated under his supervision. While this certainly is the case, it also is fair to wonder if anyone else in his situation could have accomplished more. Throughout virtually his entire career, Dellinger had a full teaching load. He also served as chair of the zoology department for over 30 years, which saddled him with considerable administrative responsibilities. He was finally curator of the museum, which involved fundraising and building the collections in other areas in addition to archaeology, and lacked a regular paid assistant until his last decade of service. Thus it is more appropriate to be amazed at how much Sam Dellinger *was* able to accomplish. He left a remarkable, enduring legacy that can be appreciated by the people of Arkansas and beyond for many, many years.

NOTES

1. "S. C. Dellinger, Museum Founder, Dies at Age 81," *Northwest Arkansas Times,* 13 August 1973, 2. Dellinger had four sisters and three brothers; see 1910 U.S. Population Census, Lincolnton Ward 2, Lincoln County, North Carolina, Roll T624–117, p. 13A, Enumeration District 72, Image 1094, Dwelling 231. Additional genealogical information on the Dellinger family may be found at: <http://wc.rootsweb.com/cgibin/igm.cgi?op=REG&db=michaelt&id=I206299> (viewed 10 October 2006).
2. Charles J. Finger, (untitled), *Field Notes* (of the Arkansas Archeological Society) 108 (1973): 10.
3. *Arkansas Alumnus* 10(7): 7.
4. Hester A. Davis, "Being some notes from memory and from the museum records on Sam Dellinger, the university museum, and Arkansas archeology," *Field Notes* 108 (1973): 12.
5. Vitae Brief (Samuel C. Dellinger), University of Arkansas Library, Special Collections, MC 1425, Box 1, Folder 1; "S. C. Dellinger," *Arkansas Alumnus* 3(7) (1926): 13. The 1918 Hendrix College yearbook (*The Troubadour,* 20), however, lists Dellinger as "Assistant in Science."
6. Emily Tucker, *Faulkner County, Arkansas Marriages, 1873–1925* (Conway, 2004), 2; *Arkansas Alumnus* 3(7): 13.
7. Davis, "Dellinger," 12; Vitae Brief (Samuel C. Dellinger).
8. *Arkansas Traveler,* 6 October 1921, 1; Davis, "Dellinger," 12.
9. *Arkansas Alumnus* 1(3) (1924): 7.
10. "S. C. Dellinger."
11. Samuel D. Dickinson, "A Relic Looks Back," *Arkansas Archeologist* 30 (1991): 4.
12. "University of Arkansas Museum," *Arkansas Alumnus* 3(7) (1926), 7; "S. C. Dellinger," *Arkansas Alumnus* 3(7) (1926): 13; University of Arkansas, *Annual Catalog of the University of Arkansas* (Fayetteville, 1925), 8; Official appointment letters (Samuel C. Dellinger), University of Arkansas Library, Special Collections, MC 204, Box 3, Folder 8.
13. "Many New Specimens for University Zoo," *Fayetteville Daily Democrat,* 28 November 1925, 1:4.
14. Charles R. McGimsey, "Museum anecdotes," Office of the Registrar, Arkansas Archeological Survey.
15. "University of Arkansas Museum," *Arkansas Alumnus* 3(7) (1926): 7.
16. "New Finds Added to Museum," *Arkansas Alumnus* 10(6) (1933): 5–6.
17. *University of Arkansas Catalog* (1923:72), (1924:74), (1925:108); see also Dellinger to Dean G. D. Nichols, 10 May 1957, MC 204, Box 8, folder 9, Mullins Library, University of Arkansas.
18. Dickinson, "Relic."
19. "Faculty and Students at the Front in Early Anti-Evolution Battle," *Arkansas Alumnus* 4(8): 15.
20. Robert A. Leflar, *The First 100 Years* (Fayetteville, 1972), 152.
21. "UA Zoologist May Have 'Retired,' But . . . ," *Arkansas Gazette,* 9 June 1968, 5E.
22. "Geologists to Explore Newton County Caves," *Harrison Weekly Times,* 26 December 1924, 3.
23. "Find of Rare Relics Made by Zoologist in Old Cotton Field," *Arkansas Traveler,* 20 January 1928, 4.
24. Couch was one of the most important Arkansans of the twentieth century. Perhaps his most important accomplishment was in the development of rural electrification. In 1930, President Herbert Hoover appointed him state relief chairman. See Stephen Wilson, *Harvey Couch: An Entrepreneur Brings Electricity to Arkansas* (Little Rock, 1986).
25. "Dellinger's Efforts to Preserve Indian Remains in Arkansas Recognized," *Arkansas Alumnus* 7(4) (1930): 12; "Arkansas Caveman Relics Dug Up by Prof. Dellinger for Museum," *Arkansas Traveler,* 31 January 1930, 1, 3.
26. The term "salvage archaeology" refers to archaeology conducted in advance of construction or other activities that will damage or destroy archaeological sites. Today, various federal and state laws require salvage archaeology in some situations, but this was not the case in Dellinger's day.

27. Dellinger to Couch, 11 December 1929, MC 204, Box 8, folder 4, Mullins Library, University of Arkansas.

28. Dickinson, "Relic," 4.

29. *Arkansas Alumnus* 8(7) (1931): 14; "S. C. Dellinger, Member of U.A. Faculty since 1921, Active in Several Fields," *Northwest Arkansas Times,* 6 June 1957, 8.

30. *Arkansas Alumnus* 14(6) (1937): 2.

31. *Arkansas Alumnus* 8(5) (1931): 5.

32. Dellinger to Guthe, 17 March 1934, Carl E. Guthe correspondence file, University of Arkansas Museum. Guthe was a professor of anthropology at the University of Michigan and head of the National Research Council's Committee on State Archaeological Surveys.

33. *Arkansas Alumnus* 14(5) (1937): 2.

34. Haun to Dellinger, 21 July 1937, and Haun to Dellinger, 20 October 1938, Walter R. Haun correspondence file, University of Arkansas Museum.

35. Leflar, *First 100 Years,* 206.

36. Guthe to Dellinger, 13 January 1937, Carl Guthe correspondence file, University of Arkansas Museum.

37. "UA Zoologist," *Arkansas Gazette.* Rufus Garrett and Rebsamen were prominent businessmen. Winthrop Rockefeller was a philanthropist who served as Arkansas's thirty-seventh governor. Donaghey also was a very successful businessman and created a foundation to support Little Rock Junior College (now University of Arkansas at Little Rock).

38. Davis, "Dellinger," 12; "Zoology Staff Is Increased through Fund," *Arkansas Traveler,* 18 October 1934, 1. In 1933, Dellinger attempted to have the well-known Toltec Mounds site, near Little Rock, deeded to the University of Arkansas; see Dellinger to Guthe, 15 May 1933, 1 June 1933, and 7 August 1933; Guthe, Carl E. file, University of Arkansas Museum Collections Facility. He was unsuccessful, but today Toltec Mounds is a state archeological park.

39. "S. C. Dellinger, Member of U.A. Faculty since 1921, Active in Several Fields," *Northwest Arkansas Times,* 6 June 1957, 8.

40. Neil Compton, "Prof. S. C. Dellinger," *Ozark Society Bulletin* 7(3) (1973): 11.

41. Edwin A. Lyon, *A New Deal for Southeastern Archaeology* (Tuscaloosa, 1996).

42. Dellinger to Futrall, 30 September 1936, Univ. Affairs Misc. Correspondence file, University of Arkansas Museum.

43. Patterson to Dellinger, 15 June 1936; Works Progress Administration Data & Information file, University of Arkansas Museum.

44. "Archaeological Survey," *Arkansas Alumnus* 16(7) (1939): 7, 13. The excavations are mentioned in the text accompanying the "Indian Culture Map" that appeared on the back of the 1939 Arkansas state highway map, which is reproduced herein; Arkansas State Highway Commission, *Official Highway Service Map* (Little Rock, 1939).

45. Frank F. Schambach, *Pre-Caddoan Cultures in the Trans-Mississippi South,* Research Series 53, Arkansas Archeological Survey (Fayetteville, 1998).

46. Guthe to Dellinger, 14 October 1935; Carl E. Guthe correspondence file, University of Arkansas Museum.

47. Compton, "Dellinger."

48. "Prof. S. C. Dellinger" (in "This Year's Emeritus Professors"), *Arkansas Alumnus* (n.s.) 10(6) (1957): 11; Official appointment letters (Samuel C. Dellinger), University of Arkansas Library, Special Collections, MC 204, Box 3, Folder 8.

49. Davis, "Dellinger," 2, 12.

50. "UA Zoologist May Have 'Retired,' But . . ." *Arkansas Gazette,* 9 June 1968, 5E.

51. Davis, "Dellinger," 2, 12.

52. Davis, "Dellinger," 2.

53. "S. C. Dellinger," *Northwest Arkansas Times,* 13 August 1973, 2.

54. Durham, untitled.

55. Finger, untitled.

56. Samuel D. Dickinson, untitled, *Field Notes* 108 (1973): 7.

57. Davis, "Dellinger," 2.

"Arkansas for Arkansans"

ALMOST NO SOONER had Sam Dellinger been appointed curator of the University museum in 1925 than he began to denounce what he viewed as the pillaging of Arkansas by out-of-state museums:

> "Imagine my chagrin," said Mr. Dellinger, "when I visited such museums as Peabody at Harvard, the National Museum at Washington, D.C., the one at the University of Michigan, the Heye Museum of the American Indian at New York and found there that their finest and most valuable Indian displays had been sent from Arkansas. Specimens are there that can never be found again in our state. They were sold to the big museums for a nominal sum. They are not like a crop of cotton or corn that can be grown again but when these go out of the state they are lost forever. In many instances they were simply collected by expeditions of the sort that are sent into more backward states or countries. Do we want to send our University students to another university in order to learn something of the first inhabitants of Arkansas?"[1]

His concerns were neither unfounded, nor without precedent. For example in late 1879 through the spring of 1880, Edwin Curtiss, a Tennessean hired by the Peabody Museum at Harvard University, excavated at a number of late-prehistoric sites along the St. Francis River and procured over 900 complete pottery vessels; the entire collection was displayed prominently at the museum for a number of years.[2] Curtiss's work represents the earliest reported large excavation project in Arkansas. A few years before Curtiss, in 1876, retired steamboat captain Wilfred Peter Hall, representing the Davenport (Iowa) Academy of Natural Sciences, began his first excavations in Arkansas. Hall worked intermittently in the state through 1887 and obtained 742 lots of artifacts, the vast majority of which are whole pottery vessels. Traveling in a 20-foot skiff, he excavated at sites along the Mississippi, St. Francis, and White Rivers in Arkansas, but also was active in Illinois, Missouri, Tennessee, Mississippi, Louisiana, and Alabama. Hall was well liked by a number of prominent landowners, including R. W. Friend, who owned the famous Pecan Point site in Mississippi County, Arkansas.[3] Hall's collections served as the basis for William H. Holmes pioneering study of prehistoric pottery from the Mississippi Valley.[4]

Curtiss and Hall were essentially contract employees who were commissioned to obtain prehistoric Native American artifacts for their respective institutions by excavation, purchase, and trade. Curtiss received a small but regular stipend; Hall was largely left to fend for himself, though members of the Academy sent him money when he was sick or injured.

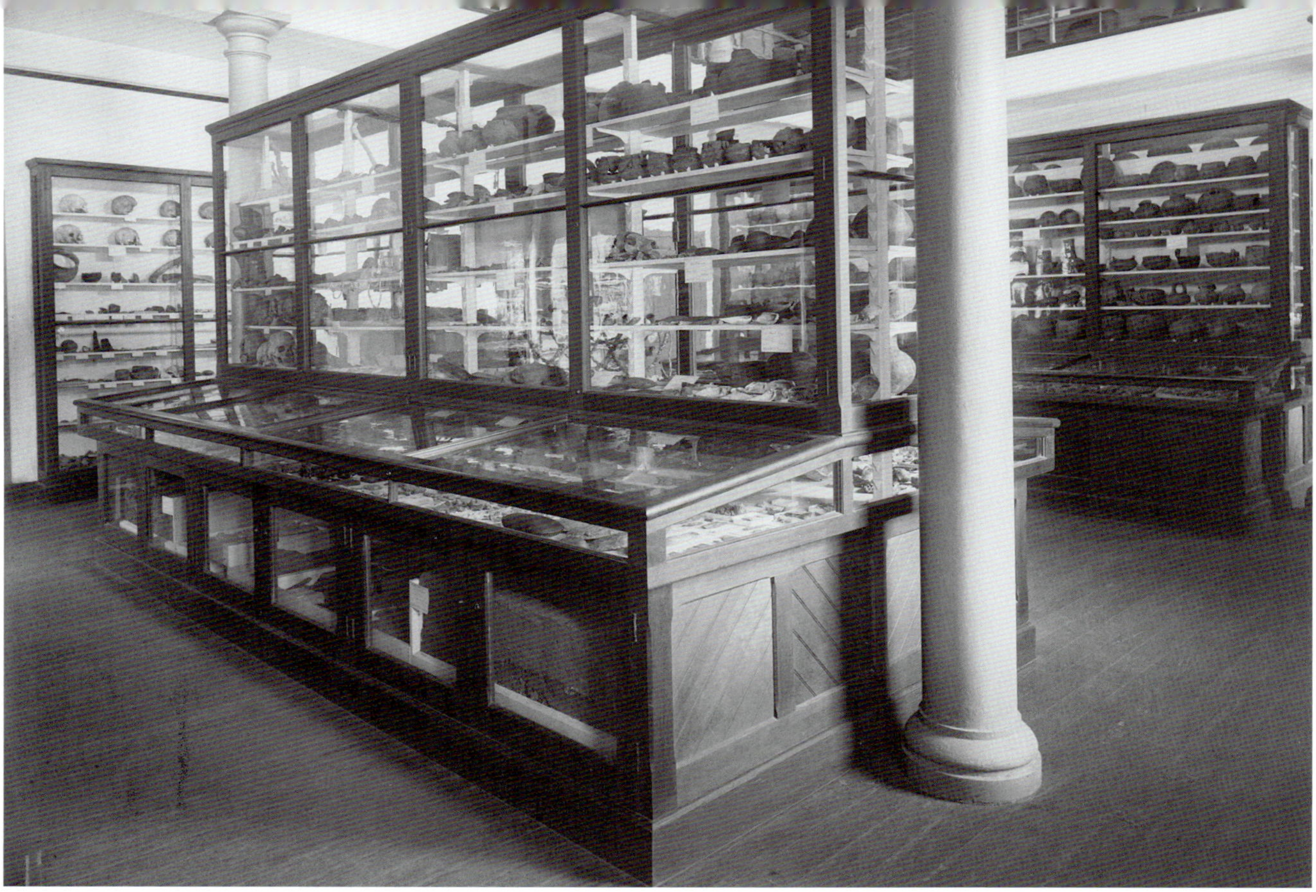

Figure 13. The "Moundbuilders room" at the Peabody Museum, Harvard University, circa 1890.
Many of the objects displayed, as well as the human remains, were collected by Edwin Curtiss in Cross County, Arkansas.

Figure 14. Another view of the "Moundbuilders room" at the Peabody Museum, Harvard University, circa 1890.

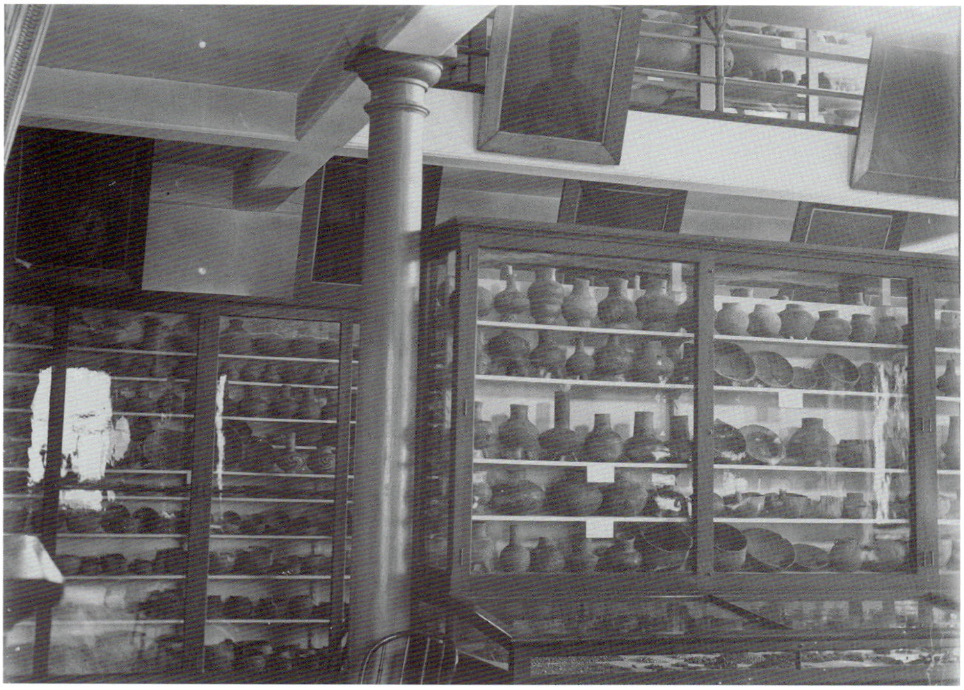

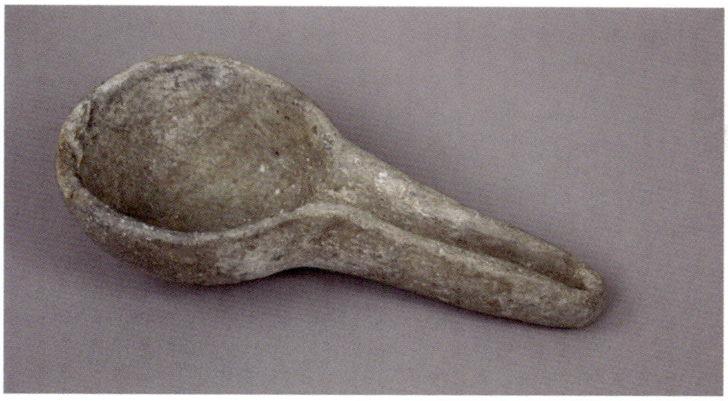

Figure 15. Ladle (OSHTL2006.004.01)
Ceramic; 13.0 x 6.2 cm
Rose Mound, Cross County, Arkansas
Late Mississippi period, A.D. 1350–1600
Collected by Edwin Curtiss

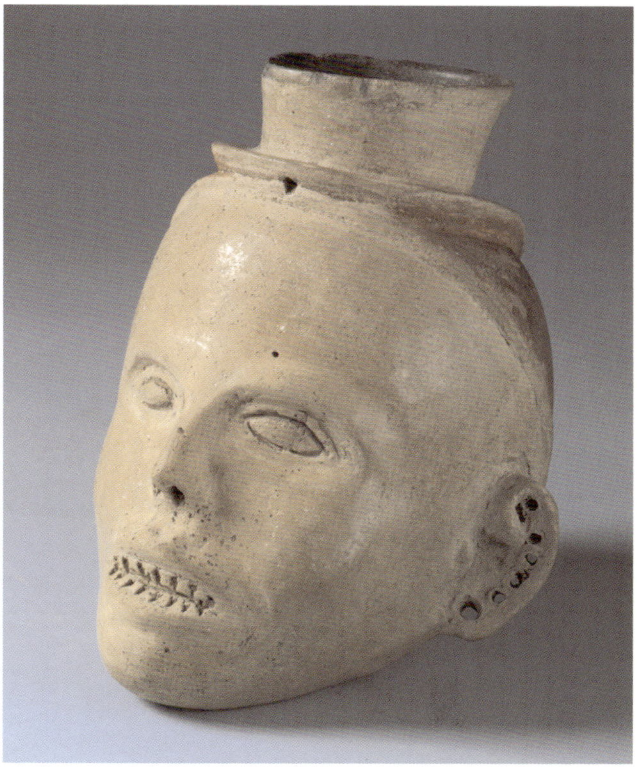

Figure 17. Red and Buff Headpot (OSHTL2006.004.03)
Ceramic; 16.4 x 19.0 cm
Fortune Mound, Cross County, Arkansas
Late Mississippi period, A.D. 1350–1600
Collected by Edwin Curtiss
Collected in 1880, this is the first reported headpot.

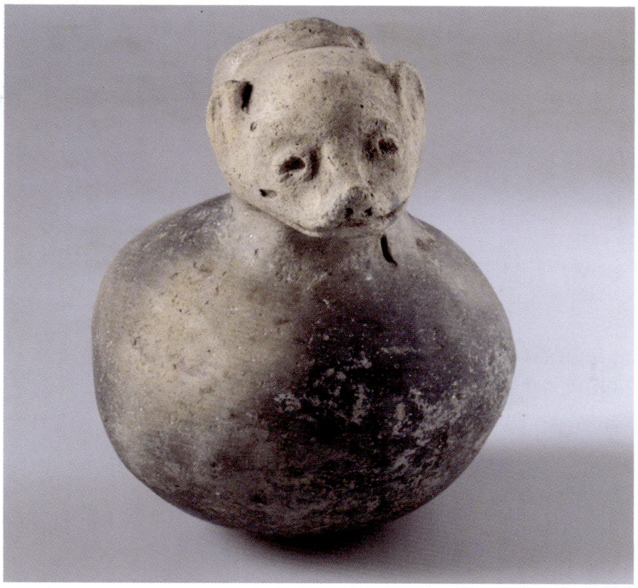

Figure 16. Opossum Effigy (OSHTL2006.004.02)
Ceramic; 11.0 x 8.8 cm
Fortune Mound, Cross County, Arkansas
Late Mississippi period, A.D. 1350–1600
Collected by Edwin Curtiss

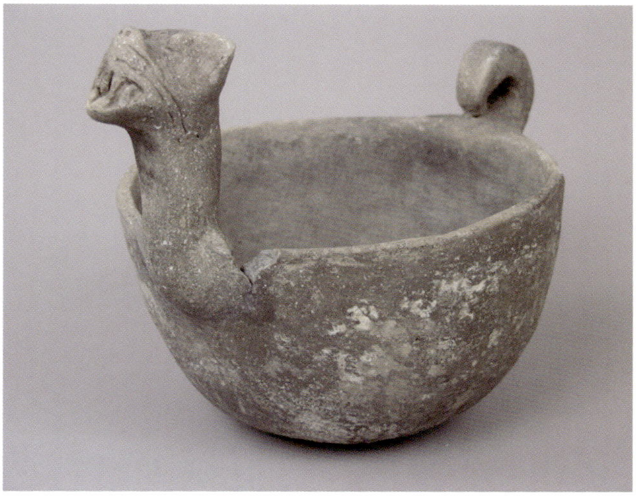

Figure 18. Cat Serpent Bowl (OSHTL2006.004.04)
Ceramic; 17.0 x 25.0 cm
Cross County, Arkansas
Late Mississippi period, A.D. 1350–1600
Collected by Edwin Curtiss
The "cat serpent" is one of the more common ceramic effigy forms found in northeast Arkansas.

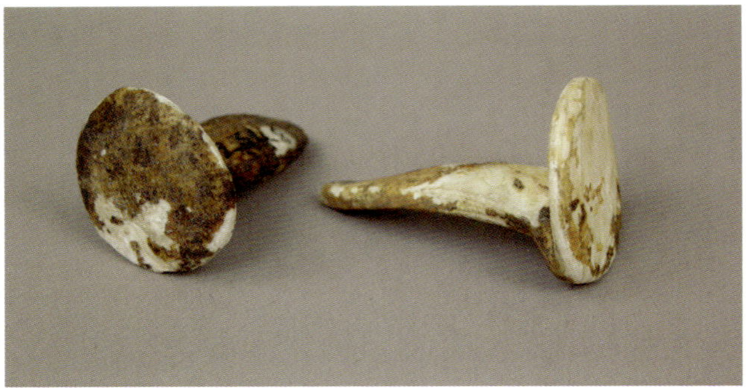

Figure 19. Ear Plugs (OSHTL2006.004.05)
Marine shell; 4.9 x 3.3 cm
Rose Mound, Cross County, Arkansas
Late Mississippi period, A.D. 1350–1600
Collected by Edwin Curtiss

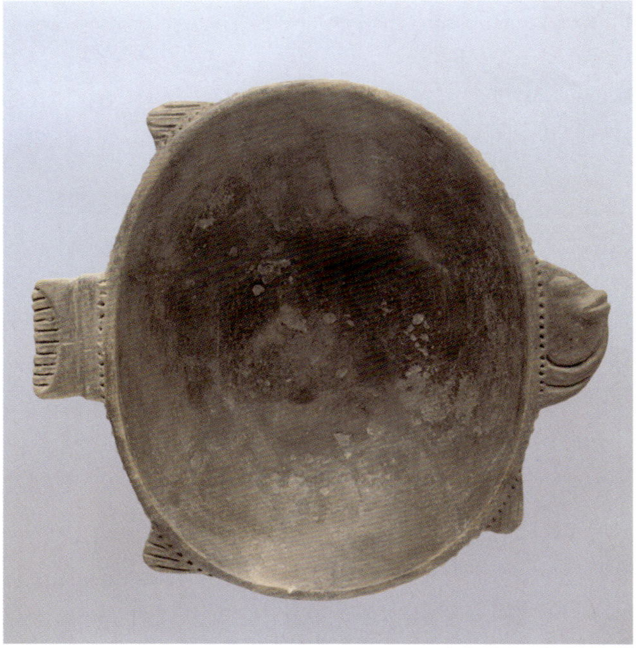

Figure 21. Catfish Effigy Bowl (OSHTL2006.004.07)
Ceramic; 9.0 x 30.7 cm
Fortune Mound, Cross County, Arkansas
Late Mississippi period, A.D. 1350–1600
Collected by Edwin Curtiss

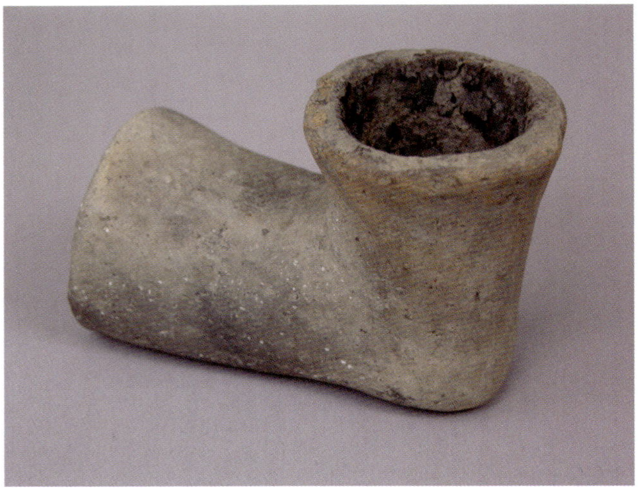

Figure 20. Smoking Pipe (OSHTL2006.004.06)
Ceramic; 6.0 x 8.9 cm
Togo site, Cross County, Arkansas
Late Mississippi period, A.D. 1350–1600
Collected by Edwin Curtiss

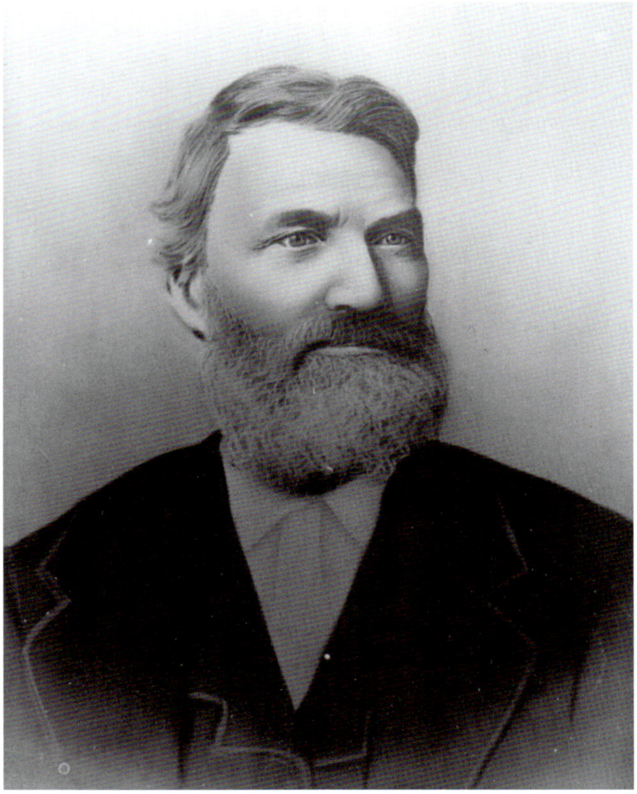

Figure 22. Wilfred Peter Hall

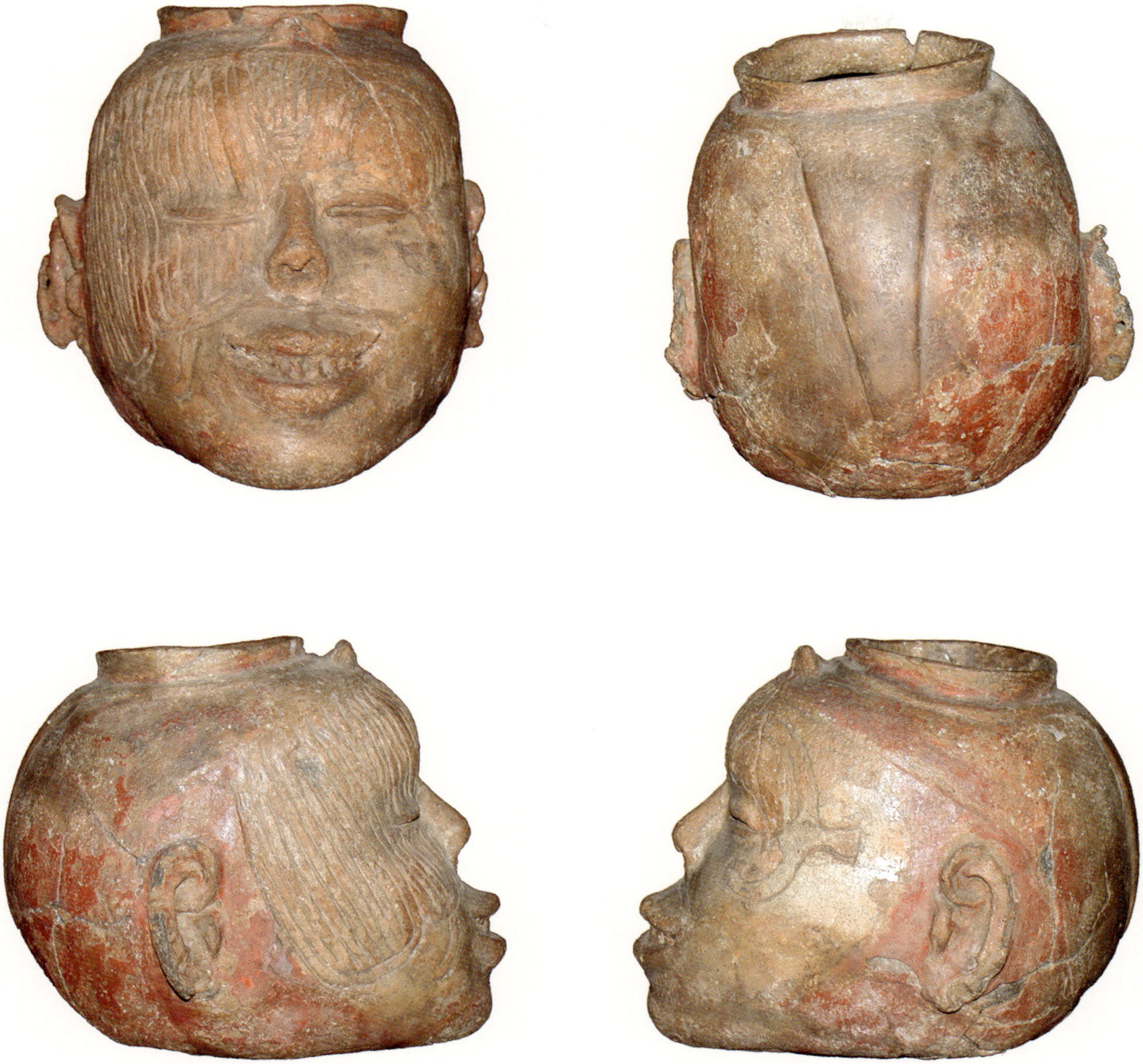

Figure 23a–d. Head pot; front, back, left side, right side
Ceramic
Big Eddy site, St. Francis County, Arkansas
Late Mississippi period, A.D. 1350–1600
Collected by W. P. Hall

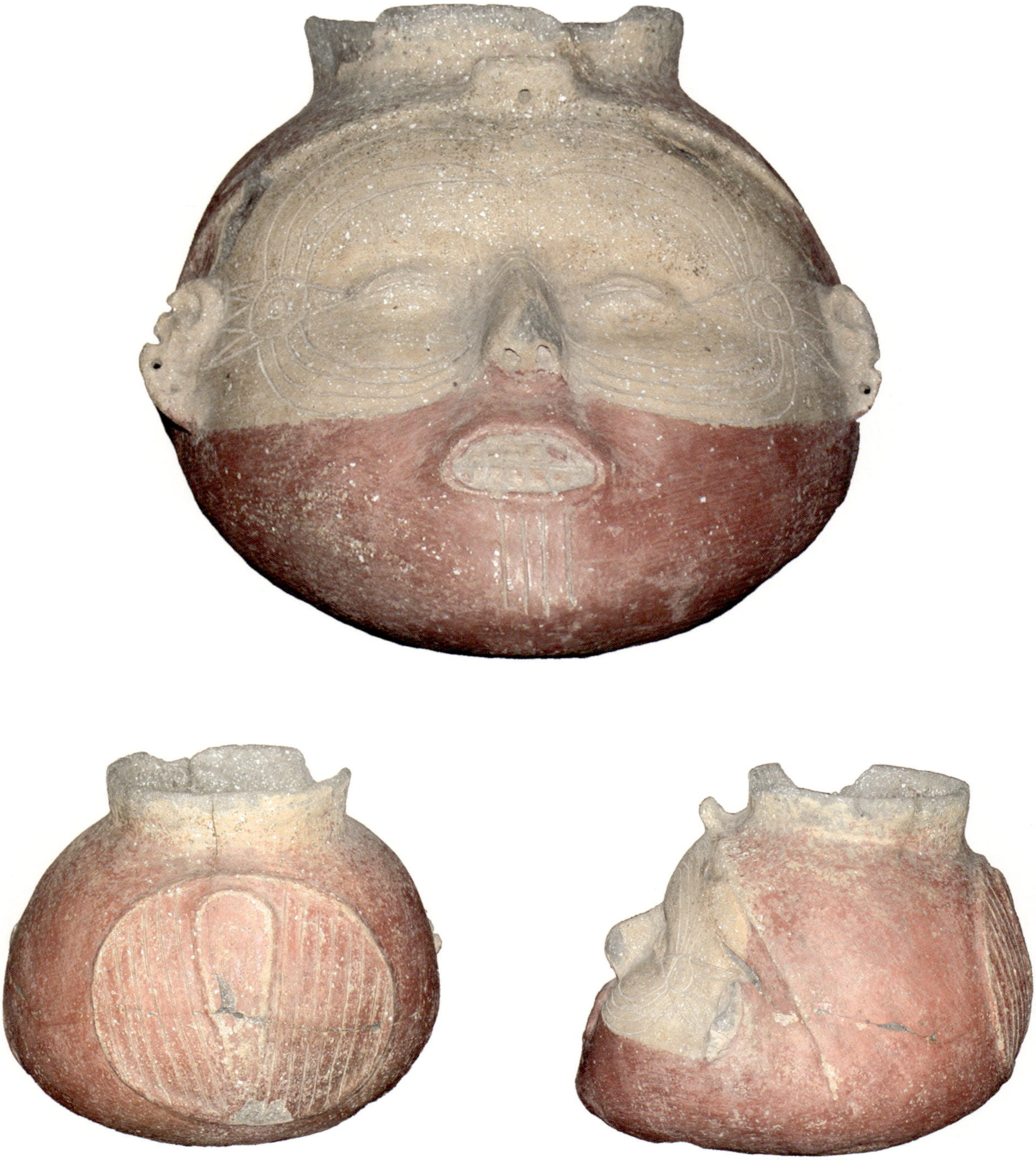

Figure 24a–c. Head pot; front, back, left side
Ceramic
Big Eddy site, St. Francis County, Arkansas
Late Mississippi period, A.D. 1350–1600
Collected by W. P. Hall

Neither recorded much information about their "finds"; in most cases all that is known about the various objects they collected is the site from which they came. After amassing a sufficient number of artifacts, Curtiss and Hall would wrap the objects in newspaper and pack them into barrels or crates for transport via train or steamboat to Cambridge or Davenport.

In contrast to Curtiss and Hall, who collected on behalf of museums, their contemporary, Chauncey Wales (more commonly, "C. W.") Riggs, excavated artifacts for his own enjoyment and personal gain. Unfortunately, little is known about Riggs. He began collecting prehistoric artifacts in 1876 and continued until roughly 1891. His collecting activities seem to have centered on Mississippi, Crittenden, Cross, and Poinsett Counties in Arkansas. During this time Riggs and his wife traveled in a 66-foot houseboat with a 50-foot cabin. At one time, Riggs's collection included roughly 3,000 pottery vessels. He also excavated in the American Southwest and purchased Native American blankets from that region.[5] Today, the Cincinnati Museum Center curates about 1,000 pottery vessels collected by Riggs, primarily from Arkansas.

Between July 1881 and June 1890, the Smithsonian Institution (Washington, D.C.) undertook an extraordinary program of archaeological excavations to definitively the question of who built the thousands of earthen enclosures and mounds encountered by settlers as they spread westward from the east coast. Under the direction of Dr. Cyrus Thomas, Smithsonian "field assistants" investigated over 2,000 mounds in 140 counties. Arkansas, particularly the alluvial lowlands, received considerable attention from the "Division of Mound Exploration," and much of the work was conducted by Dr. Edward Palmer between October 1881 and August 1884. Palmer visited a great many sites that are well known by archaeologists today, including Toltec Mounds, which is now an archaeological park.[6]

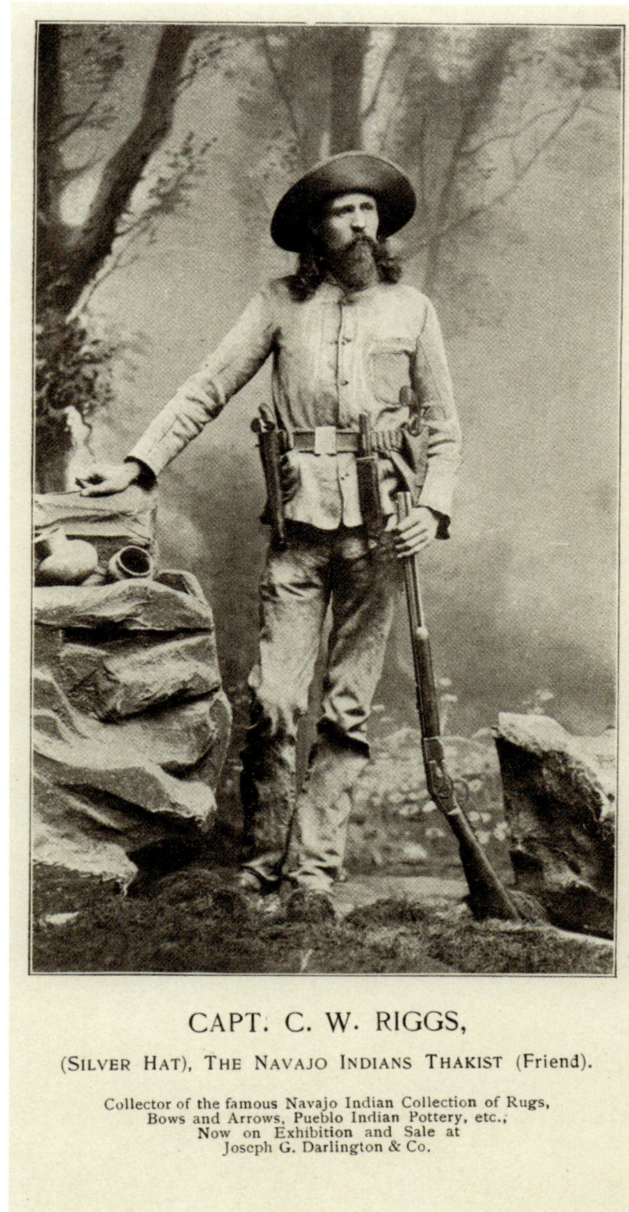

Figure 25. C.W. (Chauncey Wales) Riggs. Notice how Riggs attempts to emulate Buffalo Bill Cody in both appearance and pose. The pottery vessels are probably from northeast Arkansas.

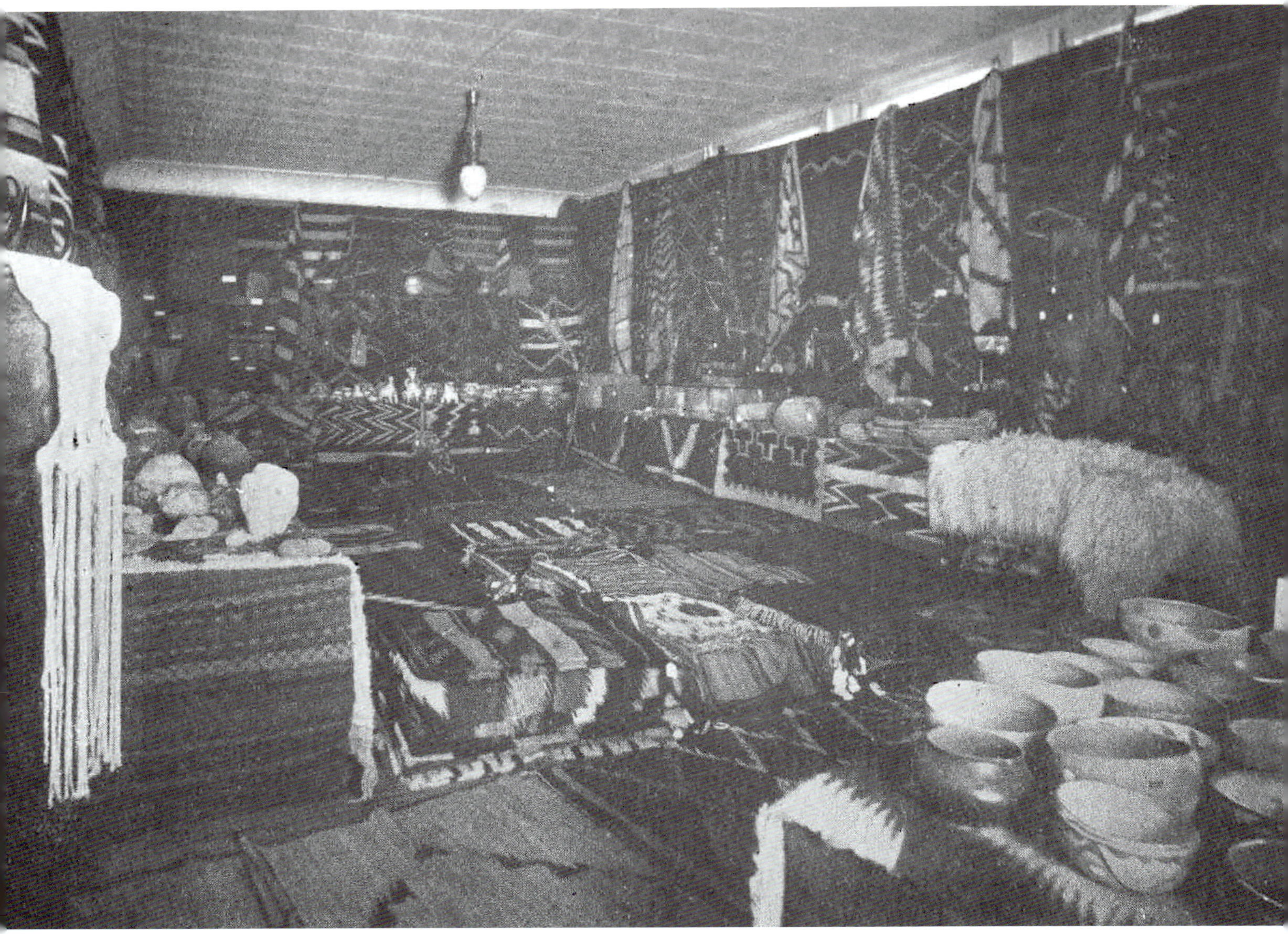

Figure 26. A portion of C.W. Riggs's collection featuring southwestern material, though a number of Mississippi Valley (probably northeast Arkansas) pottery vessels also are shown.

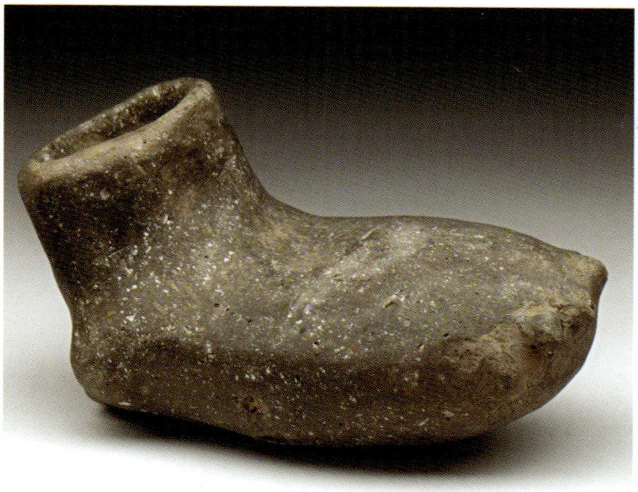

Figure 27. Foot Effigy Vessel (OSHTL2006.002.01)
Ceramic; 5.5 x 9.5 cm
Cross County, Arkansas
Late Mississippi period, A.D. 1350–1600
Collected by C. W. Riggs

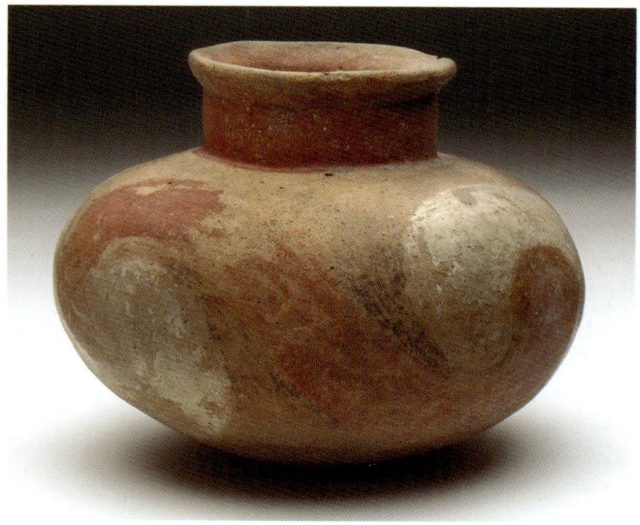

Figure 28. Bottle with Red and White Spiral Design (Nodena Red and White) (OSHTL2006.002.02)
Ceramic
Cross County, Arkansas
Late Mississippi period, A.D. 1350–1600
Collected by C. W. Riggs

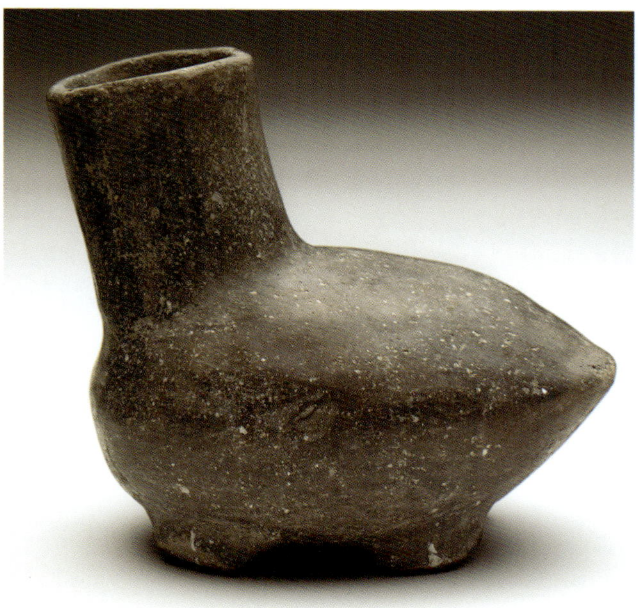

Figure 29. Waterfowl Effigy Bottle (OSHTL2006.002.03)
Ceramic
Cross County, Arkansas
Late Mississippi period, A.D. 1350–1600
Collected by C. W. Riggs

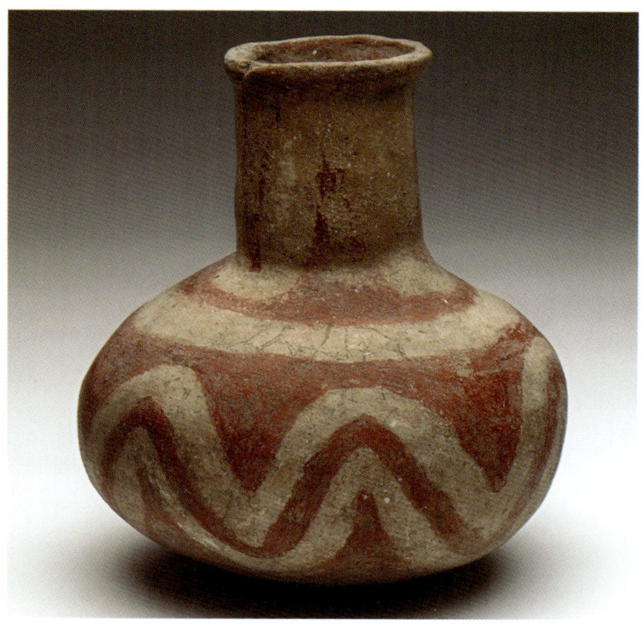

Figure 30. Red and White Bottle (Nodena Red and White) (OSHTL2006.002.04)
Ceramic
Cross County, Arkansas
Late Mississippi period, A.D. 1350–1600
Collected by C. W. Riggs

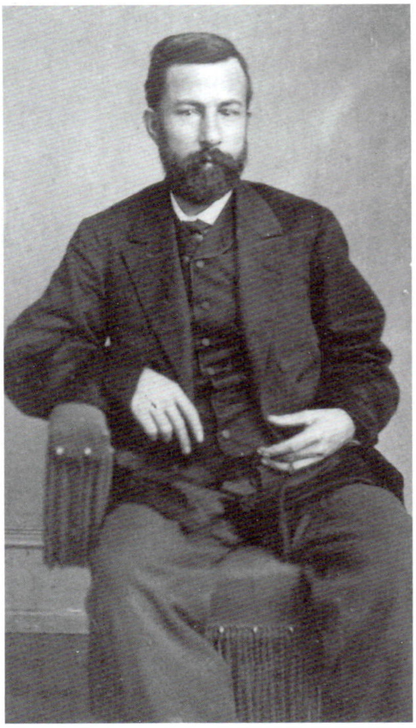

Figure 31. Edward Palmer, probably late 1867.

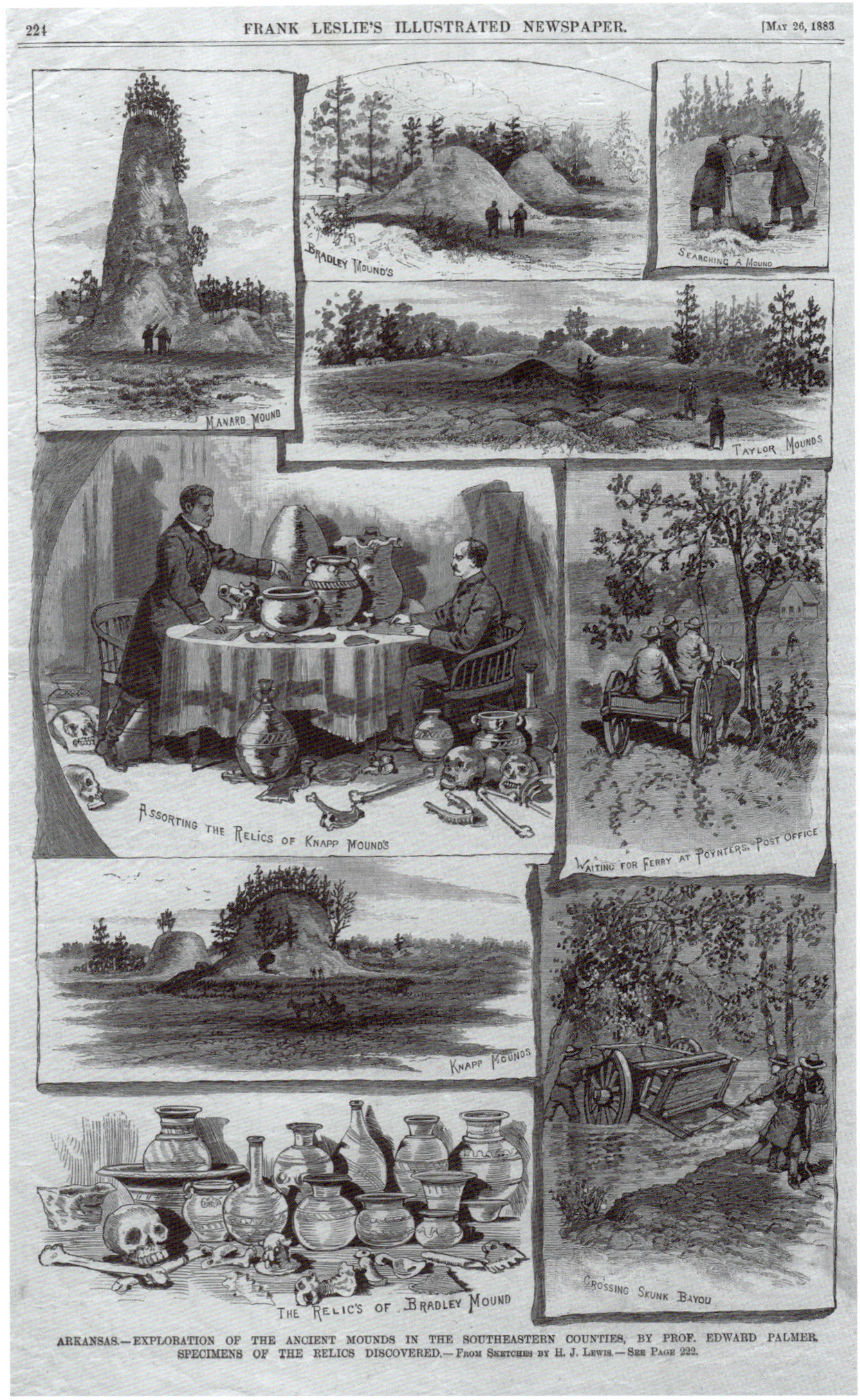

Figure 32. Stylized version of engraving by H. J. Lewis showing some of the work done by Edward Palmer in eastern Arkansas; Lewis's original engraving has been lost. As discussed by Jeter (1990), the *Leslie's* versions of Lewis's engravings often are sensationalized and inaccurate with regard to mounds and artifacts; in this case, the depictions of Lewis and Palmer do not closely resemble caricatures by Lewis himself.

During the early 1900s, Clarence Bloomfield Moore, of the Philadelphia Academy of Science, excavated over a thousand human burials (many with associated pottery vessels) at late-prehistoric sites in northeast and southern Arkansas, including 349 at the Pecan Point site (Mississippi County) alone.[7] Moore was a wealthy resident of Philadelphia who attended Harvard University. For 37 years, beginning in 1891, Moore plied the major waterways of the Southeast in his stern-wheeler, the *Gopher of Philadelphia*. In contrast to earlier excavators in Arkansas (and elsewhere), Moore took notes about individual burials and promptly published his findings in lavishly illustrated, folio-size volumes of the *Journal of the Academy of Natural Sciences of Philadelphia*. He regularly consulted with experts in such fields as human osteology, geology, Native American iconography, and zoology. Moore was basically a Victorian-era natural scientist, and he clearly viewed himself and his work as much better than the collectors that preceded him.[8] His fieldnotes and publications, though very wanting by modern standards, remain useful to this day.

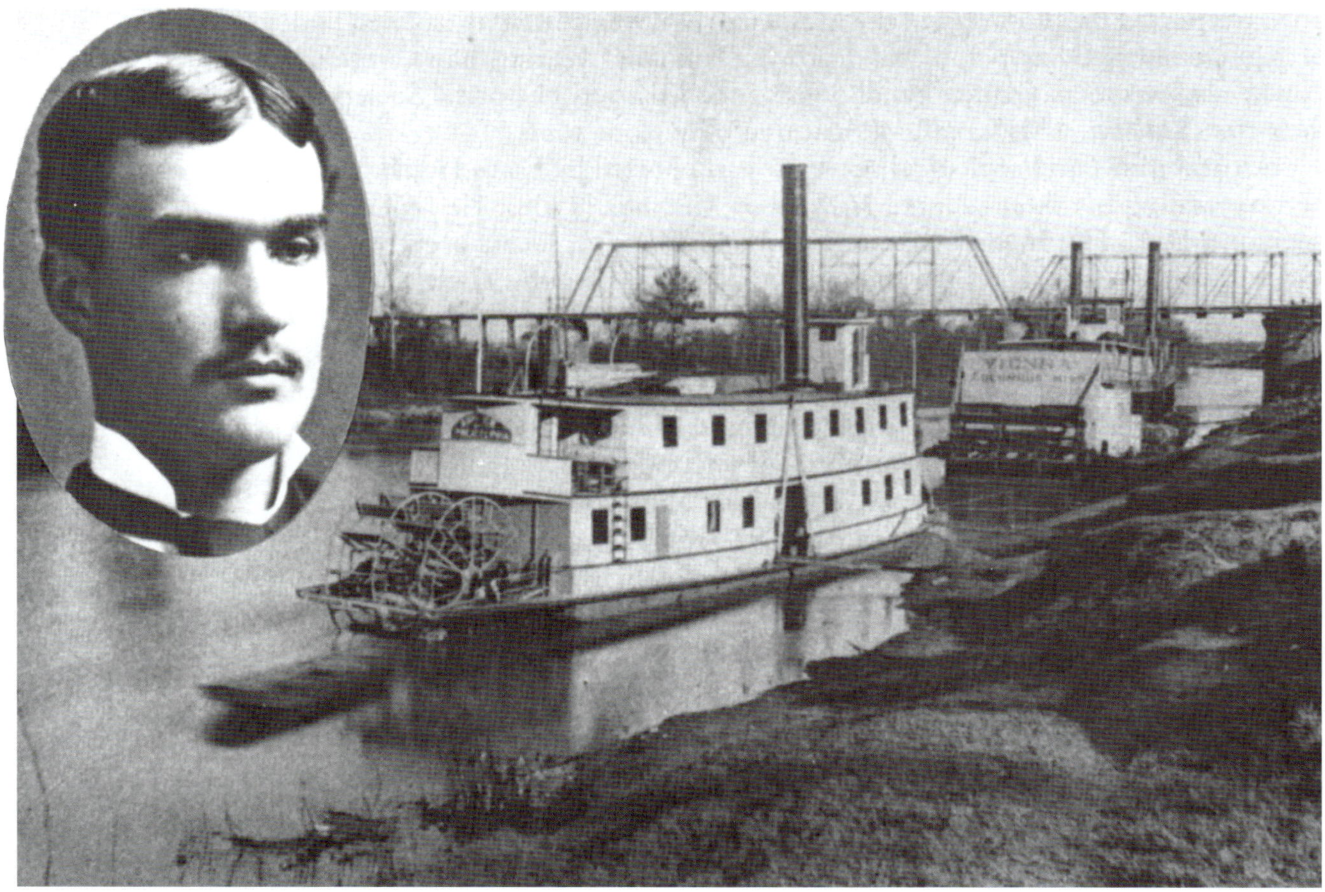

Figure 33. C. B. (Clarence Bloomfield) Moore and his steamboat.

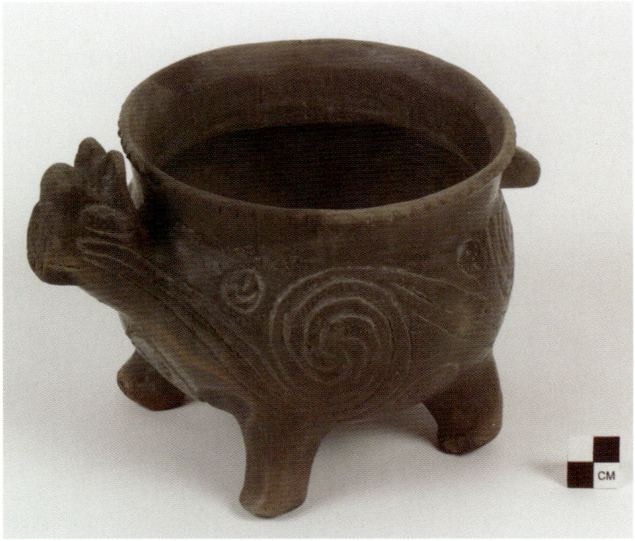

Figure 34. Feline Effigy Jar with Incised Spirals (OSHTL2006.008.31)
Ceramic; 6.2 x 11.0 cm
Rose Mound, Cross County, Arkansas
Late Mississippi period, A.D. 1350–1600

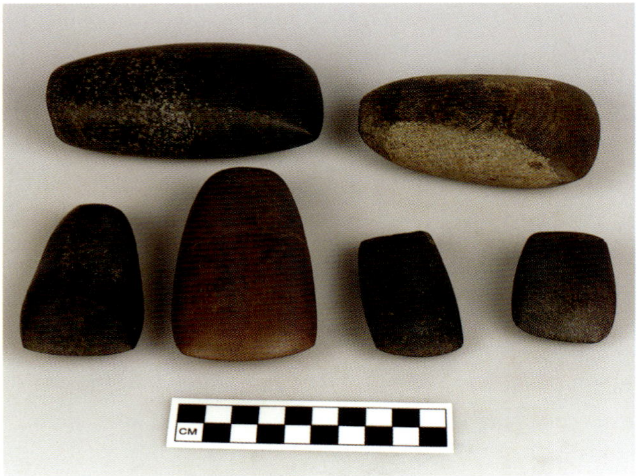

Figure 35. Celts (OSHTL2006.008.32)
Unidentified stone; various sizes
Rose Mound, Cross County, Arkansas
Late Mississippi period, A.D. 1350–1600
Collected by C. B. Moore

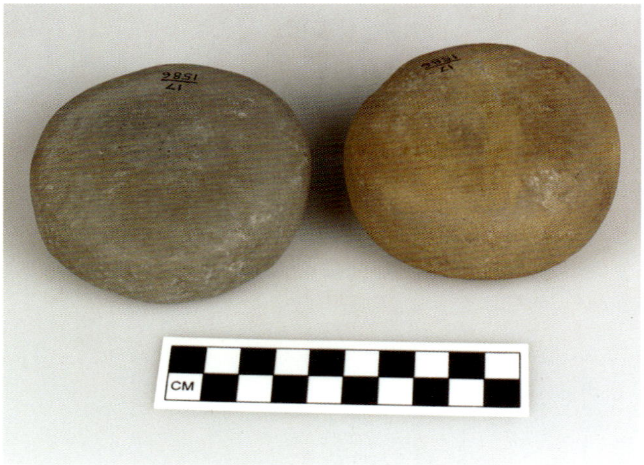

Figure 36. Discoidals (OSHTL2006.008.33)
Unidentified stone; diameter, apx. 8.0 cm
Rose Mound, Cross County, Arkansas
Late Mississippi period, A.D. 1350–1600
Collected by C. B. Moore

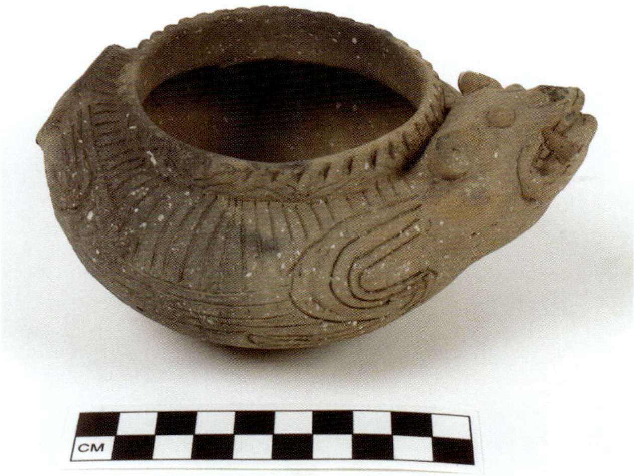

Figure 37. Zoomorphic Effigy Jar with Incising (OSHTL2006.008.37)
Ceramic; 6.4 x 14.0 cm
Rose Mound, Cross County, Arkansas
Late Mississippi period, A.D. 1350–1600
Collected by C. B. Moore
Ceramic portrayals of the same creature are shown in Figures 72 and 95.

After C. B. Moore's expedition up the Ouachita River 1908, Senator Roy Rasco prepared a bill entitled "An act to prohibit non-residents from entering the state for the purpose of acquiring the antiquities of the state."[9] It is not clear if Rasco actually introduced this bill to the Arkansas Senate, and there is no indication that Sam Dellinger knew Rasco and was aware of the proposed bill. Nonetheless, the proposed bill suggests that as early as 1909 there was some resentment among prominent Arkansans about the removal of antiquities. In fact, such sentiment was by no means limited to Arkansas. For instance, in 1915 Alabama passed a State Antiquities Law that made it unlawful for nonresidents to excavate an archaeological site or to take any archaeological objects out of the state.[10]

In 1916 and 1917, Mark R. Harrington, an archaeologist with the Heye Foundation Museum of the American Indian in New York City, investigated a number of late-prehistoric Caddo sites in southwest Arkansas. In the early 1920s, Harrington returned to Arkansas, excavating in several Ozark bluff shelters and obtaining a number of pottery vessels from the Carden Bottom area in the Arkansas River valley.[11]

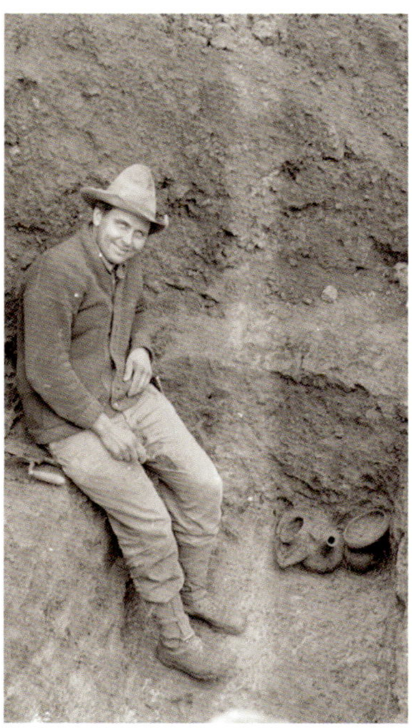

Figure 38. Mark R. Harrington at a mound near Ozan, Hempstead County, Arkansas, in 1916.

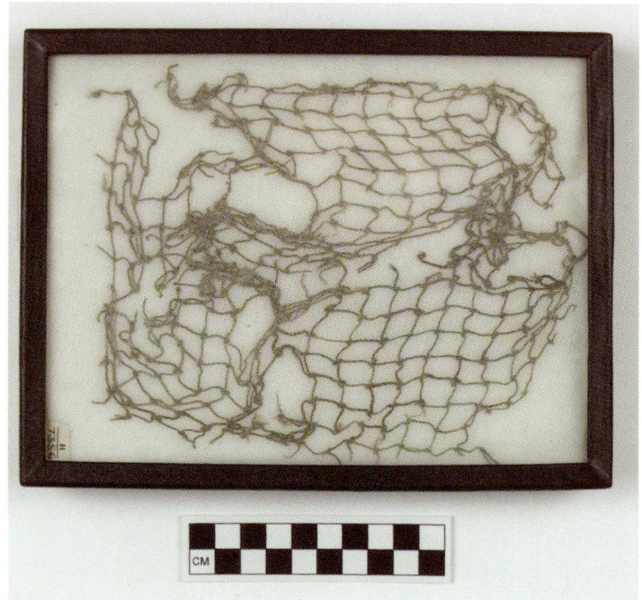

Figure 39. Net (OSHTL2006.008.01)
Vegetal fiber; 19.5 x 16.0 cm
Allred Bluff, Benton County, Arkansas
Probably Woodland period, 200 B.C.–A.D. 900

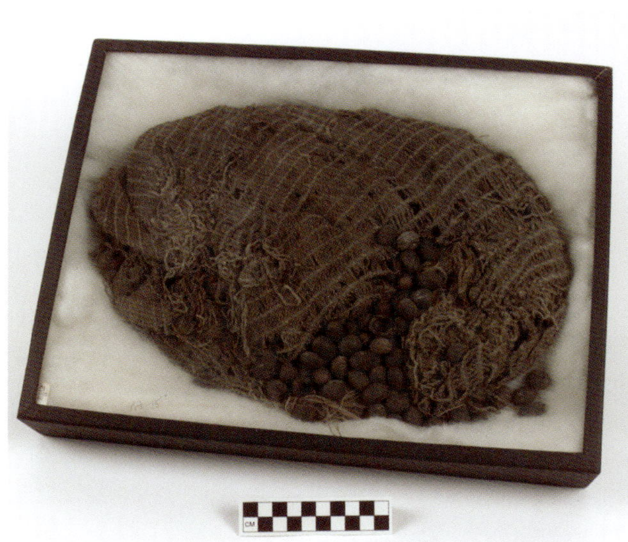

Figure 40. Twined Fabric Bag Containing Acorns (OSHTL2006.008.02)
Vegetal fiber; 32.5 x 20.0 cm
Bushwhack Shelter, Benton County, Arkansas
Probably Woodland or Mississippi period, 200 B.C.–A.D. 1600

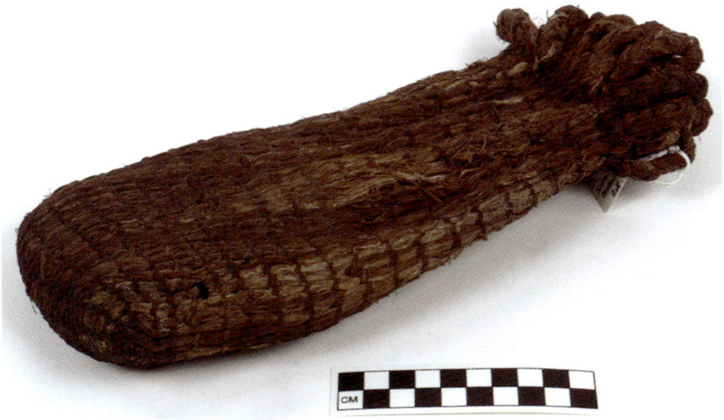

Figure 41. Twined Fiber Bag (OSHTL2006.008.03)
Vegetal fiber; 26.0 x 8.0 cm
Judian Bluff, Benton County, Arkansas
Probably Woodland or Mississippi period, 200 B.C.–A.D. 1600

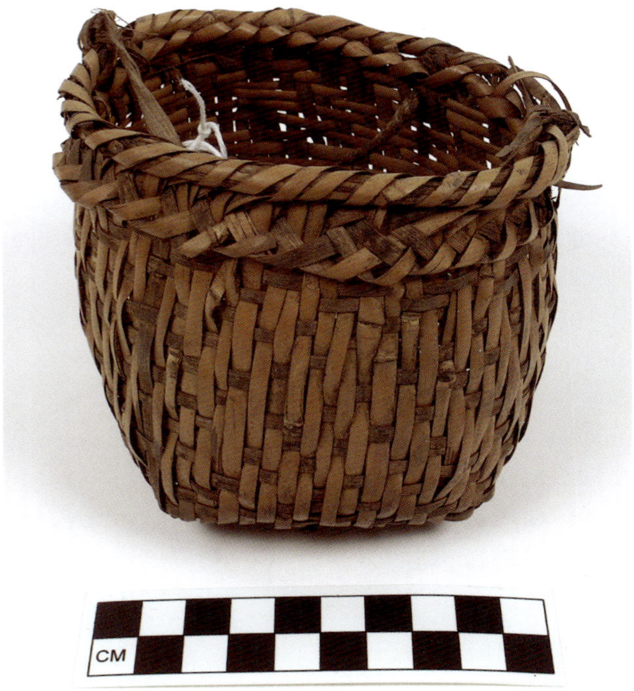

Figure 42. Small Plain Weave Basket (OSHTL2006.008.04)
Cane; 11.5 x 11.5 cm
Judian Bluff, Benton County, Arkansas
Probably Woodland or Mississippi period, 200 B.C.–A.D. 1600

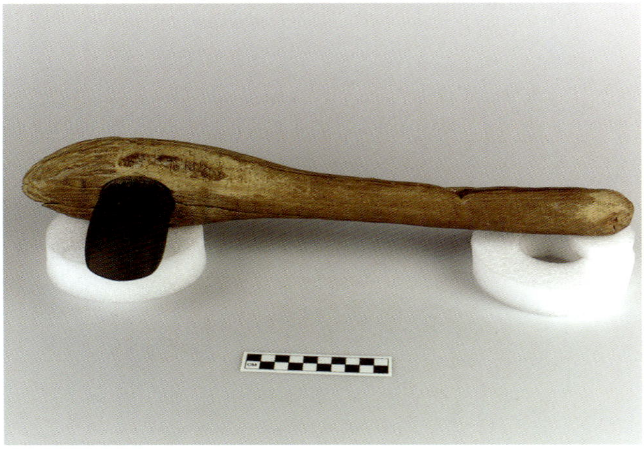

Figure 43. Hafted Celt (OSHTL2006.008.05)
Unidentified ground stone and wood; 42.2 x 11.0 cm
Buffalo River near Yellville, Marion County, Arkansas
Age unknown

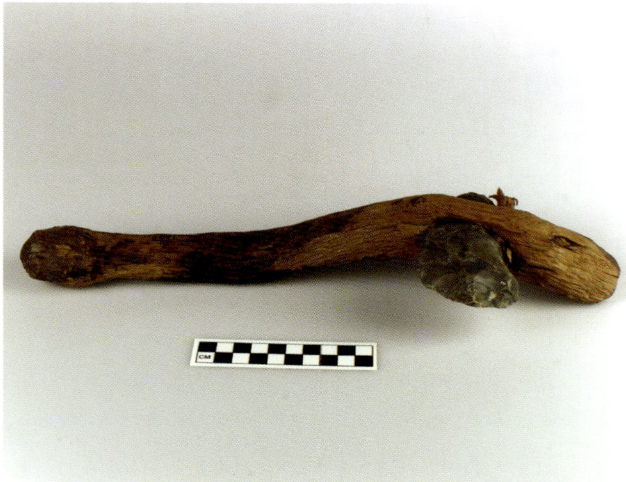

Figure 44. Hafted Axe (OSHTL2006.008.06)
Unidentified chipped stone and wood; 31.4 x 6.5 cm
Allred Bluff, Benton County, Arkansas
Probably Woodland or Mississippi period, 200 B.C.–A.D. 1600

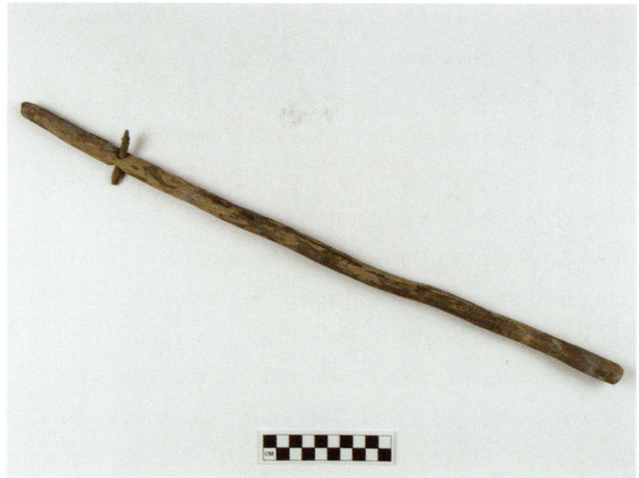

Figure 45. Atlatl (Throwing Stick) (OSHTL2006.008.07)
Unidentified wood; 49.3 x 3.0 cm
Allred Bluff, Benton County, Arkansas
Probably Woodland period, 200 B.C.–A.D. 1600

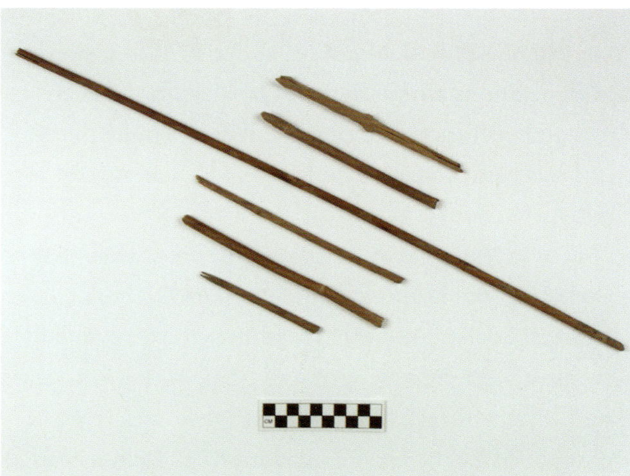

Figure 46. Arrow Shafts (OSHTL2006.008.14)
Unidentified wood; 11 to 57 cm long
Bushwhack Shelter, Benton County, Arkansas
Late Woodland or Mississippi period, A.D. 700–1600

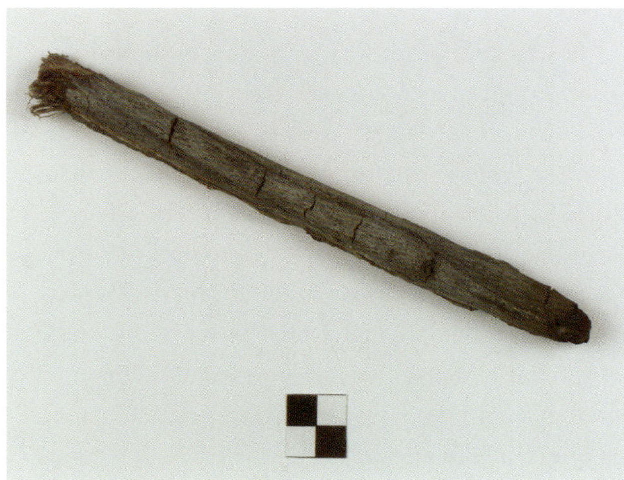

Figure 47. Stick (OSHTL2006.008.15)
Unidentified wood; 19.0 x 1.5 cm
Bushwhack Shelter, Benton County, Arkansas
Age unknown

There was nothing unethical or underhanded about any of the excavations, and at the time they were conducted, there was no state-sponsored archaeology program in Arkansas. In fact, much of the material collected by the eastern institutions might never have been available for study and to the public if not for these early excavations. Arkansas clearly was, however, one of the favorite destinations for archaeological projects conducted by the well-established museums in the East, and this fact clearly was not lost on Dellinger.

Particularly galling to Dellinger, who was working furiously to develop an archaeological research program at the University of Arkansas Museum, were the 1926 excavations by the Oklahoma Historical Society at several caves and/or bluff shelters in Boone County.[12] In fairness, it should be noted that the historical society might have been unaware of Dellinger and his new-found interest in archaeology, though a representative could have contacted the university as a matter of courtesy.

In 1926, Dellinger was catapulted to some degree of national prominence for his views regarding Arkansas's archaeological heritage when the prestigious *Christian Science Monitor* published a moderately long article based on an interview with him. The article noted that Dellinger was "making an effort to keep Arkansas' historic antiques within the State at a place where they can be studied. Dr. Dellinger is now endeavoring to raise funds to buy a valuable collection of antiques from J. W. Bailey of Atkins, Ark. He is appealing principally to alumni of the University of Arkansas who are interested in archeology to contribute money toward making the purchase possible." And, "As a further effort to preserve the historic treasures of the State, Dr. Dellinger is considering methods of preventing the lamentable effects of excavating by inexperienced relic seekers. Careless digging into historic mounds is destroying many valuable archeological specimens of the State, he says." Quoting Dellinger, "The State of Arkansas is rich in archeological material, but many owners of relics value their findings as curios and prefer to keep them rather than let them be taken to the university museum or some other suitable place for valuable study. We wish to preserve as many antiques [*sic;* antiquities] as possible in the university museum, where they will not be retained solely for exhibition purposes, but can be used for studying prehistoric inhabitants."[13]

Dellinger received some high-profile support for his efforts to preserve Arkansas's archaeological heritage within the state from the flamboyant and controversial adventurer/archaeologist Count Byron Khun de Prorok, who presented public lectures at the University of Arkansas in 1926 and 1929. Dellinger almost certainly met de Prorok at the time of his first visit to Fayetteville because when he returned in 1929, the Count donated "about 100 objects," "which is almost priceless as it contains specimens of the Chellean, Mousterian, Solutrean and Magdalean [*sic*] periods."[14] Moreover, de Prorok told the local press that "Arkansas has the most interesting and promising pre-historic mounds in America. She should take steps in her wealth of previous civilizations within her own borders for her students and visitors for all time."[15] It seems quite likely that Dellinger persuaded de Prorok to speak out on his (Dellinger's) behalf.

In a 1930 article in *Arkansas Alumnus,* Dellinger railed about the Peabody Museum, the Oklahoma Historical Society, and other institutions excavating in Arkansas and removing artifacts, going so far as to state that ". . . the [Ozark bluff] shelters we are studying were robbed by the Heye Foundation."[16] Dellinger used the occasion to ask university alumni for assistance in getting permission to excavate on private land and also to donate objects to the museum.

In the early 1930s, Dellinger had further and perhaps more justified cause for annoyance when the Alabama Museum of Natural History (AMNH) conducted excavations at several late prehistoric sites in northeast Arkansas in the early 1930s. These included the well-known Upper and Middle Nodena sites, at which the University of Arkansas Museum also excavated.[17] The museum's correspondence files contain some rather pointed letters between Dellinger, Walter B. Jones (director, AMNH), and Dellinger's archaeological mentor, Carl Guthe (director of the Museum of Anthropology, University of Michigan, and head of the Committee on State Archaeological Surveys). By this time, Dellinger had begun an active excavation program in the same region, and this was well known to Walter Jones. Moreover, the Alabama Museum of Natural History was involved concurrently in proprietary excavations at the magnificent Moundville archaeological site near Tuscaloosa. After discussions that lasted several years, Guthe came to sympathize with Dellinger about the Alabama excavations.[18] In all, the AMNH field crews excavated over 1,000 human burials and a large number of associated funerary objects in northeast Arkansas.

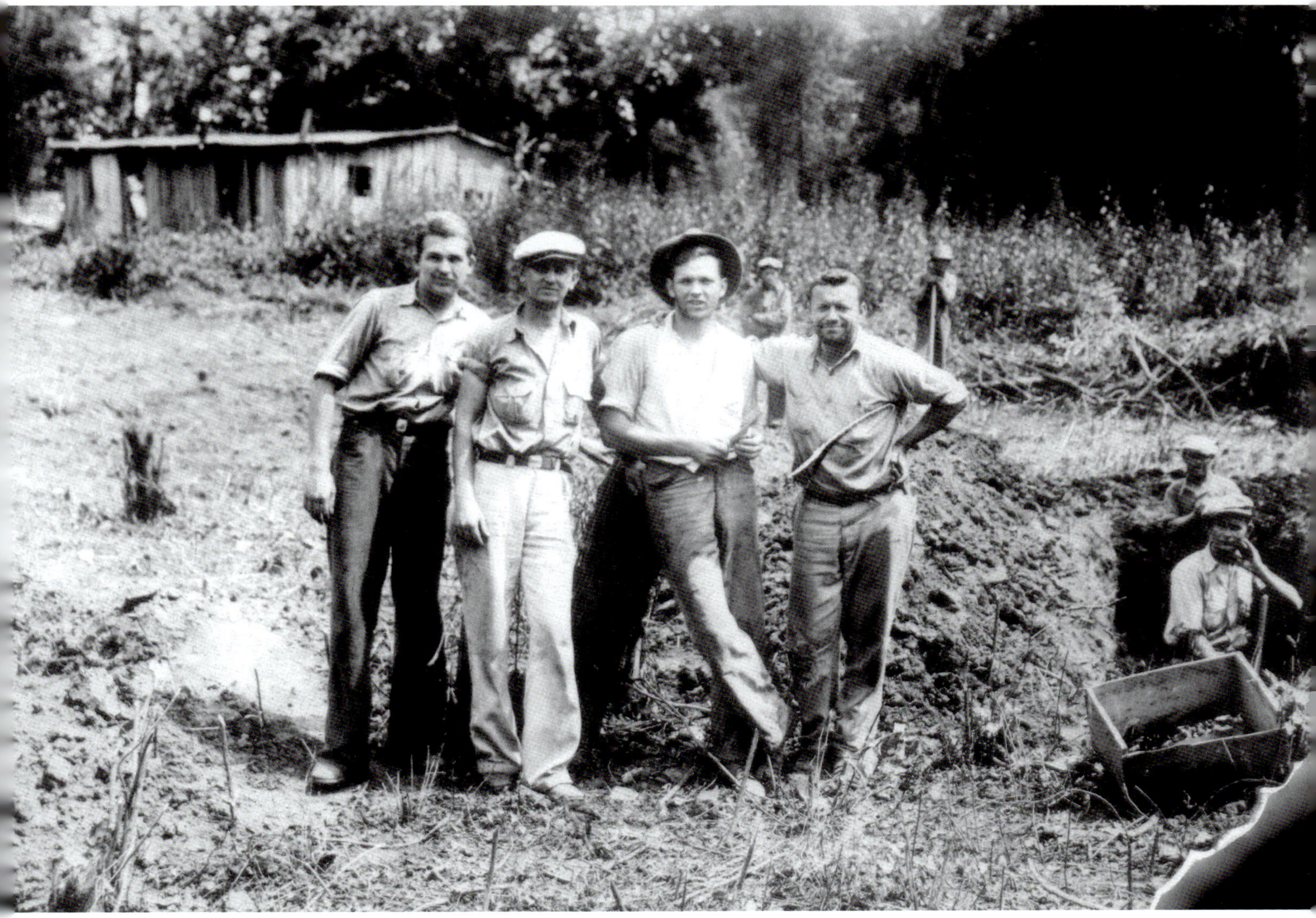

Figure 48. *Left to right:* John Dodd, David DeJarnette, Jimmy Hays, and Walter B. Jones during the Alabama Museum of Natural History excavations at Walnut Mound (Floodway), Mississippi County, Arkansas, August 25, 1931.

Figure 49. Alabama Museum of Natural History excavations at Upper Nodena, 1932.

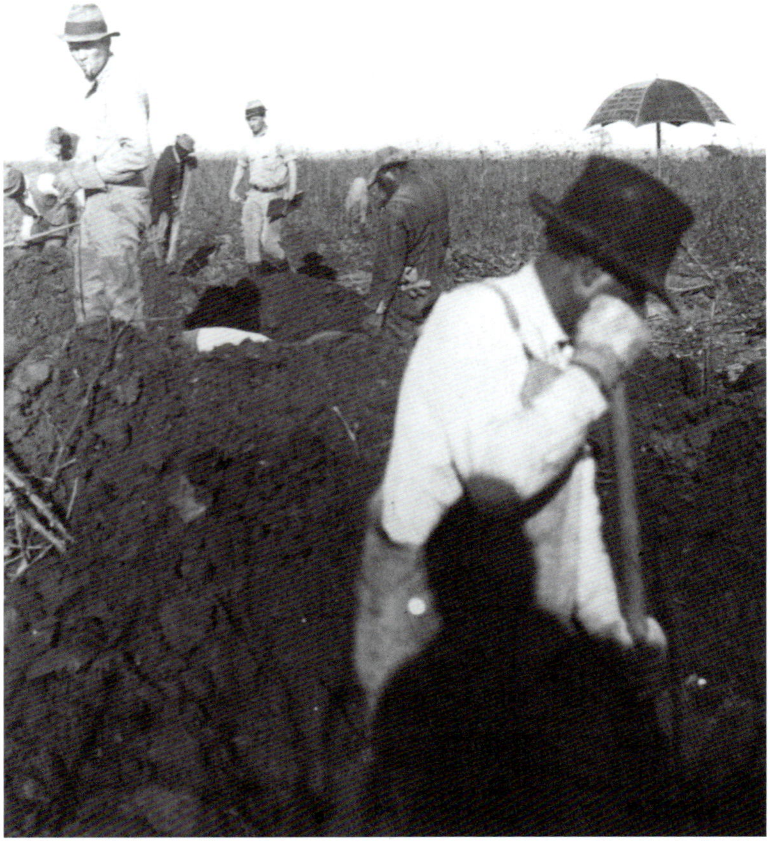

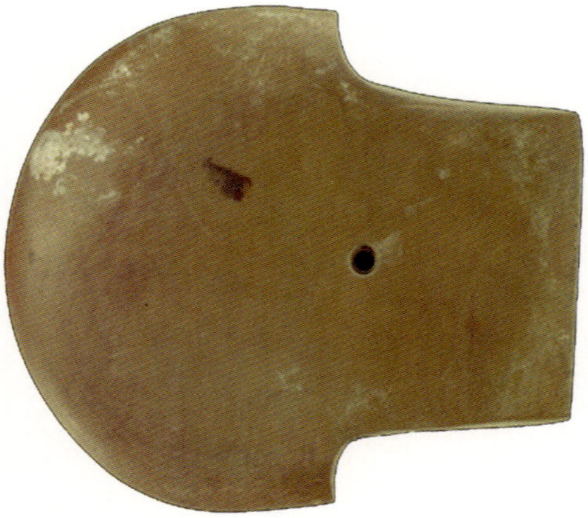

Figure 50. Spatulate Celt (OSHTL2006.006.01)
Concretionary siderite; 14.0 x 12.2 cm
Upper Nodena, Mississippi County, Arkansas
Late Mississippi period, A.D. 1350–1600

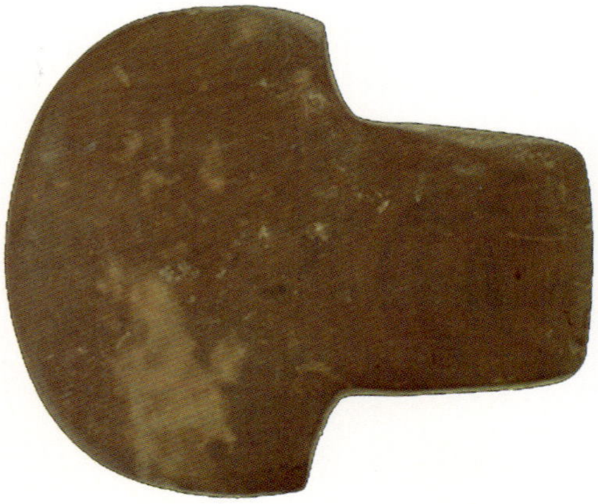

Figure 51. Spatulate Celt (OSHTL2006.006.02)
Concretionary siderite; 14.5 x 12.0 cm
Upper Nodena, Mississippi County, Arkansas
Late Mississippi period, A.D. 1350–1600

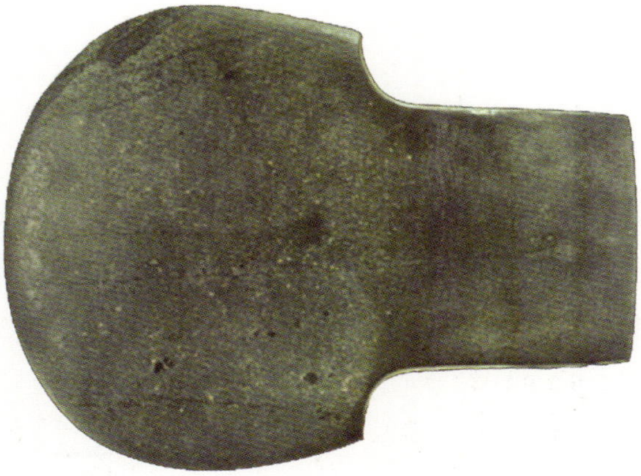

Figure 52. Spatulate Celt (OSHTL2006.006.03)
Greenstone (Hillabee metabasite); 17.5 x 12.8 cm
Upper Nodena, Mississippi County, Arkansas
Late Mississippi period, A.D. 1350–1600
Hillabee metabasite outcrops in the Hatchet Creek valley in eastern-central Alabama. This spatulate celt probably was fashioned in Alabama, perhaps at Moundville.

Figure 53. Disk Pipe with Incised Figure (OSHTL2006.006.04)
Catlinite; 9.8 x 6.2 cm
Upper Nodena, Mississippi County, Arkansas
Late Mississippi period, A.D. 1350–1600

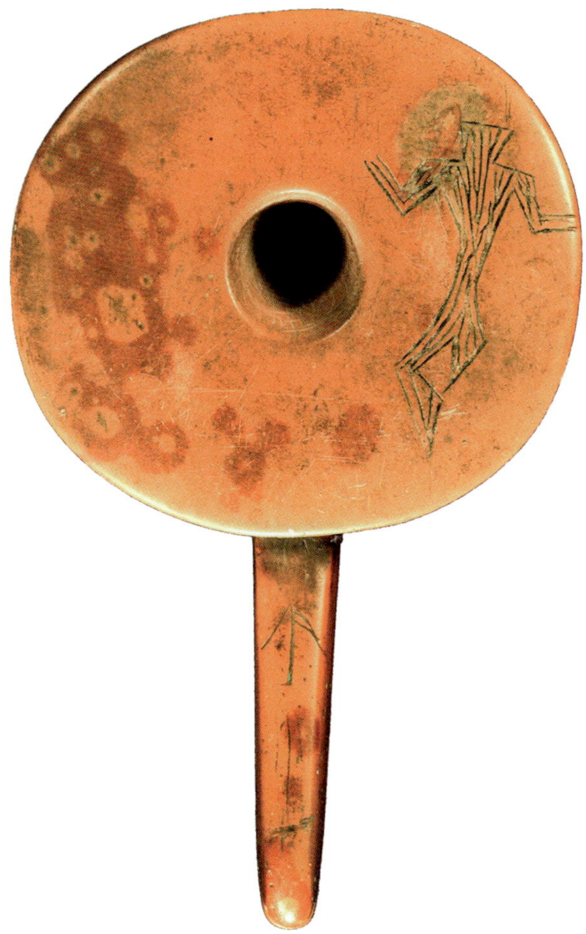

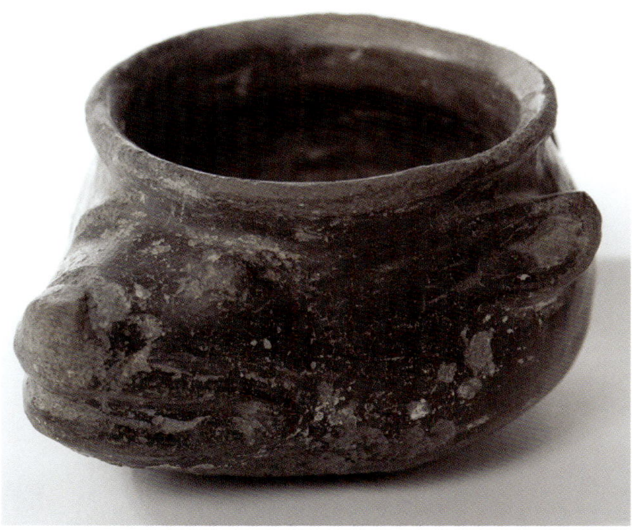

Figure 54. Bear(?) Effigy Jar (OSHTL2006.006.05)
Ceramic; 14.0 x 12.4 cm
Upper Nodena, Mississippi County, Arkansas
Late Mississippi period, A.D. 1350–1600

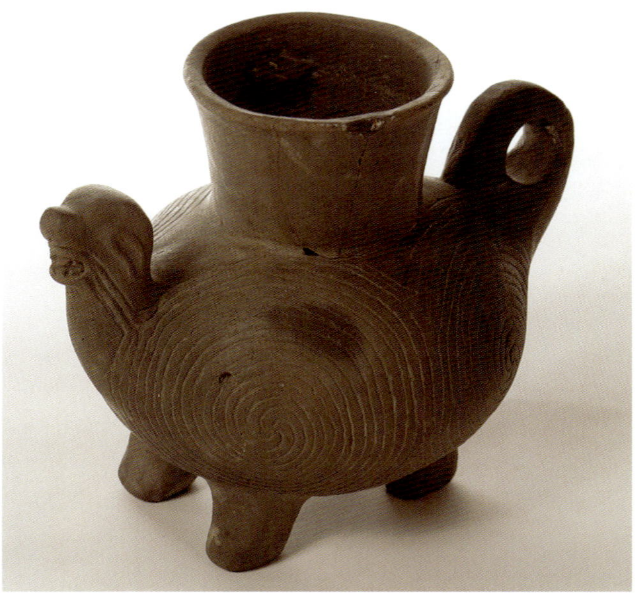

Figure 55. Cat Serpent Bottle with Legs (OSHTL2006.006.06)
Ceramic; 21.6 x 14.3 cm
Upper Nodena, Mississippi County, Arkansas
Late Mississippi period, A.D. 1350–1600

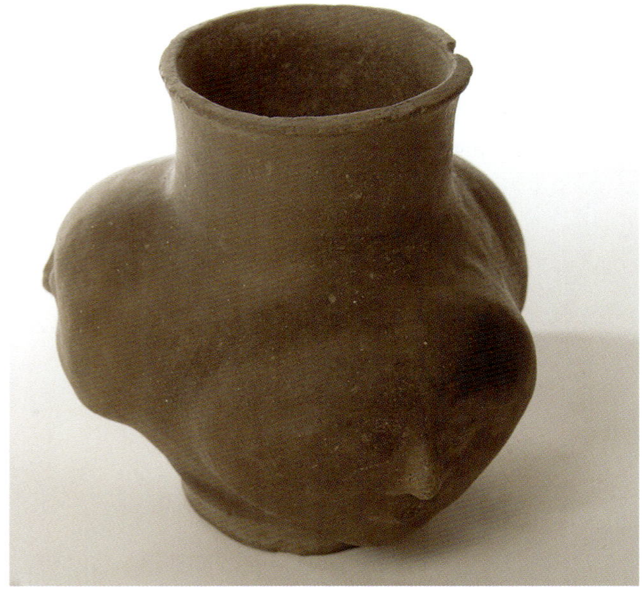

Figure 56. Triune Bottle (OSHTL2006.006.07)
Ceramic; 16.8 x 15.9 cm
Upper Nodena, Mississippi County, Arkansas
Late Mississippi period, A.D. 1350–1600
Several bottles with three human faces (hence the term "triune," which typically refers to a being with three aspects) have been reported from northeast Arkansas and southeast Missouri.

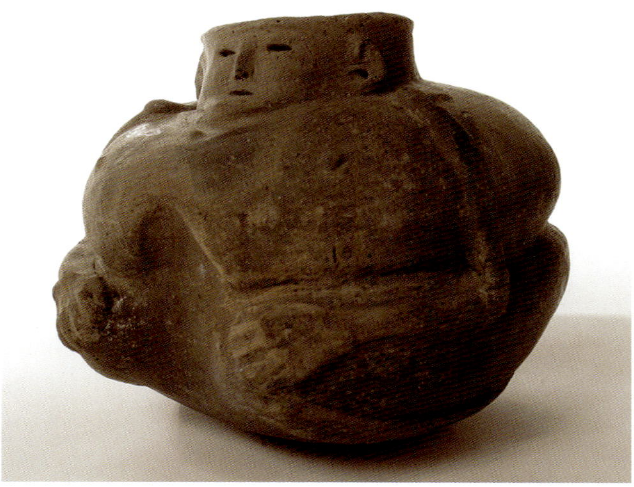

Figure 57. Kneeling Human Effigy Bottle (OSHTL2006.006.08)
Ceramic; 15.2 x 20.3 cm
Middle Nodena, Mississippi County, Arkansas
Late Mississippi period, A.D. 1350–1600

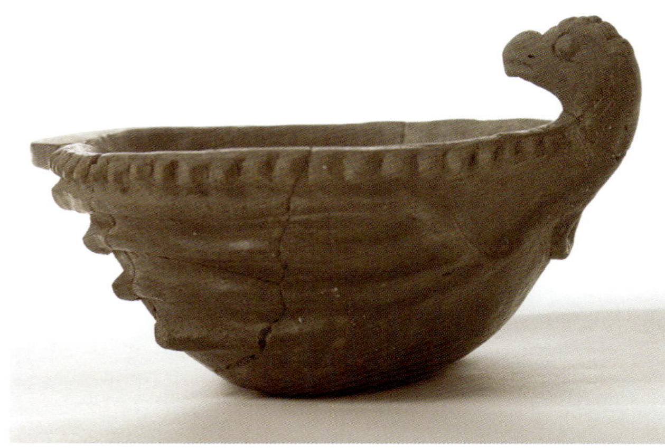

Figure 58. Bird Effigy Bowl (OSHTL2006.006.09)
Ceramic; 12.7 x 20.3 cm
Middle Nodena County, Arkansas
Late Mississippi period, A.D. 1350–1600

Dellinger also was sharply critical of excavations and collections by untrained individuals, as illustrated in a 1933 article:

> "Remaining prehistoric sites in Arkansas that will assist in interpreting past civilizations should be explored by trained archaeologists, according to Prof. S.C. Dellinger, curator of the University museum in a plea to Arkansans to discontinue the practice of removing and selling archaeological specimens to dealers in these objects. The tangible remains of past civilizations have no value in themselves.
>
> "Individual collections are valueless," said Prof. Dellinger. "The owners of two of the largest private collections are now trying to dispose of their wares, which cost them thousands of dollars to collect. The collection of artifacts destroyed volumes of our richest pre-history, yet these treasures of our ancient races are now worthless from a scientific and historical viewpoint."
>
> Prof. Dellinger suggests to those wanting to make a collection of some sort to collect postage stamps or old coins. These have all the data stamped on them so their value cannot be destroyed.
>
> One cannot over-estimate the importance of leaving the few remaining Indian sites in Arkansas for competent hands to explore. This point was forcibly brought out at the Plains Conference of Archaeology at Lincoln, Nebraska, last September, at which I was informed that my work here in Arkansas would indicate that the roaming plains tribes were once peaceful agriculturalists in this region. Later they migrated into the least favorable agricultural areas of the plains and gave up their agricultural life, becoming nomads, and depending for their food on the buffalo rather than corn crops. The statement made at the Southern Conference on Pre-history in Birmingham, Alabama, in December that the archaeology of Arkansas was the very keystone for the whole Mississippi region, because the evidence pointed to this area as the most probable for the highest culture on the North American continent.[19]

Among many archaeologists, Dellinger is perhaps best remembered as an individual who opposed what is arguably the most famous archaeological project ever conducted in eastern North America.[20] This was the archaeological survey of the lower Mississippi alluvial valley conducted during the 1940s by Philip Phillips (Harvard University), James B. Griffin (University of Michigan), and James A. Ford (Louisiana State University) with funding from the National Park Service. The survey was an extraordinarily ambitious attempt to record and make collections at archaeological sites throughout the lower Mississippi River valley, from the confluence of the Ohio River to the Gulf of Mexico, and the resulting publication is one of the true classics of American archaeology.[21] The artifact collections almost exclusively were obtained from the ground surface; the few excavations were very limited in extent.

Of course, the researchers wanted and needed to include eastern Arkansas as part of the area to be surveyed. Dellinger objected to their work, stating in a letter to the acting secretary of the Smithsonian Institution that: "On February 22, I wrote to [James] Ford, in Louisiana, and protested his coming. My reason being the fact that they could skim over in a hasty survey and take the cream off what I had been doing for a number of years."[22] This letter (and perhaps others) led Phillips and his colleagues to remark: "We have been accused of coming in as outsiders and 'skimming the cream' off the archaeology of the region. The metaphor is imprecise. The cream, in the sense of the topmost layer, had long ago been skimmed and safely removed to the collectors' shelves. It was the less attractive material that lay underneath that we were after."[23] In his letter to Wetmore, Dellinger forcefully stated that: "Under no condition will we cooperate with Phillips, Ford, or Griffin."

Taken at face value, the above would suggest that Dellinger was simply a proprietary ("Arkansas for Arkansans") obstructionist. The actual situation, which has not been reported heretofore, was a bit more complicated and, while not completely exonerating Dellinger of excessive protectionism, it at least provides a better context for his feelings. First, it is important to appreciate that Dellinger had been extraordinarily generous to Dr. Phillips in 1938–1939 by allowing him to photograph and make drawings of many of the pottery vessels in the University of Arkansas Museum collections. Further, Dellinger assisted Phillips when the latter wanted to conduct an archaeological survey of the Ouachita River drainage—an area in which Dellinger had conducted his own excavations a decade earlier.[24]

As to the proposed archaeological survey in eastern Arkansas, Dellinger was legitimately annoyed that he had not been consulted during the planning stage. But what especially upset Dellinger stemmed from difficulties he was experiencing in obtaining money for and implementing his own archaeological survey in Arkansas using funds from the Works Progress Administration (WPA). After over a year of wrangling, Dellinger's proposed survey was approved for funding in February 1939. The total amount of funding was $115,383, including matching funds provided by the University of Arkansas.[25] Once the project got underway, problems arose with several on-site field supervisors, resulting in their dismissals. WPA administrators probably had a dim view of the situation, and Dellinger's efforts to hire a new field supervisor for the project were rebuffed by the WPA for over half a year.[26]

Thus, news of the impending archaeological survey by Phillips, Ford, and Griffin arrived at a time that Dellinger's WPA project, including his own survey efforts, was essentially on hold, pending approval of a new field supervisor. Dellinger's reaction to Phillips et al., therefore, was to some degree borne of frustration. But Dellinger would receive a major insult in June 1940 when Acting Secretary Wetmore recommended to WPA officials that Dellinger hire Phillips, Ford, or Griffin "to supervise an archaeological survey in the state of Arkansas."[27] Needless to say, Dellinger did not hire any of these individuals. His plans for a statewide archaeological survey never did materialize, but the overall project was reactivated, resulting in extensive excavations at several village sites along the Ouachita River. Nearly three decades later, the records and collections from two of these sites provided the basis for an important doctoral dissertation on cultures that existed between about 2000 B.C. and A.D. 1000.[28]

Phillips et al. were, in fact, correct that much of the "cream" had been "skimmed" many years earlier, though to this day there are exciting finds being made in eastern Arkansas. But Phillips and company limited their Arkansas investigations almost exclusively to surface collections, with a very limited excavation at a single archaeological site.[29] The bags of broken pottery that they collected certainly did not detract from past or future efforts by the University of Arkansas. Dellinger seems not to have held a grudge, however, as he permitted Phillip, Ford, and Griffin to publish photographs of a number of pottery vessels in the university's museum collections,[30] and some years later he was to ask Phillips to recommend promising Harvard graduate students as candidates to become the new curator of the University of Arkansas Museum.

With the benefit of hindsight, it is possible to appreciate Dellinger's desire to keep archaeological material from Arkansas in the state. He was appointed curator of the University of Arkansas Museum at a time when the collections were quite small and included virtually no archaeological specimens. His appointment also coincided with rampant looting of human graves in the Arkansas River valley, which resulted in the sale of numerous funerary objects to out-of-state parties. Moreover, several outside institutions—notably the Heye Foundation and the Oklahoma Historical Society—were conducting excavations at some of Arkansas's remarkable bluff shelters. All this occurred at a time when Dellinger had only begun to build an archaeology program at the university museum. Nor was Dellinger alone in his desire to "protect" his own state.[31] Trained as a zoologist, Dellinger recognized his insufficient knowledge of archaeology and museum management and sought help from one of the most prominent archaeologists in the eastern United States, Carl Guthe.

Though protective, Dellinger nonetheless permitted outside researchers to photograph unpublished pottery vessels in the museum collection and helped a doctoral student at Harvard University with an archaeology project in southern Arkansas. Dellinger's attitude certainly never detracted from our understanding of Arkansas archaeology. Far from it, in fact, as it was his concern about Arkansas's archaeological heritage that spurred Dellinger to obtain the research grants that built the archaeology collection of the University of Arkansas Museum into one of the finest in the nation. To this day, the collection and associated records continue to be an important source of information about the prehistory of Arkansas and eastern North America in general.[32]

NOTES

1. "University of Arkansas Museum," *Arkansas Alumnus* 3(7): 7, 12.
2. Robert C. Mainfort Jr. and Sarah R. Demb, "Edwin Curtiss' Archaeological Explorations along the St. Francis River, Northeast Arkansas," *Arkansas Archeologist* 41 (2001): 1–28.
3. *The W. P. Hall Mississippian Collection at the Putnam Museum,* Putnam Museum (1985); Captain Wilfred Peter Hall correspondence, Putnam Museum of History and Natural Science, Davenport, Iowa.
4. William H. Holmes, "Ancient Pottery of the Mississippi Valley," *Proceedings of the Davenport Academy of Natural Sciences* 4 (1886): 123–196.
5. David S. Brose, "How Capt. C. W. Riggs Hunts for Mound Builders' Relics: An Historical Investigation of Some Contemporary Influences on C. B. Moore," *Southeastern Archaeological Conference Bulletin* 22 (1980): 145–152; C. W. Riggs, *How We Find Relics* (Philadelphia: W. B. Conkey, 1893); Althea May Riggs, *Among the Indians* (Philadelphia: Ketterlinus, 1897).
6. Marvin D. Jeter, *Edward Palmer's Arkansas Mounds* (Fayetteville: University of Arkansas Press, 1990); Cyrus Thomas, Report on the Mound Explorations of the Bureau of Ethnology. Twelfth Annual Report of the Bureau of Ethnology, pp. 3–742 (reprinted in 1985 as No. 7 in the "Classics of Smithsonian Anthropology" series by the Smithsonian Institution Press, Washington, D.C.
7. E.g., Clarence B. Moore, "Antiquities of the Ouachita Valley," *Journal of the Academy of Natural Sciences of Philadelphia* 14 (1909): 7–170; "Antiquities of the St. Francis, White and Black Rivers, Arkansas," *Journal of the Academy of Natural Sciences of Philadelphia* 14 (1910): 255–364; "Some Aboriginal Sites on Mississippi River," *Journal of the Academy of Natural Sciences of Philadelphia* 14 (1911): 367–478; "Some Aboriginal Sites on Red River," *Journal of the Academy of Natural Sciences of Philadelphia* 14 (1912): 481–644.
8. Vernon J. Knight, "Introduction: The Expeditions of Clarence B. Moore to Moundville in 1905 and 1906." In V. J. Knight (editor), *The Moundville Expeditions of Clarence Bloomfield Moore* (Tuscaloosa: University of Alabama Press, 1996), 1–20.
9. "To Keep Indian Relics in State," *Arkansas Gazette,* 25 January 1909, 8.
10. Knight, "Introduction," 14.
11. Mark R. Harrington, *Certain Caddo Sites in Arkansas,* Museum of the American Indian Notes and Monographs No. 10 (New York: Heye Foundation, 1920); "A Pot-Hunter's Paradise," *Indian Notes and Monographs* (New York: Heye Foundation, April 1924), vol. 1(2), 85; *The Ozark Bluff-Dwellers,* Museum of the American Indian Notes and Monographs No. 12 (New York: Heye Foundation, 1960). For a brief biography of Harrington, see: <http://encyclopediaofarkansas.net/encyclopedia/entry-detail.aspx?entryID=576> (viewed 10 October 2006).
12. "Boone County Caves Yield Relics of Bluff Dwellers: Expedition Sent by Historical Society of Oklahoma Carrying on Extensive Study in Habitat of Ancient Race," *Arkansas Gazette,* 3 March 1926 (page number missing).
13. "Making Archeological Relics Available for Study," *Christian Science Monitor,* 24 November 1926.
14. "Noted Archeologist Gives Vivid Lecture," *Arkansas Traveler,* 28 January 1926, 1.
15. "Priceless Objects of Ancient World Given to UA Museum by Count DeProrock: Explorer Interested in Ark. Mounds," *Fayetteville Daily Democrat,* 29 January 1929, 1:3.
16. "Indian Remains in Arkansas Should Be Preserved in State Museum," *Arkansas Alumnus* 7(5) (1930): 5–6.
17. Rita Fisher-Carroll, *Mortuary Behavior at Upper Nodena,* Research Series 59 (Fayetteville: Arkansas Archeological Survey, 2001); "Dr. Dellinger Doesn't Approve of 'Bama Professor Digging His Arkansas Archeological Mounds," *Fayetteville Daily Democrat,* 21 February 1934, 6:3. .
18. Guthe to Dellinger, 24 February 1934; Carl E. Guthe correspondence file, University of Arkansas Museum.
19. "Dellinger Makes Plea for Prehistoric Sites," *Arkansas Alumnus* 10(7) (1933): 4.
20. Edwin A. Lyon, *A New Deal for Southeastern Archaeology* (Tuscaloosa: University of Alabama Press, 1996).
21. Philip Phillips, James A. Ford, and James B. Griffin, *Archaeological Survey in the Lower Mississippi Alluvial Valley, 1940–1947,* vol. 25. Papers of the Peabody Museum of American Archaeology and Ethnology (Cambridge: Harvard University, 1951) .
22. Dellinger to Alexander Wetmore, 31 July 1940, Dellinger correspondence file, University of Arkansas Museum.
23. Phillips et al., *Archaeological Survey,* 40.

24. Dellinger to Alexander Wetmore, 31 July 1940, Dellinger correspondence file, University of Arkansas Museum; "Visiting Scientists Study Museum Relics," *Northwest Arkansas Times,* 15 July 1938, 1:3.

25. "Archeological Survey Soon," *Northwest Arkansas Times,* 13 February 1939, 1:8; "Archaeological Survey," *Arkansas Alumnus* 16 (7) (1939): 7, 13.

26. Dellinger to Florence Kerr (national director, Professional and Service Division, WPA, Washington), 31 July 1940.

27. Wetmore to Bevens, 18 June 1940, May Blevins (*sic*) correspondence file, University of Arkansas Museum.

28. Frank F. Schambach, *Pre-Caddoan Cultures in the Trans-Mississippi South,* Research Series 53 (Fayetteville: Arkansas Archeological Survey, 1998).

29. Phillips et al., *Archaeological Survey.*

30. Phillips et al., *Archaeological Survey.*

31. Lyon, *New Deal.*

32. A bibliography of publications, theses, and dissertations that focus primarily on or make extensive use of Dellinger's archaeological collections appears later in this volume.

Human Burials and the Law

MANY OF THE archaeological specimens obtained under Dellinger's direction, including most of those in the exhibit, were found in the graves of pre-Columbian Native Americans. During the 1930s, when most of the University of Arkansas Museum excavations were conducted, professional archaeologists throughout the United States routinely excavated the graves of pre-Columbian Native Americans as simply another kind of archaeological feature—just like a house or a storage pit. Thus, the museum excavations were by no means unusual and, in fact, the records kept by the excavators were better than those kept by other institutions.

Until the 1970s, archaeologists and other scientists generally regarded Native American human remains and associated funerary objects as scientific specimens to be stored in museums. In contrast, when graves of Euroamericans were excavated, this usually was done by a funeral home and the remains were promptly reburied. Not surprisingly, this double standard caused considerable resentment among Native Americans.

Today, professional archaeologists and museologists recognize that modern Native Americans have rightful and appropriate interests in the buried remains of their ancestors, including those that were excavated many years ago. Moreover, federal and state legislation has recognized the interests of Native Americans. At the federal level, the Native American Graves Protection and Repatriation Act (NAGPRA) requires consultation with Native American tribes prior to the excavation of graves located on federal lands. NAGPRA also provides a process for museums and federal agencies to return certain Native American cultural items—human remains, funerary objects, sacred objects, and objects of cultural patrimony—to lineal descendants, culturally affiliated Indian tribes, and Native Hawaiian organizations.

The state of Arkansas has enacted strong legislation that protects human remains in unregistered cemeteries, as well as prohibiting the trade or commercial display of human skeletal remains and associated funerary objects. Act 1533 of 1999, which amends Act 753 of 1991, is presented below, along with the actual criminal penalties for violations.

Act 1533 of 1999
AN ACT TO AMEND ARKANSAS CODE ANNOTATED "13-6-406, 13-6-407, AND 13-6-408 TO INCREASE THE CRIMINAL PENALTIES FOR DISPLAYING HUMAN SKELETAL BURIAL REMAINS AND DESECRATING BURIAL GROUNDS; AND FOR OTHER PURPOSES."
Subtitle: "AN ACT TO INCREASE CRIMINAL PENALTIES FOR DISPLAYING HUMAN SKELETAL BURIAL REMAINS AND DESECRATING BURIAL GROUNDS."

Be it Enacted by the General Assembly of the State of Arkansas:

SECTION 1. Arkansas Code Annotated 13–6–406 is amended to read as follows:

"13–6–406. Trade or collecting of remains.

(a) Anyone who knowingly buys, sells, or barters human skeletal burial remains or their associated burial furniture is committing a Class D felony for the first offense and a Class C felony on the second and subsequent offenses.

(b) Artifacts as defined in this subchapter and private collections legally acquired prior to July 15, 1991, are exempted from this section.

(c) Nothing in this subchapter prohibits the collecting of such artifacts by landowners or others who do so with the landowner's permission."

SECTION 2. Arkansas Code Annotated 13–6–407 is amended to read as follows:

"13–6–407. Display of remains.

Anyone who knowingly displays human skeletal burial remains for profit or to aid and abet a commercial enterprise is committing a Class C felony with each day of display being a separate offense."

SECTION 3. Arkansas Code Annotated 13–6–408 is amended to read as follows:

"13–6–408. Desecration of burial grounds and burial furniture.

(a) Anyone who intentionally or knowingly desecrates or permits desecration of a burial ground and associated burial furniture is committing on the first offense a Class D felony and on the second or subsequent offenses, a Class C felony.

(b) The presence in the ground of grave markers, caskets, or casket hardware creates a rebuttable presumption that these are burial furniture and of the existence or presence of a human burial ground.

(c) Exempted from this section is disturbance of human skeletal burial remains or burial furniture by landowners or agricultural tenants as a consequence of agricultural activity."

SECTION 4. All provisions of the Act of a general and permanent nature are amendatory to the Arkansas Code of 1987 Annotated and the Arkansas Code Revision Commission shall incorporate the same in the Code.

SECTION 5. If any provision of this Act or the application thereof to any person or circumstance is held invalid, such invalidity shall not affect other provisions or applications of the Act which can be given effect without the invalid provision or application, and to this end the provisions of this Act are declared to be severable.

SECTION 6. All laws and parts of laws in conflict with this Act are hereby repealed.

FELONIES FOR UNMARKED BURIAL ACT VIOLATIONS:

* The penalty for a Class D felony is no more than 6 years in a State prison. The minimum penalty could be as light as probation.

* The penalty for a Class C felony is a prison term of no less than 3 years nor more than 10 years.

History of the University of Arkansas Museum

SAMUEL DELLINGER SERVED as curator of the University of Arkansas Museum for over 30 years, and a large portion of the museum's collections was obtained under his leadership. He was not, however, the "founder" of the museum, nor even the first curator.[1] In fact, the museum had been established nearly 50 years prior to Dellinger's arrival at the university.

The first published reference to the University of Arkansas Museum appears in the *First Report of the Arkansas Industrial University*, published in 1873.[2] In extolling the building now known as Old Main, scheduled for completion by September 1875, the structure was described as containing "five large halls for library, cabinets and museums."[3] Further: "The institution being yet in its infancy, the collection of mineralogical specimens in the museum of the University is as yet rather small, but is being increased as rapidly as possible, and gives earnest of being not only very interesting but also highly instructive ere long."[4] Insofar as the university at this time consisted of only two wooden frame buildings, use of the term "museum" might have been a bit overstated, but the passage makes clear that the need for a museum was recognized at the founding of the university. The 1876 catalogue notes: "The collections in these [i.e., the "Cabinet and Museum"] are as yet inconsiderable, but are slowly increasing," and that the state geologist "has kindly consented to forward to the University duplicates of the specimens obtained by him."[5]

In his history commissioned for the one hundredth anniversary of the University of Arkansas, Robert Leflar stated that: "Professor Francis L. Harvey, who taught biology and geology at the University from 1875 to 1885 and did a tremendous amount of original scientific investigation and reporting on the state's natural history during that period, was actually the founder of the museum. His specimens, carefully labeled, gave the little collection a professional character."[6] Leflar's statement is confirmed by information in the university catalogues of the time period.

Born in 1850 near Ithaca, New York, Francis Leroy Harvey was the second son of Daniel and Amanda Harvey. His family moved to Iowa when he was a teenager, and Harvey attended the Iowa Agricultural College (now Iowa State University), receiving his bachelor of science degree in 1872. In 1875, he was hired to chair the chemistry and natural science programs at the University of Arkansas.[7]

The 1877 university catalogue records that Professor Harvey offered a prize of $10 for the best biology collection (of birds, insects, or plants) and a $10 prize for the best "set of chemical compounds used

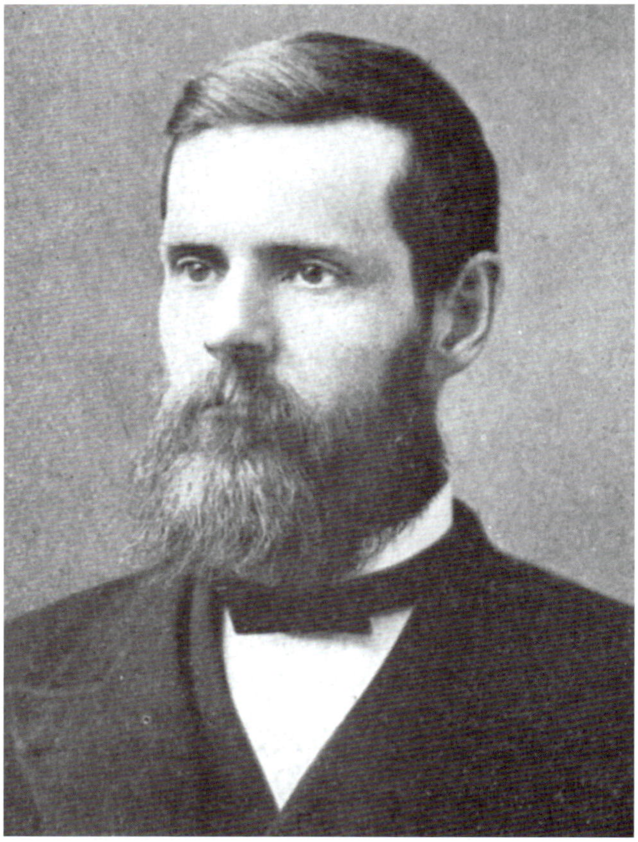

Figure 59. Francis Leroy Harvey, the founder of the University of Arkansas Museum.

in the arts and manufactured from native minerals found in the State" and that the specimens were "to be left as an accession to the museum of the University." [8] In year 2006 dollars, Harvey's prizes would be worth roughly $130 each! The following year Harvey offered prizes for the best pressed and mounted collection of plants; the best unmounted collection of *Graminae* [grasses] and *Compositae* [various flowering plants with composite heads, including goldenrod, ragweed, and sunflower]; the best collection of reptiles; and the "best consideration of the Geology of Washington County." [9]

Harvey continued with his student prizes in 1879, and the university catalogue for that year notes that contributions to the "Museum and Cabinets during the year" included minerals, birds, and plants to the herbarium.[10] Harvey also "distributed at his own expense one hundred thousand native plants to schools and colleges of the State."[11]

The 1880 catalogue noted that the recently completed local railroads provided passes "by means of which the Professors can visit other portions of the State, and collect material for the Museum." [12] More important, the new railroads greatly facilitated travel to and from northwest Arkansas, including the university.

Professor Harvey's key role with the museum is made clear in the 1881 university catalogue: "Any one desiring information about plants, animals or fossils, which they have procured in the State, are solicited to send specimens to Prof. F. L. Harvey, Fayetteville, Arkansas. Desirable specimens will be placed to the credit of the donor in the University museum, and due acknowledgment made in the catalogue." [13]

The same university catalogue also supplies, for the first time, considerable information about the museum and its collection. At that time, Professor Cuthbert P. Conrad (adjunct professor of chemistry and natural science) was making a collection of "State Minerals for the University."[14] Contributions to the "General Cabinet" during the previous year included minerals and ores, while contributions to the "Biology Department" included Indian relics, fossils, wood specimens, a rattlesnake, and a human fetus.[15] Further: "The private collections of the Professors, amounting to several hundred specimens, are at the disposal of students for study"; "The University has but few specimens from outside the State"; "The College has no Herbarium. The collection of the Professor, amounting to 1200 specimens, is used to illustrate Botany"; "There are about 500 species of Animal Specimens, to illustrate the various departments of Zoology"; "The collections for illustrating the subject of Geology, are meagre"; "Collections in all the departments are slowly accumulating."[16] This rather lengthy discussion in the catalogue indicates that the museum was playing an increasingly important and visible role within the young university.

By 1882, there had "been constructed an herbarium case large enough to hold the indigenous plants of North America,"[17] and the catalogue for that year specifically identifies Professor Harvey as the individual "who has charge of the General Cabinet and Museum,"[18] confirming his role as "founder" of the University of Arkansas Museum. Importantly, 1882 marked the first year of a formal appropriation by the board of trustees to "enable the Professor to make many valuable collections during the coming year."[19]

In 1884, Harvey donated 750 species of botanical specimens from his private collection to the university,[20] but unfortunately, Harvey's hard work and donations did not protect him from the blanket dismissal of the entire University of Arkansas faculty in 1885.[21] His remaining personal collection of plant specimens, "embracing more than 2,500 specimens,"[22] was purchased by the university shortly after his termination.[23]

In their 1910 *History of the University of Arkansas*, Reynolds and Thomas state that Professor Harvey "was zealous in the work of collecting specimens. The botanical and mineralogical collections of Professor Harvey were especially good . . . the specimens remain part of the permanent equipments of the university."[24] This remains true today, as there are a number of mineral specimens in the museum's collections with old "Harvey" numbers and numerous historically important "Harvey" specimens in the university herbarium.[25] It is worth noting that Harvey's *The Minerals and Rocks of Arkansas* was published in 1886—a year after his termination.[26]

By 1891, the museum collections had grown appreciably: "The cabinet of minerals consists chiefly of a collection of State minerals, contributed by various parties of the State, and by the professors; but it has been recently enlarged by purchase, and embraces also specimens of value from other States. There has been constructed an herbarium case large enough to hold the indigenous plants of North America and such exotics as are of economic value. It will be the work of years to complete a collection of the plants of North America, but the work is progressing; and the collection is large and valuable. There are about 500 specimens of animals, illustrating the various parts of zoology. Mr. C. W. Wentworth's donation of his collection furnishes us the nucleus for an entomological collection. Collections in all departments are slowly accumulating. Contributions of minerals, fossils, Indian relics and rare curiosities are solicited."[27]

The first mention of the actual space occupied by the museum appears in the 1892 university catalogue, which notes that "on the fourth floor [of Old Main] are the commodious and well-furnished halls of the literary societies and the Museums."[28] Two pages later, the catalogue states that the university's "aim is to make the Museum of more practical and educational value."[29]

The remarkably spacious exhibit hall of "The Museum of Natural History" was photographed for the 1894 university catalogue.[30] The exhibit hall was located in the south wing of the fourth floor of University Hall (Old Main). "Adjoining [the exhibit hall] are two rooms, one being used for the storage of alcoholic specimens, the other for taxidermy."[31] With the completion of University Hall, space for the museum could have been available as early as 1875, the year Professor Harvey was hired, and it seems likely that the museum occupied a portion of the fourth floor beginning that year or soon thereafter.

An untitled 1894 note in the *Fayetteville Weekly Democrat* specifically identifies Professor Seth Eugene Meek as "Curator of the Museum,"[32] marking the first known use of that title in print. Meek also is the first individual specifically mentioned in connection with the museum after the dismissal of Francis Harvey in 1885. The article goes on to state: "The A. I. U. [Arkansas Industrial University] museum is being rapidly enlarged under the management of Prof. Meek and it is now a very interesting feature of the University. Geological

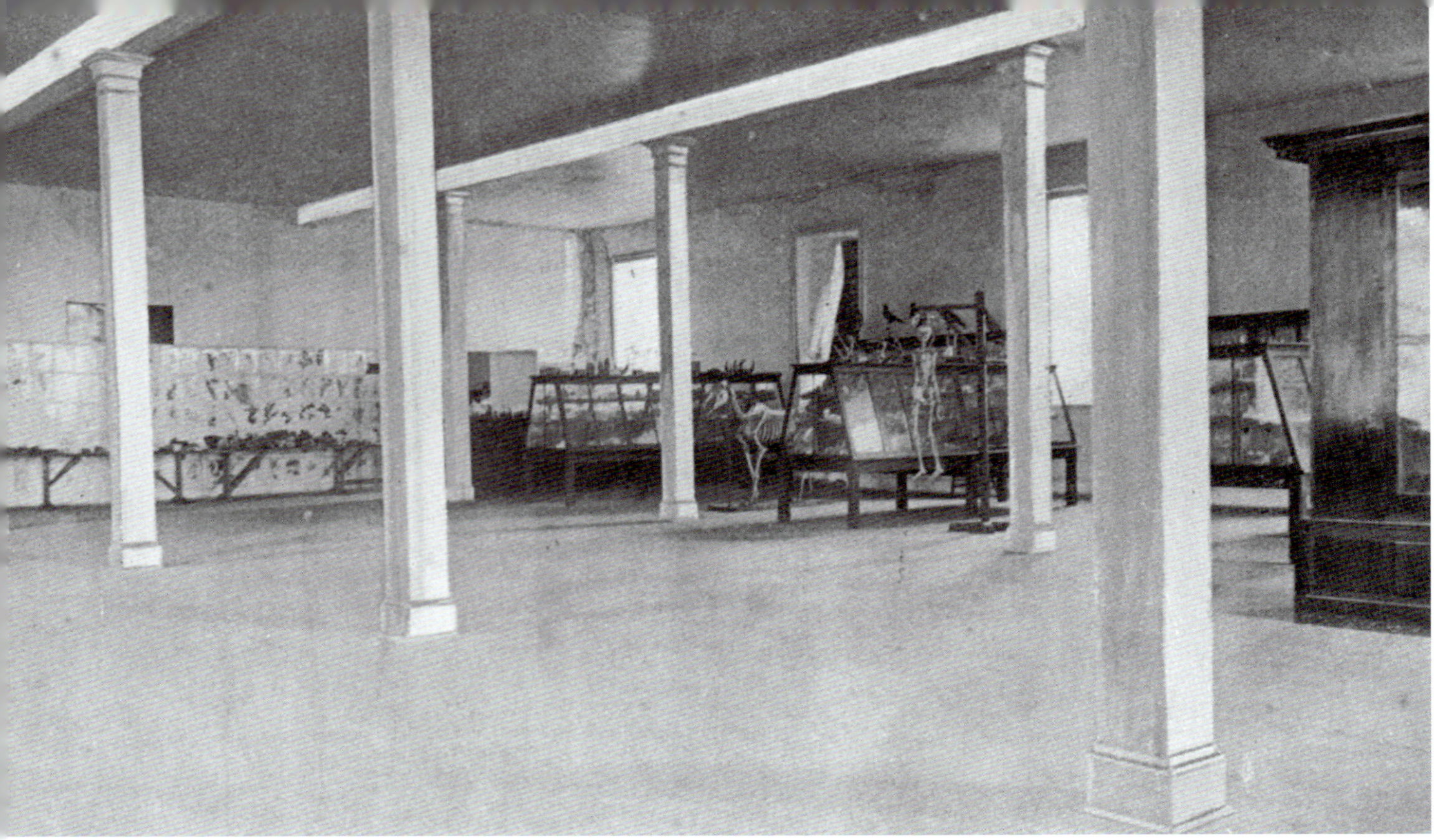

Figure 60. The University of Arkansas Museum, circa 1894.

specimens, historical relics, reptiles, birds, mammals &c are desired and those who can make donations of this kind will be gratefully remembered."

Meek was an adjunct and associate professor of biology and geology from 1891 until 1896.[33] His *A List of Fishes and Mollusks Collected in Arkansas and Indian Territory* was published in 1894, and he donated his private collections of about 250 species, mostly lower invertebrates, to the museum.[34] Into the 1890s, "Through the kindness of the 'Frisco and Eureka Springs Railroad the curator [i.e., Meek] has been much aided in making collections in northwestern Arkansas, these roads having furnished him with free transportation over their lines in Arkansas."[35]

In 1896, Meek was succeeded as curator by Professor Albert Homer Purdue, who was "elected associate professor of geology and curator of the museum" that year and was promoted to full professor two years later.[36] Purdue was also the *de facto* state geologist of Arkansas, and he remained at the University of Arkansas until 1912, when he left to become the state geologist of Tennessee. Around 1900, his office was on the fourth floor of University Hall (Old Main)—also the location of the museum.[37] Growth of the museum continued under Purdue's direction, and in 1898 "several new sloping-top cases with drawers beneath have recently been added."[38] These are shown in a circa 1902 photograph of the exhibit hall.

The 1902 university catalogue notes that the museum "occupies the fourth floor of the south wing of the main building," and that some "large additions" were recently made to equipment "to facilitate instruction in geology and biology, and also to make it of increased interest to the visiting public."[39] At the time, the museum collections included minerals, a petrographic collection, a paleontology collection, the Major Earle collection (minerals and fossils), as well as zoology and botanical collections.[40] Today, the University of

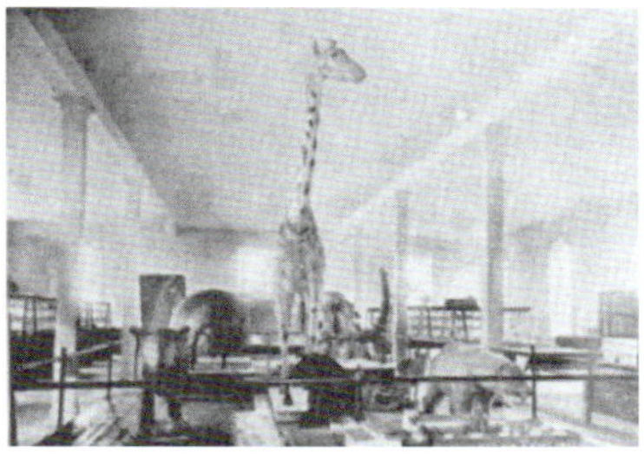

Figure 61. "Corner of the museum" in 1902.

Arkansas Museum also curates Major Earle's ceremonial sword.

By 1912, the museum's zoological collections had grown to include 200 birds and mammals, 200 reptiles and amphibians, 1,500 fishes, 1,000 insects and other invertebrates, and several skeletons.[41] The growth of the zoological collections may account for Dellinger's statement decades later that the museum was started through the Department of Zoology (i.e., Professor Harvey), and that many fine specimens were collected. Dellinger also said that during the time that Geology "had control" of the museum (probably referring to the time of Professor Purdue onward), the zoological specimens were in such a bad state of preservation that they had to be discarded.[42]

Noah Fields Drake, professor of geology, succeeded Purdue as curator of the museum,[43] holding both titles until he left the University of Arkansas in 1920 after eight years of service.[44] Drake collected some archaeological specimens and a human skull from Denny Cave, northeast of Huntsville, in 1915.[45]

Following the departure of Professor Drake, another geologist, George Haven Cady, was appointed curator, but he seems to have served in that capacity for only one year.[46] For several years, the museum lacked a titled curator until Dellinger's appointment in 1925, as mentioned earlier. In the interim, responsibility for the museum probably rested with the geology department, and it was during this period that the zoological specimens suffered such neglect that they had to be discarded.[47] Nonetheless, the museum clearly was not forgotten, as the fiftieth anniversary issue of the University of Arkansas yearbook included several photographs of the museum exhibits, including a "mineralogy exhibit," a mastodon skull with tusks, a "baby hippo" (probably in a storage room), and a glyptodon.[48]

Although Sam Dellinger came to the University of Arkansas in 1921, he was not appointed curator of the museum until 1925, following completion of his PhD coursework and research at Columbia University and Woods Hole, Massachusetts.[49]

In the same issue that introduced Dellinger to university alumni as the new curator of the museum, the *Arkansas Alumnus* 3(7) also published an overview of the museum:

> No mention had been made of any special appropriations for the museum by the state legislature previous to 1895, when $500.00 was appropriated. In 1897 this amount was increased to $1000.00, but dropped in 1901, according to data in the History of Arkansas [i.e., *History of the University of Arkansas,* 1910] by Thomas and

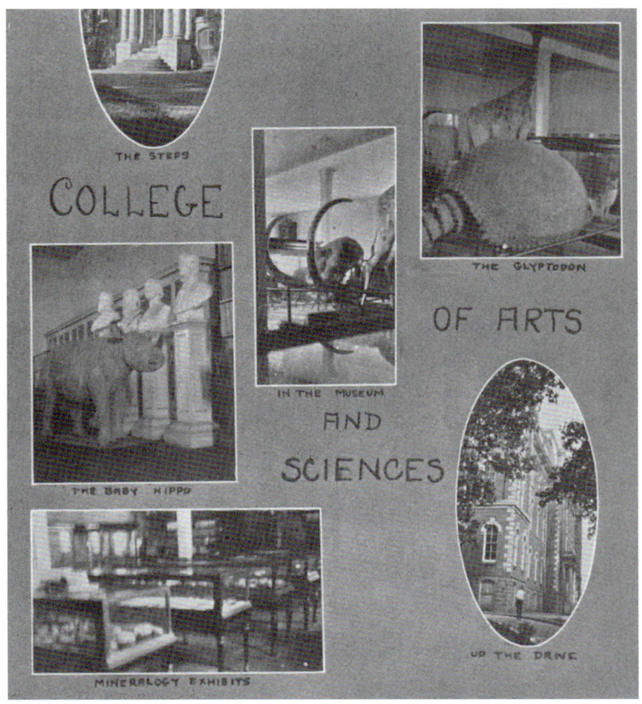

Figure 62. Photographs of the museum in 1922.

Reynolds. The appropriations have been made since then as follows: 1903, $1000.00; 1905, $700.00; 1907, $500.00; 1909, $500.00.

For years through the loyalty of professors in charge of the department of geology and biology, through gifts from University of Arkansas alumni, purchase and exchange the museum contains some valuable collections.

In one of the display cases is a set of the original specifications for the main building, University Hall, which were drawn up by W. Z. Mayes, builder and contractor. Mrs. Ida Mayes Carlisle, daughter of the contractor, presented this to the University.

The mineral collections on display are very fine. The collection of rocks, which were given by H. D. Miser, an alumnus, now state geologist of Tennessee, is good, but a larger one is needed.

An unusual and valuable collection of swords and guns was lent to the University recently by Mr. B. H. Stone.

One of the largest collections of Indian relics in the museum is the one given by Lt. C. H. Metcalf of the U. S. Marines, a graduate of the University. The material of this collection came from an old Indian mound just south of the city of Vera Cruz, Mexico. The collection consists of several fine images of Toltec or Aztec workmanship.

Another good collection was given to the University by Miss Carrie Pace. The collection includes pieces of pottery, arrow heads and other stone tools, and bones. This material was found in a mound in St. Francis county.[50]

Dellinger's appointment as curator marked the beginning of a major research program at the museum, and increased interest in the museum by the university community and the general public. During the 1926–27 academic year, only a year after Dellinger became curator, there were 2,841 visitors to the museum, a number "larger by far" than in any year since the museum was established in the "early seventies."[51]

In April 1930, the museum still was located on the fourth floor of Old Main, occupying the hall and rooms 401 and 407. Room 401 housed various skeletons of vertebrates. Among the exhibits was a collection of

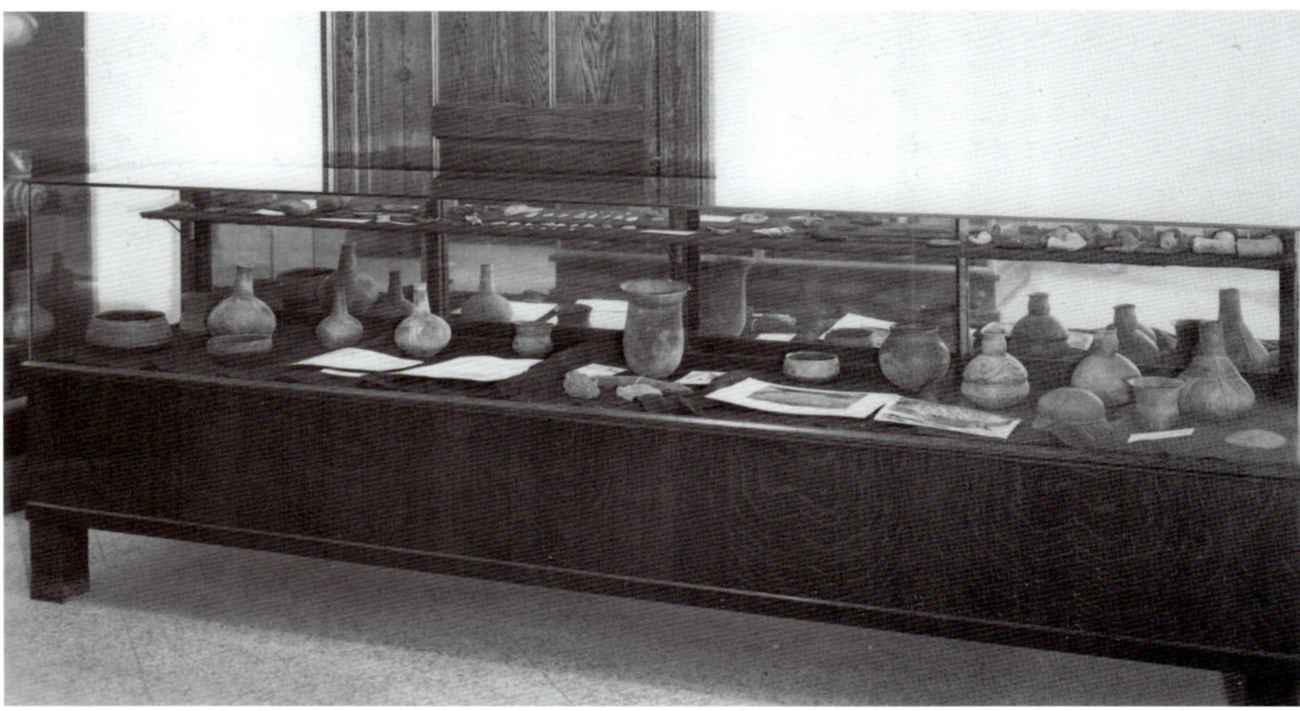

Figure 63. University of Arkansas Museum exhibits in the basement of Vol Walker Hall, circa 1950.

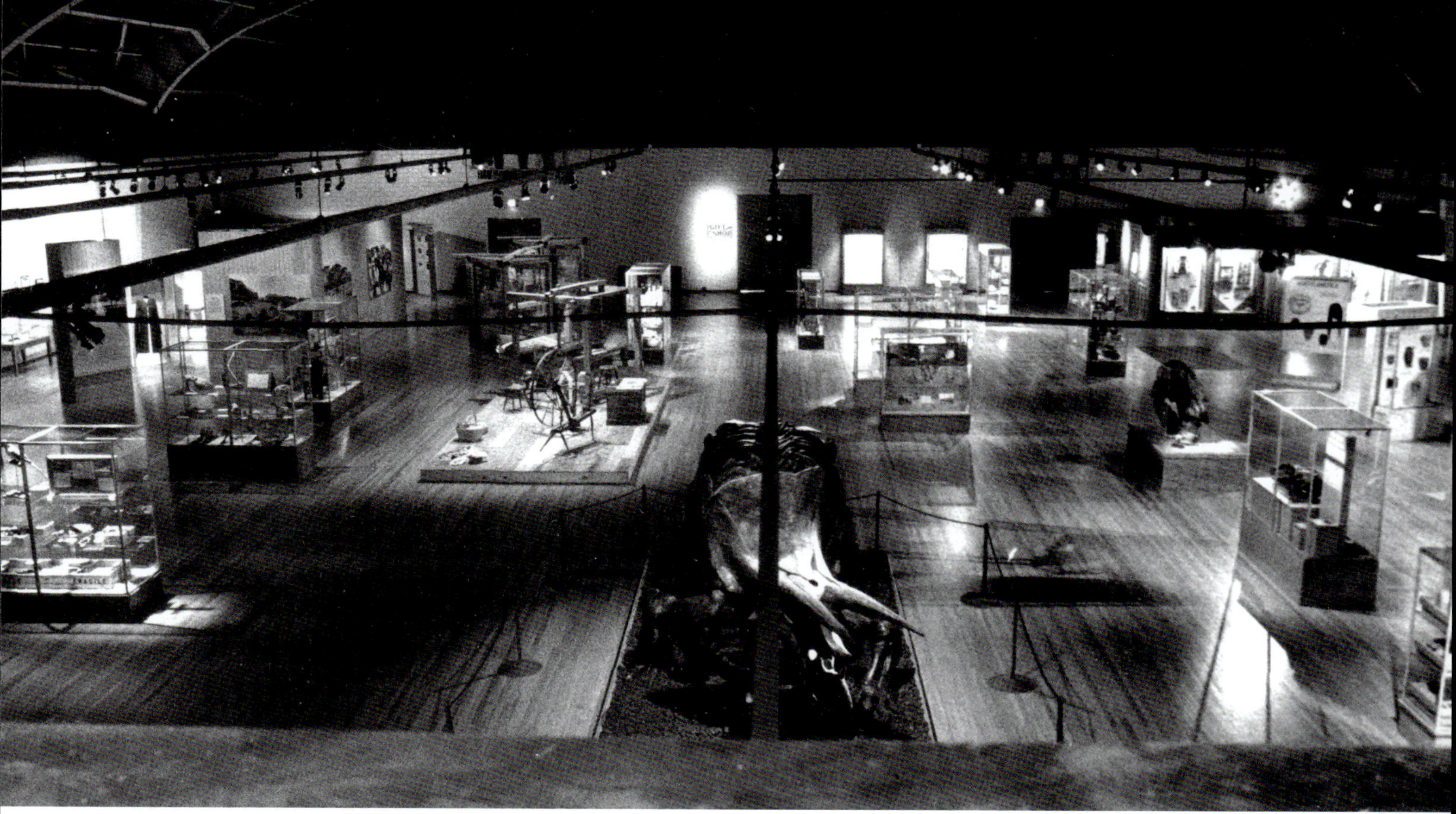

Figure 64. University of Arkansas Museum exhibits in the old Men's Gymnasium, circa 1988.

Australian mammals including a duckbilled platypus and a spiny anteater, which remain in the museum collections today.[52]

In the fall of 1930, the most valuable material in the museum collections was moved to the new fireproof Agriculture Building,[53] and additional exhibit space was provided in Room 301 of the new building, where big game animals (including some shot in Wyoming by a party led by President Futrall), prehistoric Native American pottery vessels, and fossils were displayed.[54] Items of historical interest also were added to the exhibits, and Dellinger specifically asked alumni to donate such items, especially articles made of corn shucks during reconstruction and a genuine Bowie knife.[55]

With the completion of the new library (Vol Walker Hall) in 1935, the museum exhibits were moved to the basement, where they remained for over three decades.[56] The museum also was given workrooms and storage space in the library.[57] The spacious new exhibit hall, which permitted display of more of the outstanding archaeological collections, attracted a record number of visitors during the 1939–40 academic year—a total of 8,882, up from 7,868 the previous year.[58]

Five years after the museum moved to the new library, Old Main suffered a serious fire. At that time, all that remained of the old museum exhibits was an "old pelican" and a "disreputable buffalo's head" on the fourth floor.[59]

In 1955, increasing demands for space in Vol Walker Hall caused the museum exhibits to be moved back to the renovated fourth floor of Old Main,[60] where the museum allocated the entire floor comprising about 18,000 square feet. Much of this space was devoted to exhibits, but there also were offices, workrooms, and storage areas. In June 1957, Sam Dellinger formally retired from the University of Arkansas, though he continued to work part-time through the 1959–60 academic year.[61] Dellinger hired his successor, Charles R. ("Bob") McGimsey, in 1957 and presumably continued to work to help McGimsey "learn the ropes." McGimsey initially held the title of assistant curator, but in 1960 he was given the title of director of the museum.[62] Although Dellinger had, in effect, served as director of the University of Arkansas Museum for over 30 years, he never held the title of director.

With the completion of Mullins Library in 1969, most of the museum collections were moved back to Vol Walker Hall,[63] and in the mid-1970s the museum exhibits were moved to Hotz Hall. This was especially unfortunate not only because exhibit space had to be created out of former dormitory rooms, but also because the museum was removed from the main part of campus and, hence, away from most students and faculty. The exhibits were moved into the old Men's Gymnasium on Garland Avenue in 1983,[64] where they remained for 20 years until the university, for financial reasons, closed the exhibits in October 2003.[65] Today the University of Arkansas Museum collections, including objects formerly on display, are curated in a new state-of-the-art facility located north of campus, where the collections continue to be used for research, teaching, and as a source of objects used for exhibits developed by other institutions.

NOTES

1. "S. C. Dellinger, Museum Founder, Dies at Age 81," *Northwest Arkansas Times,* 13 August 1973, 2.
2. *Contra* John H. Reynolds and David Y. Thomas, *History of the University of Arkansas* (Fayetteville, 1910), 317.
3. Arkansas Industrial University, *First Report of the Arkansas Industrial University* (Little Rock, 1873), 16.
4. *First Report,* 45.
5. Arkansas Industrial University, *Fourth Report and Catalogue of the Arkansas Industrial University* (Little Rock, 1876), 38.
6. Robert A. Leflar, *The First 100 Years* (Fayetteville, 1972), 328.
7. Reynolds and Thomas, *History,* 468–469.
8. Arkansas Industrial University, *Fifth Report and Catalogue of the Arkansas Industrial University* (Little Rock, 1877), 41.
9. Arkansas Industrial University, *Sixth Catalogue of the Arkansas Industrial University* (Little Rock, 1878), 41.
10. Arkansas Industrial University, *Seventh Catalogue of the Arkansas Industrial University* (Little Rock, 1879), 63.
11. Reynolds and Thomas, *History,* 469.
12. Arkansas Industrial University, *Eighth Catalogue of the Arkansas Industrial University* (Little Rock, 1880), 64.
13. Arkansas Industrial University, *Ninth Catalogue of the Arkansas Industrial University* (Little Rock, 1881), 58.
14. *Ninth Catalogue,* 63.
15. *Ninth Catalogue,* 64.
16. *Ninth Catalogue,* 66.
17. Arkansas Industrial University, *Tenth Catalogue of the Arkansas Industrial University* (Little Rock, 1882), 58.
18. *Tenth Catalogue,* 60.
19. *Tenth Catalogue,* 59.
20. Arkansas Industrial University, *Twelfth Catalogue of the Arkansas Industrial University* (Little Rock, 1884), 57.
21. Reynolds and Thomas, *History,* 130–132.
22. Arkansas Industrial University, *Seventeenth Catalogue of the Arkansas Industrial University* (Little Rock, 1889), 96.
23. Arkansas Industrial University, *Fourteenth Catalogue of the Arkansas Industrial University* (Little Rock, 1886), 65.
24. Reynolds and Thomas, *History,* 113.
25. Johnnie Gentry (curator, university herbarium), personal communication 2004.
26. A year after his dismissal from the University of Arkansas, Harvey was appointed chair of natural history at the University of Maine in Orono—a position he held until his death in 1900. The same year, he received his MS degree from the Iowa Agricultural College. In 1890, the University of Arkansas awarded him the degree of PhD for a thesis on the apple maggot. Harvey's research specialty was dragonflies (Odonata), but he also published on plants and forestry. An obituary appears in *Entomological News and Proceedings of the Entomological Section of the Academy of Natural Sciences of Philadelphia* (April 1900), 451–452.
27. Arkansas Industrial University, *Nineteenth Catalogue of the Arkansas Industrial University* (Little Rock, 1891), 97–98.

28. Arkansas Industrial University, *Twentieth Catalogue of the Arkansas Industrial University* (Little Rock, 1892), 19.

29. Arkansas Industrial University, *Twentieth Catalogue,* 21.

30. Arkansas Industrial University, *Twenty-second Catalogue of the Arkansas Industrial University* (Little Rock, 1894), 19.

31. Arkansas Industrial University, *Twenty-second Catalogue,* 17.

32. *Fayetteville Weekly Democrat,* 8 March 1894, 3:2.

33. Arkansas Industrial University, *Twentieth Catalogue;* Arkansas Industrial University, *Twenty-second Catalogue.*

34. Arkansas Industrial University, *Twenty-second Catalogue,* 17.

35. Arkansas Industrial University, *Twenty-second Catalogue,* 18.

36. Reynolds and Thomas, *History,* 244; University of Arkansas, *Catalogue of the University of Arkansas, Thirteenth Edition* (1902–1903) (Fayetteville 1902), 29.

37. Label for photograph 17, MC 214, Manuscript Oversize Box 1, Mullins Library, University of Arkansas.

38. Arkansas Industrial University, *Catalogue of the Arkansas Industrial University* (Fayetteville, 1898), 17.

39. University of Arkansas, *Catalogue of the University of Arkansas, Thirteenth Edition,* 29.

40. University of Arkansas, *Catalogue of the University of Arkansas, Thirteenth Edition,* 29–30.

41. University of Arkansas, *University of Arkansas Catalogue, 1912–1913* (Fort Smith, 1912), 16.

42. Dellinger to Dean G. D. Nichols, 10 May 1957, MC 204, Box 8, folder 9, Mullins Library, University of Arkansas.

43. *University of Arkansas Catalogue, 1912–1913;* University of Arkansas, *University of Arkansas Catalogue, 1919–1920* (Fayetteville, 1920); "Interesting Relics at University Museum," *Fayetteville Daily Democrat,* 12 April 1919, 1:4.

44. Leflar, *First 100 Years,* 218.

45. "Pottery Found by Students in Huntsville Cave," *Fayetteville Daily Democrat,* 5 January 1925, 1.

46. *Annual Catalog, 1920–1921* (Fayetteville, 1921); *Annual Catalog, 1921–1922* (Fayetteville, 1922).

47. Dellinger to Dean G. D. Nichols, 10 May 1957, MC 204, Box 8, folder 9, Mullins Library, University of Arkansas.

48. Junior Class, University of Arkansas, *The "Golden" Razorback* (Jefferson City, 1922).

49. "S. C. Dellinger," *Arkansas Alumnus* 3(7) (1926): 13.

50. "University of Arkansas Museum," *Arkansas Alumnus* 3(7) (1926): 6.

51. (Untitled), *Arkansas Alumnus* 4(5) (1927), 15.

52. "Rare Collection of the University Greatly Enlarged," *Fayetteville Daily Democrat,* 7 April 1930, 8:3.

53. "Museum Valuables to be Moved to Fireproof Building," *Fayetteville Daily Democrat,* 17 August 1930, 2:2.

54. "Museum Enlarged," *Arkansas Alumnus* 8(3) (1930): 7.

55. "Growth in Museum," *Arkansas Alumnus* 10(2) (1932): 5.

56. "Ozark Bluff Dwelling Relics to Be Put in New Museum," *Arkansas Traveler,* 23 May 1935, 2; "Outstanding Relics to Be Housed at New UA Library," *Fayetteville Daily Democrat,* 10 June 1935, 3:3.

57. Leflar, *First 100 Years,* 328.

58. "Museum Visitors," *Arkansas Alumnus* 18(2) (1940): 9.

59. "Old Main's Fire," *Arkansas Alumnus* 18(3) (1940): 7–8.

60. Hester A. Davis, "Being Some Notes from Memory and from the Museum Records on Sam Dellinger, the University Museum, and Arkansas Archeology," *Field Notes* 108 (1973): 2–6, 8, 11–13.

61. "Prof. S. C. Dellinger" (in "This Year's Emeritus Professors"), *Arkansas Alumnus* (n.s.) 10(6) (1957): 11; Official appointment letters (Samuel C. Dellinger), University of Arkansas Library, Special Collections, MC 204, Box 3, Folder 8.

62. *Annual Catalog, 1960–1961* (Fayetteville, 1960).

63. Leflar, *First 100 Years,* 329.

64. Charles R. McGimsey (director emeritus, Arkansas Archeological Survey), personal communication, 2004.

65. "UA Officials: Museum Shut to Save Money," *Arkansas Democrat-Gazette*, 17 June 2003, 1B, 3B; "Children, State Lose, Museum Employees Say," *Morning News*, 18 June 2003, 1A, 2A; "Fight Planned to Save UA Museum," *Arkansas Democrat-Gazette*, 24 June 2003, 1B, 6B; "Why UA Museum Must Close," *Arkansas Democrat-Gazette*, 7 July 2003, 5B; "Closing Up Shop," *Arkansas Traveler*, 3 November 2003, 1.

The Exhibit Collections

THIS CHAPTER PRESENTS an illustrated catalog comprising the bulk of the objects in the exhibit; objects curated by out-of-state institutions are shown in a previous chapter. The objects selected for the exhibit highlight what are arguably the major strengths of the University of Arkansas Museum's archaeological collection. They represent four regions of Arkansas and one specific archaeological site in eastern Oklahoma. The catalog is arranged accordingly.

The first of Sam Dellinger's major acquisition efforts focused on the central Arkansas River valley, particularly the Carden Bottom, east of Russellville. He acquired most, though not all, of the objects from this area through purchase, rather than excavations conducted by Dellinger. As a result, there are very few records associated with the Arkansas River collections, which limits their research potential.

With the grant funds provided by the Carnegie Corporation, Dellinger's field crews excavated extensively in the bluff shelters of northwest Arkansas and at late-prehistoric sites in northeast Arkansas. The museum field assistants prepared fairly extensive field records of these excavations. Though falling far short of modern standards, these records were better than many written by archaeologists in the early 1930s.

Although relatively small in numbers, the collections from the Spiro (Oklahoma) mound group include some of the most important objects from the site that are curated in public institutions. Like most of the best-known artifacts from Spiro, these were purchased from collectors and have little documentation.

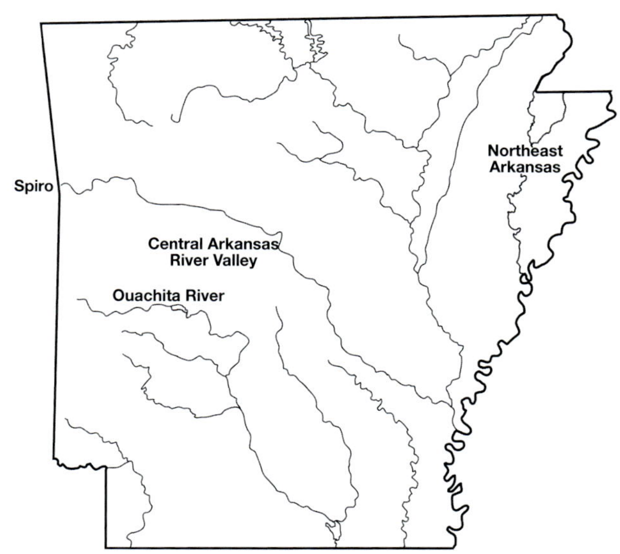

Figure 65. Map showing regions from which most of the museum's archaeological collections were obtained.

Northeast Arkansas

The rich late-prehistoric and protohistoric (between about A.D. 1350 and 1600) archaeological record of northeast Arkansas has been recognized for many years.[1] Ceramic vessels from archaeological sites in the region provide the core of several major museum collections, as well as numerous private collections, and many vessels have appeared in publications, both scholarly and popular. The density of large archaeological sites dating to this time period suggests that around A.D. 1500, northeast Arkansas supported one of the largest Native American populations in eastern North America, perhaps numbering in the tens of thousands.[2]

It is likely that the expedition of the Spanish explorer Hernando de Soto passed through northeastern Arkansas in 1541.[3] There is no record of Europeans visiting the area again until 1673, when Father Jacques Marquette descended the Mississippi River to the mouth of the Arkansas River, where he encountered several Quapaw villages, but he did not report seeing any Native Americans to the north on the Arkansas shore.[4]

Along with the Ozark bluff shelters, late prehistoric archaeological sites in northeast Arkansas were a major focus of the University of Arkansas Museum investigations that were carried out using grant money from the Carnegie Corporation. Between February 1932 and September 1933, the museum conducted large-scale excavations at 11 important archaeological sites in Mississippi, Crittenden, Cross, and Poinsett Counties. Most of the sites in the region are located on prime agricultural lands, and many had already suffered considerable damage from plowing prior to the museum's excavations. The purpose of the excavations was to obtain artifacts for the museum's collections and focused primarily, but not exclusively, on human burials. James Durham and Charles Finger Jr. supervised the fieldwork, which resulted in the excavation of approximately 1,265 individuals.[5]

The excavators located human burials using a thin steel probe. Once a burial was completely exposed, basic information about it was recorded on a standard 3 x 5 inch "burial card," which included a space for sketching the skeleton and associated objects. The locations of all burials were mapped onto large sheets of paper using a transit or alidade and plane table. Some burials were photographed, and there are some general views of sites, as well.[6] Although far below modern archaeological standards, these field records, which are preserved in the museum's files, have provided the basis for several master's theses and a PhD dissertation,[7] while the excavated ceramic vessels have been the subject of other theses.[8]

During late Mississippian times in northeast Arkansas, ceramic vessels were the most common funerary objects placed with the dead.[9] Between about A.D. 1400 and 1600, Native American ceramic artistry reached its peak in northeast Arkansas and adjacent regions. Decoration became more common and complex, including incising, punctation, painting, and modeling. A number of vessels portray various animals, birds, fish, and humans.[10] It is therefore no surprise that museums and collectors have eagerly sought ceramics from northeast Arkansas for many years.

In northeast Arkansas and throughout the central Mississippi Valley, most Native Americans of the time period lived in moderately large towns of perhaps up to 500 individuals. These towns typically included at least one rectangular, flat-topped mound that served as a platform for a shrine/temple and the house of the priest-chief. The houses of other important individuals were located on smaller mounds nearby. Houses generally were rectangular in shape and constructed by setting a series of large upright posts into an excavated trench packed with clay. Small saplings and cane were woven between the posts, and the walls were then covered with moist clay. A hearth was located in the center of the interior, with sleeping and sitting platforms along the walls. Some towns—perhaps most—were surrounded by a moat and/or wood palisade. Corn, beans, and squash were grown in fields near the town. The Mississippi River bottomlands supported large herds of deer and stands of nut-bearing trees; fish and waterfowl were plentiful in oxbow and seasonal lakes.

In northeast Arkansas, around A.D. 1500, Native Americans did not bury most of their dead in mounds, but rather throughout their towns—sometimes even under the floors of houses. Almost all individuals were buried on their back in an extended position. Roughly half of the excavated burials at these towns had no preserved funerary objects. Pottery vessels were the most common objects placed with the dead, often near the head. Other kinds of funerary objects are relatively rare; these include arrow points, shell beads and ear ornaments, bone tools, and ground stone items.[11]

Parkin Archeological State Park, managed by the Arkansas Department of Parks and Tourism, preserves the remains of a large town that was occupied between about A.D. 1250 and 1550 along the St. Francis River in Cross County. The town includes one large mound and was surrounded by a defensive moat. The park features an interpretive center housing exhibits and a research station of the Arkansas Archeological Survey. The Hampson Archeological Museum State Park, also managed by the Department of Parks and Tourism, exhibits many interesting artifacts from northeast Arkansas.

THE COLLECTIONS

Although people have been living in northeast Arkansas since around 10,000 B.C., most of the museum's collections from the region date between approximately A.D. 1350 and 1600. The first date is based on the form and decoration of the pottery vessels in the collections, while the latter date is based on the almost total lack of European beads and metal (brass and iron) objects at the excavated sites.

The museum's collections from northeast Arkansas consist primarily of pottery vessels, although there are also some objects made of bone, shell, and stone. Other objects such as basketry may have been placed with the dead, but were not preserved.

The pottery vessels from northeast Arkansas in the collections are quite similar to those found at contemporary archaeological sites in southeast Missouri, western Kentucky, western Tennessee, and northwest Mississippi. In both vessel form and surface decoration, they are very different from pottery produced along the Arkansas River at roughly during the same time period, and even more different from pottery made by contemporary Caddoan people in southwest Arkansas.

Three basic ceramic vessel forms are found at late-prehistoric sites in the lower Mississippi River valley. Bottles have a distinct body and a narrower vertical neck. Bowls lack a neck and typically have outflaring or straight sides. Jars are characterized by a generally globular body, a wide, constricted neck, and often handles. Around A.D. 1350 decoration became much more commonplace on pottery vessels, including incising (straight or curved lines), punctations (small indentations), and slipping ("painting"), as did effigy vessels. Most of the latter consist of bowls with effigy elements (such as heads) placed on the rim, but human and some other effigy forms were completely modeled. Among animal forms, fish and birds are the most common.

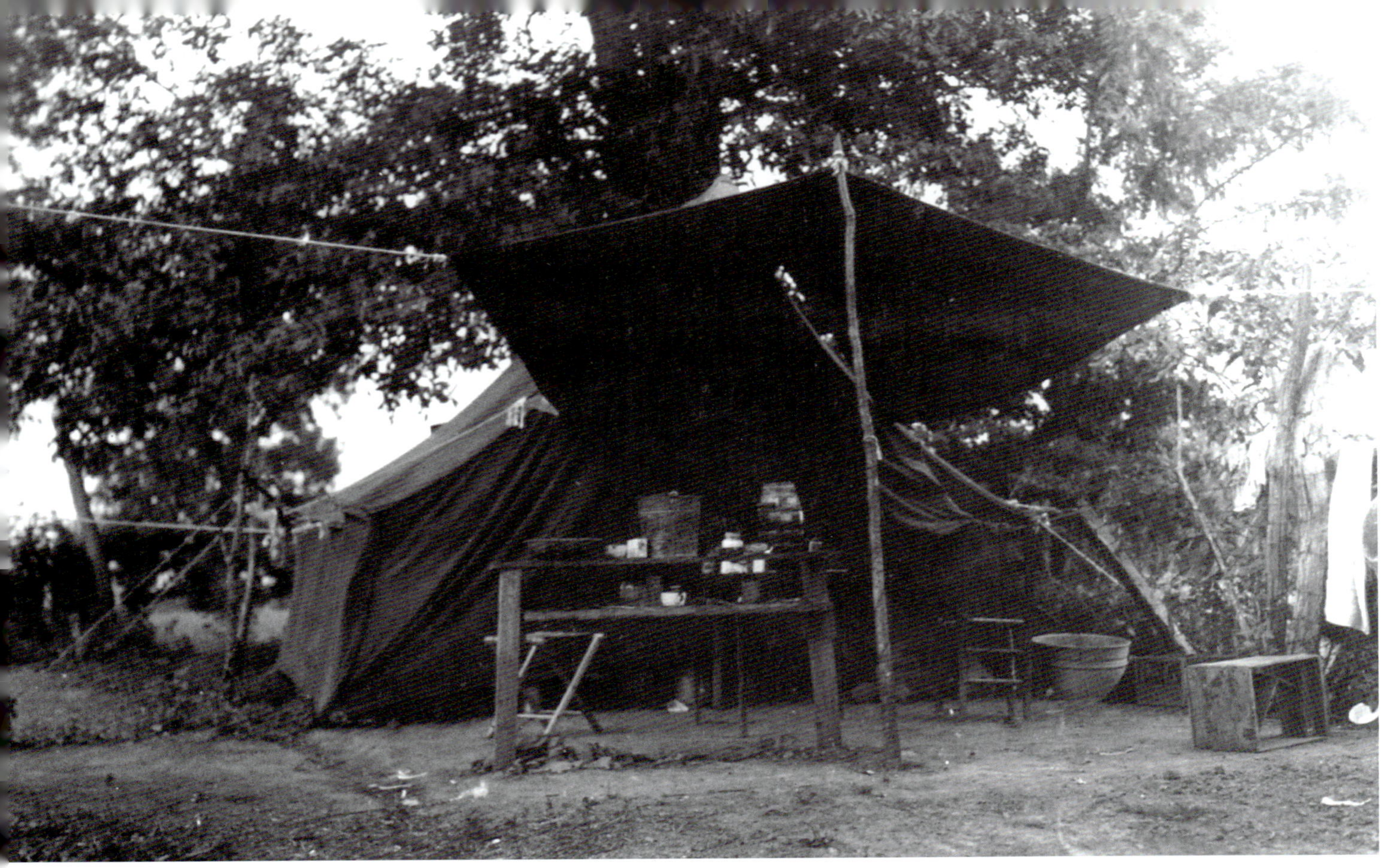

Figure 66. Museum field camp at the Vernon Paul site, 1933.

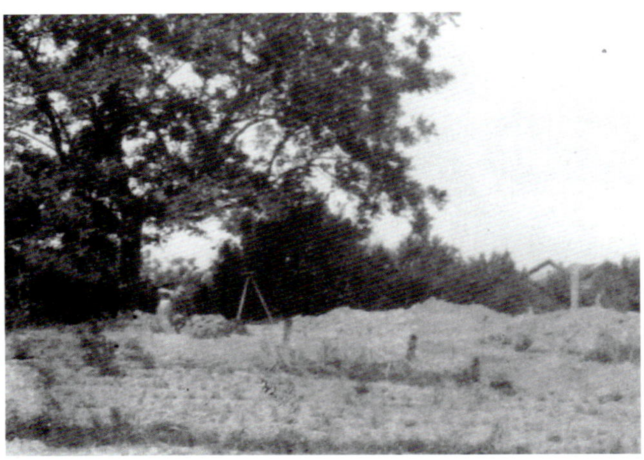

Figure 67. Museum excavations at the Vernon Paul site (Cross County, Arkansas), 1933. Note the plane table to the right of the excavator.

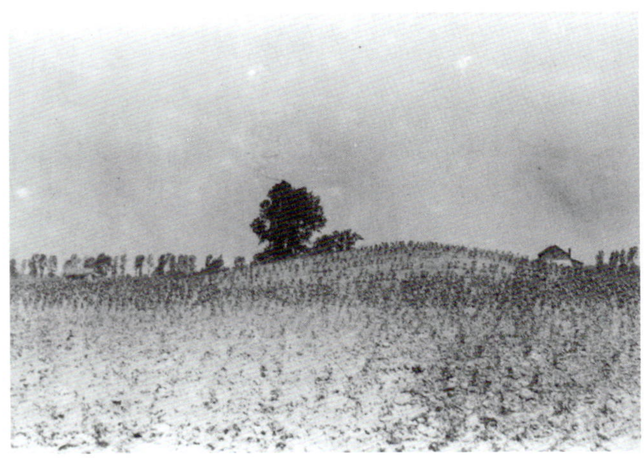

Figure 68. Mound A at Upper Nodena, circa 1932, prior to excavations at the site by the University of Arkansas Museum and the Alabama Museum of Natural History. View is to the east.

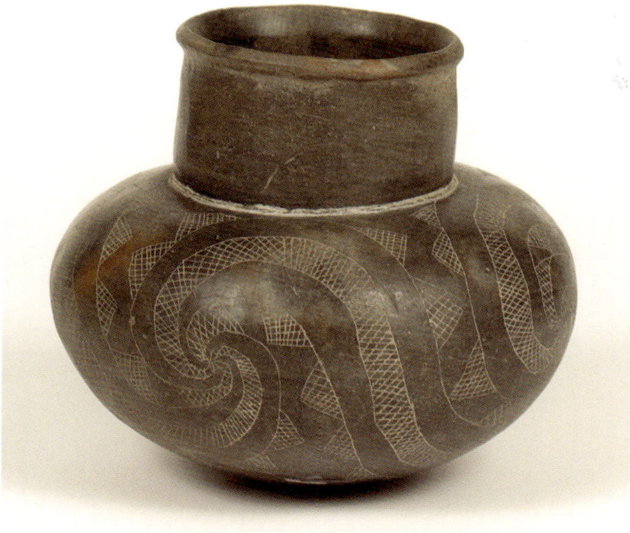

Figure 69. Engraved Bottle with Crosshatched Spirals (Walls Engraved) (OSHTL2006.003.37)
Ceramic; 20.3 x 69.9 cm
Beck Place, Crittenden County, Arkansas
Late Mississippi period, A.D. 1350–1600

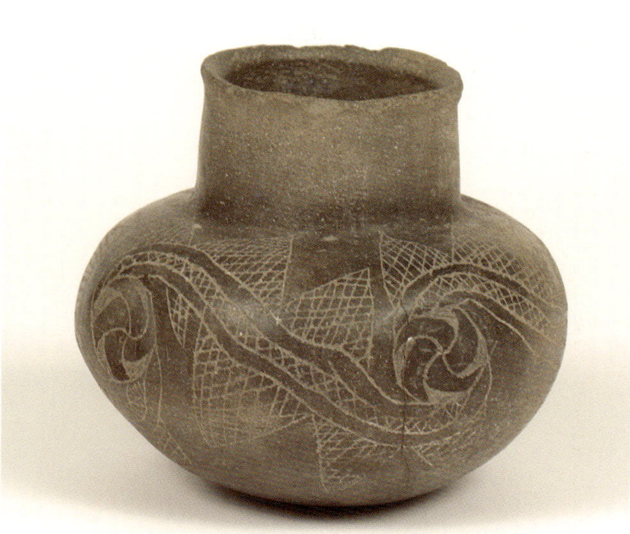

Figure 70. Engraved Bottle with Swastikas and Crosshatched Designs (Walls Engraved) (OSHTL2006.003.38)
Ceramic; 17.8 x 58.4 cm
Beck Place, Crittenden County, Arkansas
Late Mississippi period, A.D. 1350–1600

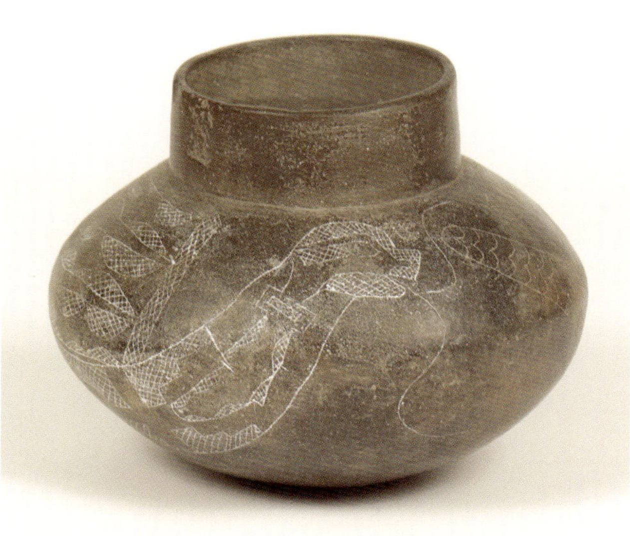

Figure 71. Engraved Bottled with Winged Rattlesnake (Walls Engraved) (OSHTL2006.003.39)
Ceramic; 17.5 x 20.5 cm
Beck Place, Crittenden County, Arkansas
Late Mississippi period, A.D. 1350–1600

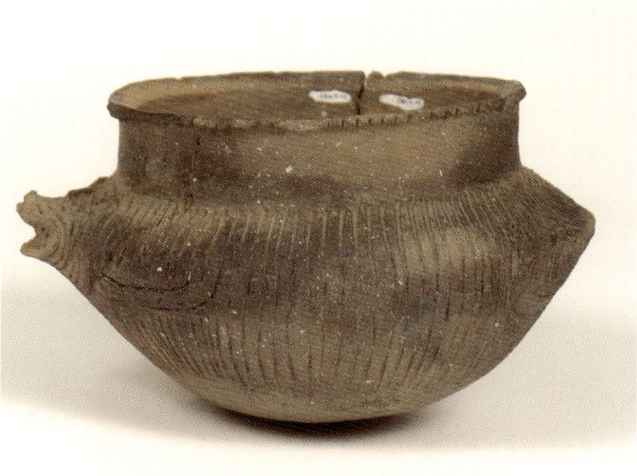

Figure 72. Incised Animal Effigy Jar (Kent Incised) (OSHTL2006.003.40)
Ceramic; 17.8 x 61.0 cm
Beck Place, Crittenden County, Arkansas
Late Mississippi period, A.D. 1350–1600
Ceramic portrayals of the same creature are shown in Figures 37 and 95.

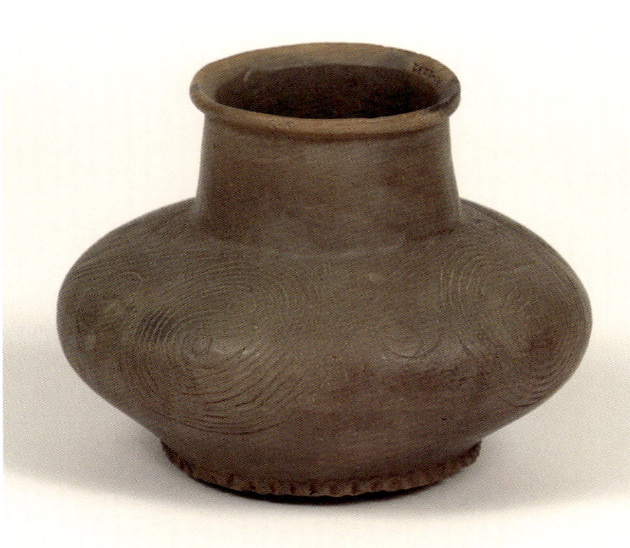

Figure 73. Incised Bottle with Swirls and Swastikas (Rhodes Incised) (OSHTL2006.003.41)
Ceramic; 14.0 x 40.6 cm
Beck Place, Crittenden County, Arkansas
Late Mississippi period, A.D. 1350–1600

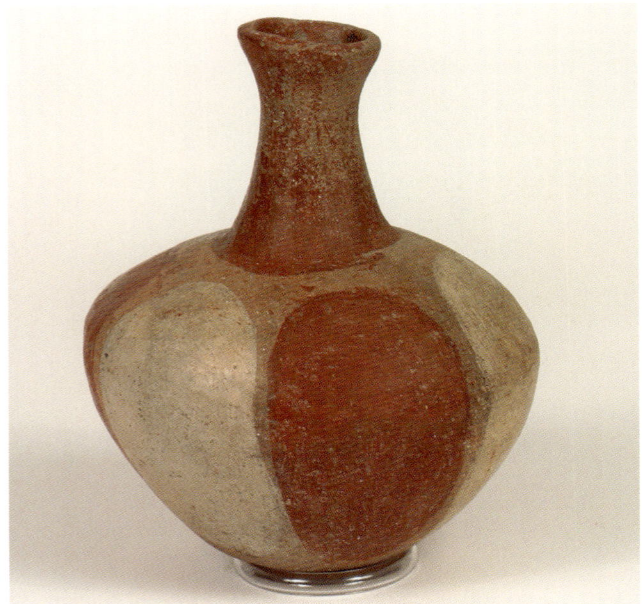

Figure 74. Red and White Slipped Bottle (Nodena Red and White)
(OSHTL2006.003.42)
Ceramic; 22.9 x 63.5 cm
Beck Place, Crittenden County, Arkansas
Late Mississippi period, A.D. 1350–1600

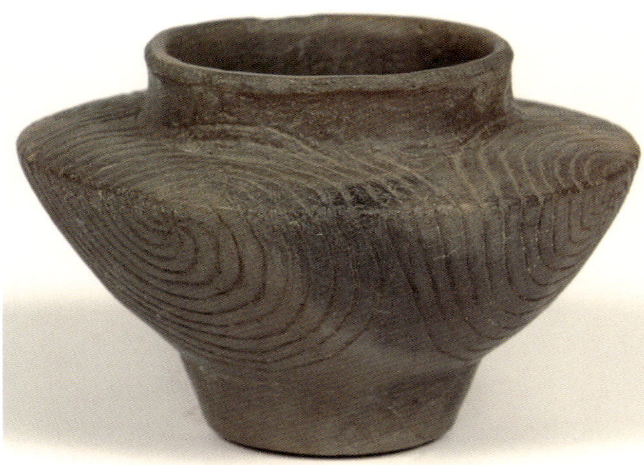

Figure 75. High Shouldered Jar with Incised Spirals (Rhodes Incised)
(OSHTL2006.003.43)
Ceramic; 19.1 x 25.4 cm
Beck Place, Crittenden County, Arkansas
Late Mississippi period, A.D. 1350–1600

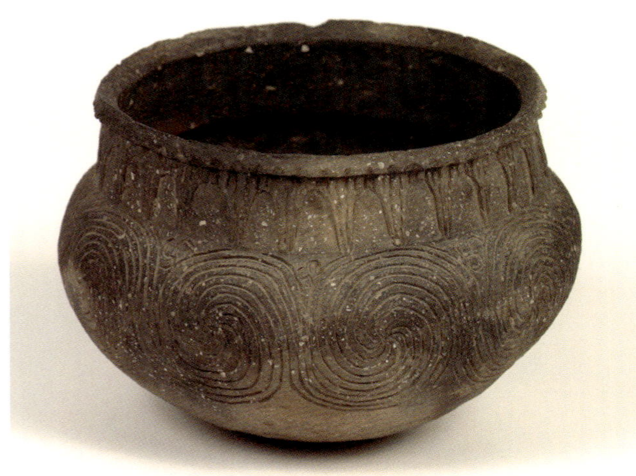

Figure 76. Jar with Incised Spirals (Rhodes Incised) (OSHTL2006.003.44)
Ceramic; 17.8 x 66.7 cm
Beck Place, Crittenden County, Arkansas
Late Mississippi period, A.D. 1350–1600

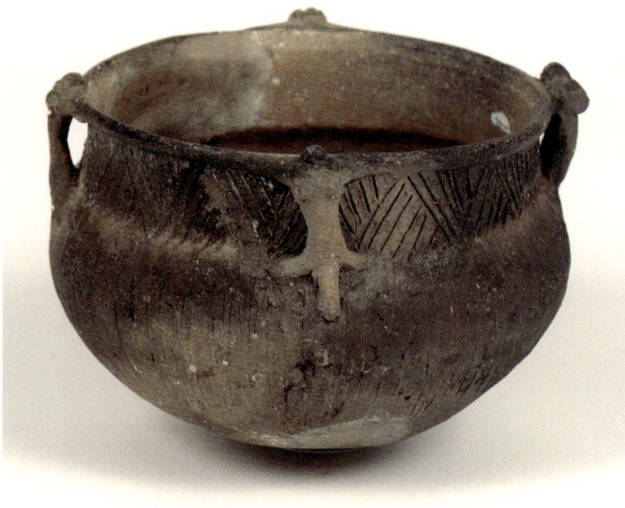

Figure 77. Incised Jar with Applied Effigy Handles (Barton Incised/Kent Incised) (OSHTL2006.003.45)
Ceramic; 19.1 x 62.2 cm
Beck Place, Crittenden County, Arkansas
Late Mississippi period, A.D. 1350–1600

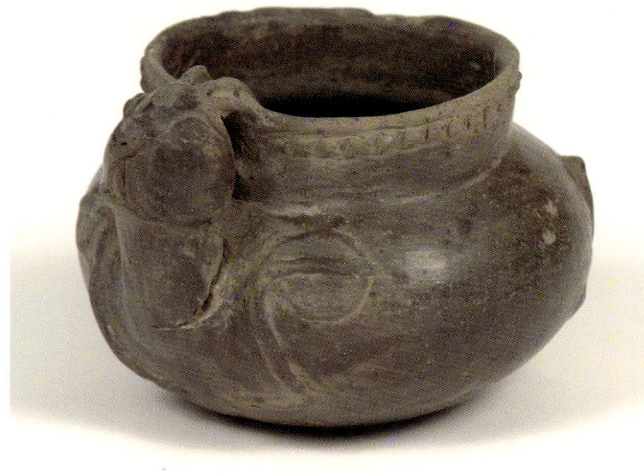

Figure 78. Swamp Rabbit Effigy Jar (Bell Plain) (OSHTL2006.003.48)
Ceramic; 14.0 x 50.8 cm
Upper Nodena, Mississippi County, Arkansas
Late Mississippi period, A.D. 1350–1600
The swamp rabbit (*Sylvilagus aquaticus*) is larger than the common cottontail and inhabits wetland areas in the Southeast.

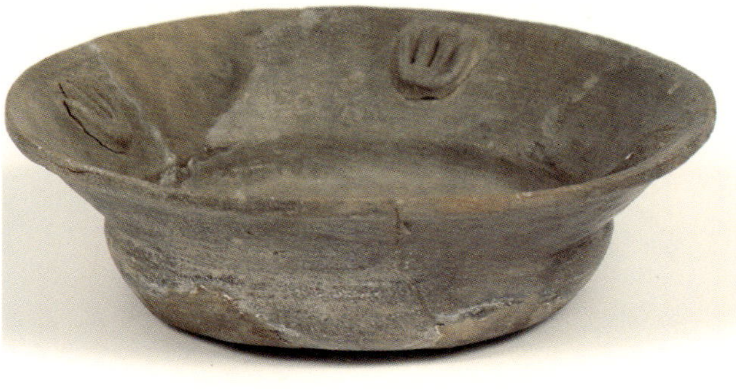

Figure 79. Flared Rim Bowl with Appliqué Hands (Bell Plain) (OSHTL2006.003.50)
Ceramic; 8.5 x 28.3 cm (restored)
Middle Nodena, Mississippi County, Arkansas
Late Mississippi period, A.D. 1350–1600

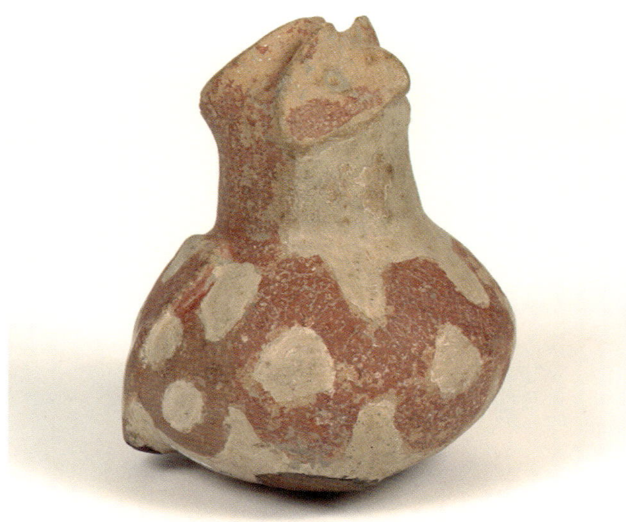

Figure 80. Red and White Owl Effigy Bottle (Nodena Red and White) (OSHTL2006.003.51)
Ceramic; 18.4 x 45.7 cm
Liddon Place, Pecan Point Bend, Mississippi County, Arkansas
Late Mississippi period, A.D. 1350–1600

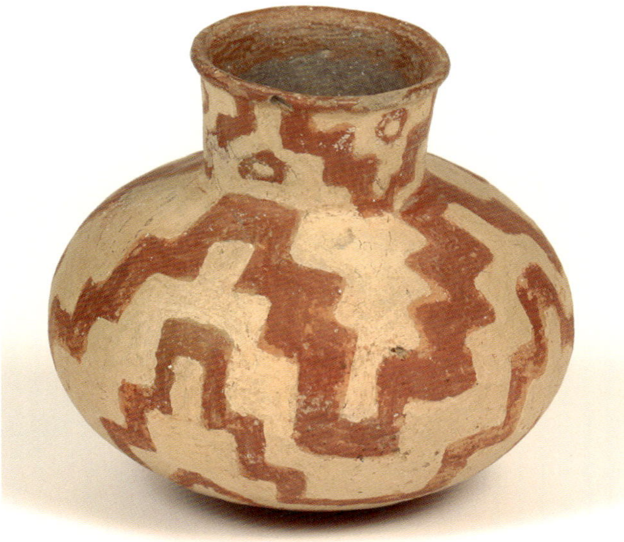

Figure 81. Red and White Bottle with Stairstep Designs (Nodena Red and White) (OSHTL2006.003.52)
Ceramic; 17.1 x 19.7 cm
Neeley's Ferry, Cross County, Arkansas
Late Mississippi period, A.D. 1350–1600

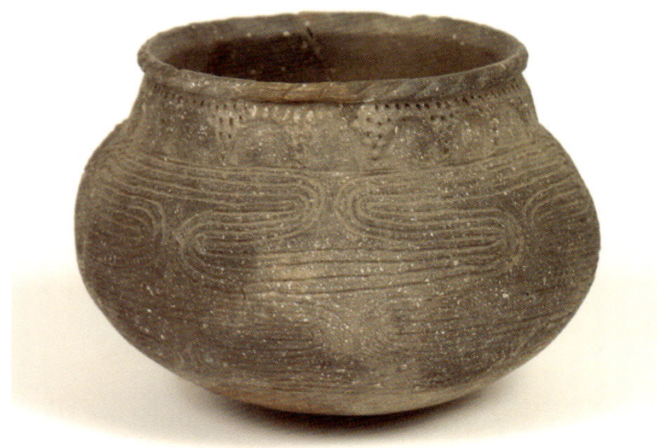

Figure 82. Incised Jar (Leland Incised, *var. Leflore*) (OSHTL2006.003.54)
Ceramic; 11.5 x 17.2 cm
Upper Nodena, Mississippi County, Arkansas
Late Mississippi period, A.D. 1350–1600

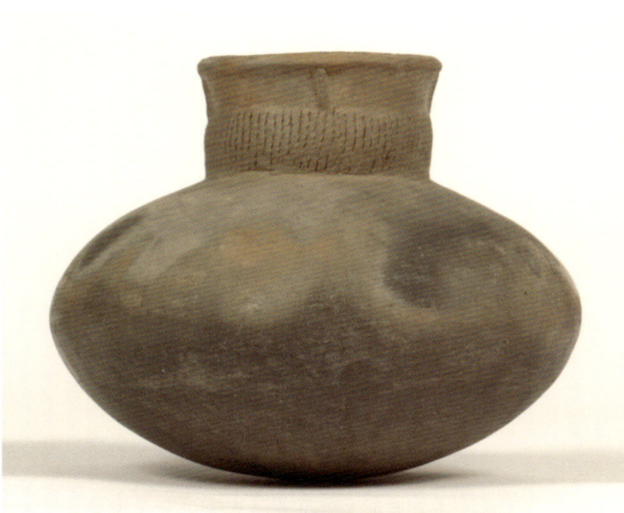

Figure 83. Compound ("Jar-Necked") Bottle (Bell Plain with punctations on neck) (OSHTL2006.003.55)
Ceramic; 16.7 x 20.4 cm
Middle Nodena, Mississippi County, Arkansas
Late Mississippi period, A.D. 1350–1600

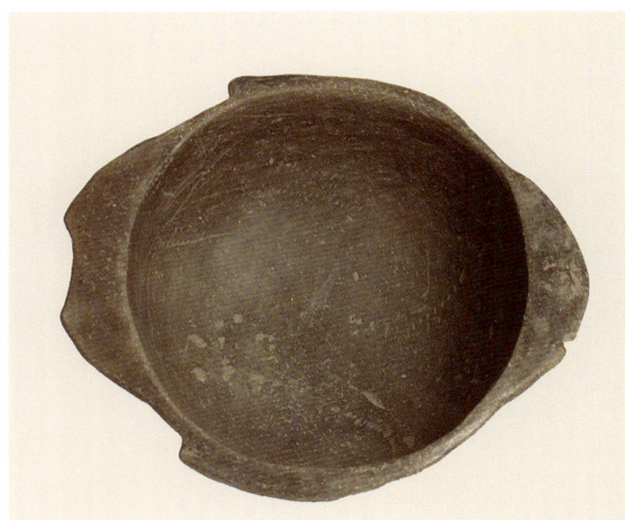

Figure 84. Fish (Bowfin) Effigy Bowl (Bell Plain) (OSHTL2006.003.56)
Ceramic; 10.0 x 24.0 cm
Hazel site, Poinsett County, Arkansas
Late Mississippi period, A.D. 1350–1600

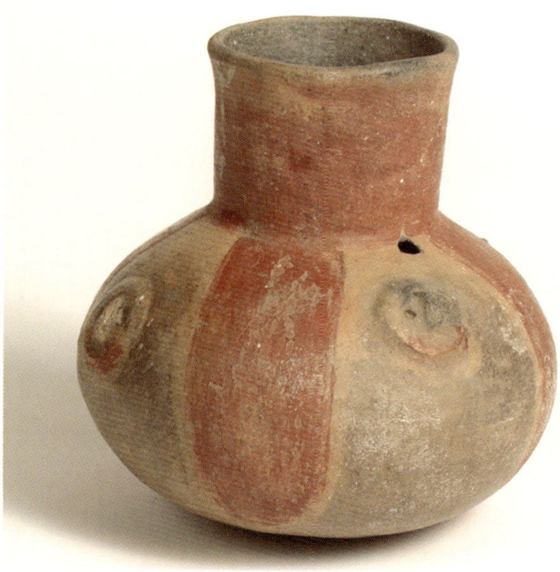

Figure 85a. Red on Buff Bottle with Four Appliqué Faces (Carson Red on Buff) (OSHTL2006.003.57)
Ceramic; 18.4 x 25.4 cm
Hazel site, Poinsett County, Arkansas
Late Mississippi period, A.D. 1350–1600

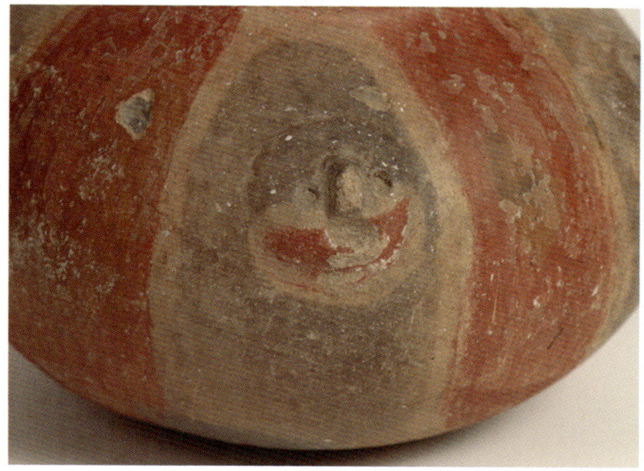

Figure 85b. Detail of Appliqué Head (OSHTL2006.003.57)

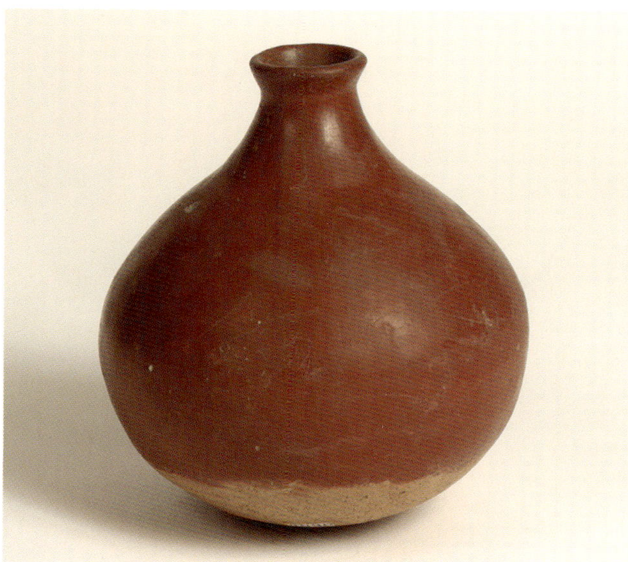

Figure 86. Red Slipped Bottle with Flared Mouth (Old Town Red) (OSHTL2006.003.58)
Ceramic; 16.5 x 16.5 cm
Cross County, Arkansas
Late Mississippi period, A.D. 1350–1600

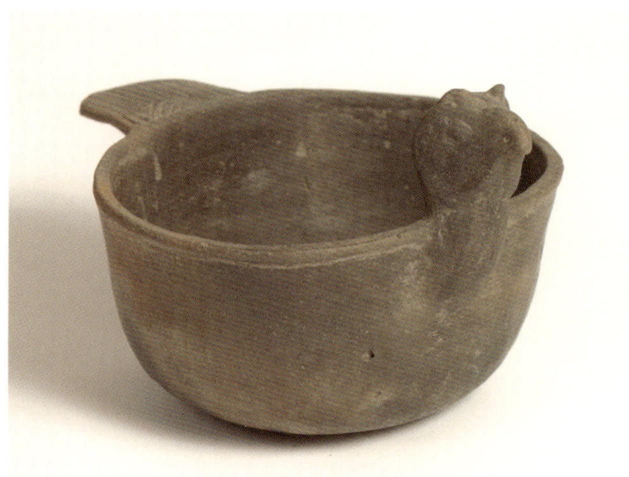

Figure 87. Bird Effigy Bowl (Bell Plain) (OSHTL2006.003.59)
Ceramic; 14.0 x 23.2 cm
Middle Nodena, Mississippi County, Arkansas
Late Mississippi period, A.D. 1350–1600

Figure 88. Red and White Turtle Effigy Bottle (Nodena Red and White) (OSHTL2006.003.60)
Ceramic; 16.8 x 22.8 cm (neck removed prehistorically)
Near Marked Tree (probably Hazel site), Poinsett County, Arkansas
Late Mississippi period, A.D. 1350–1600

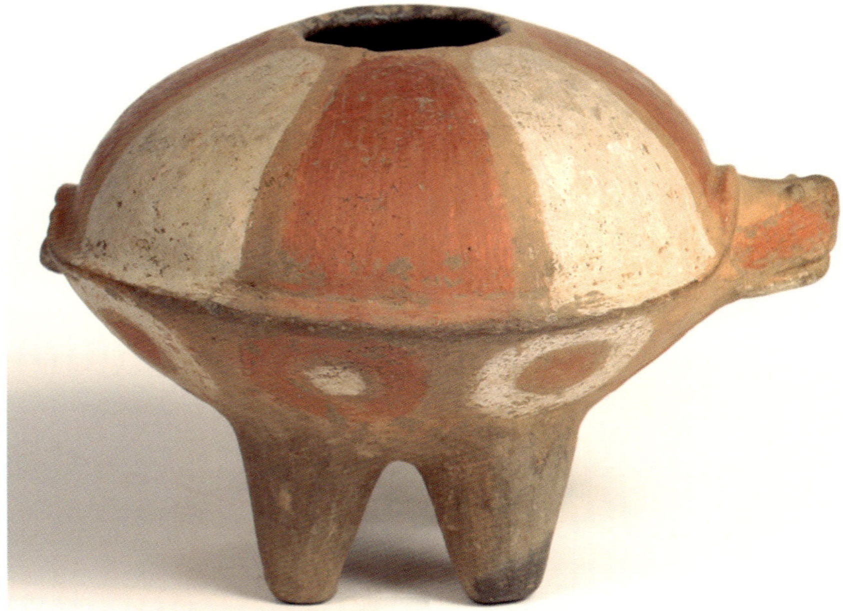

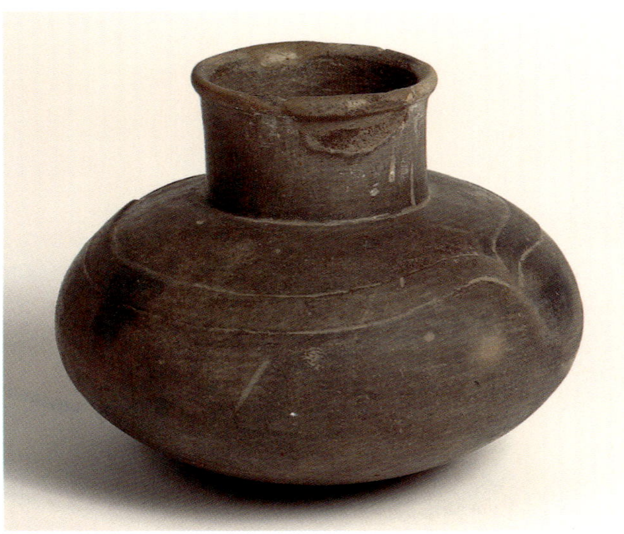

Figure 89. Bottle with Appliqué Ogee Design (Bell Plain) (OSHTL2006.003.61)
Ceramic; 15.8 x 20.5 cm
Middle Nodena, Mississippi County, Arkansas
Late Mississippi period, A.D. 1350–1600

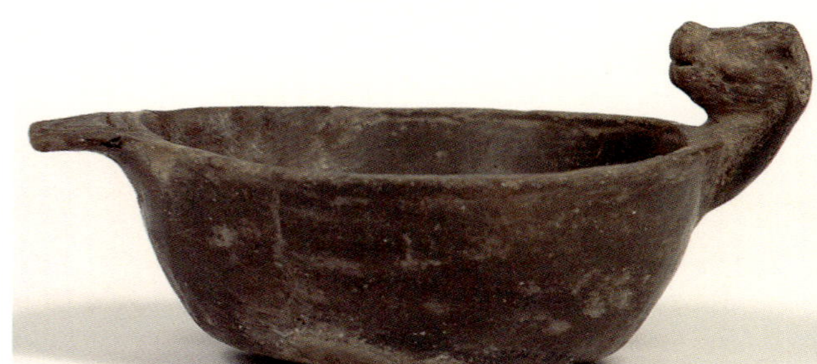

Figure 90. Animal Effigy Bowl (Bell Plain) (OSHTL2006.003.62)
Ceramic; 16.5 x 52.1 cm (restored)
Upper Nodena, Mississippi County, Arkansas
Late Mississippi period, A.D. 1350–1600

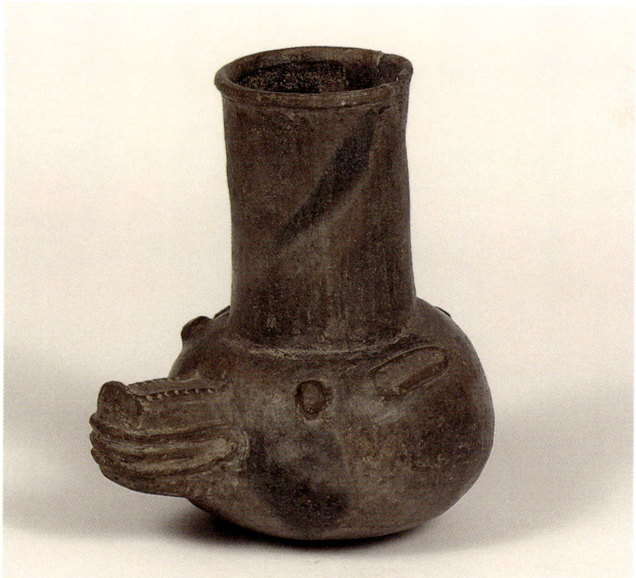

Figure 91. Bear Effigy Bottle (Bell Plain) (OSHTL2006.003.63)
Ceramic; 20.3 x 50.8 cm
Beck Place, Crittenden County, Arkansas
Late Mississippi period, A.D. 1350–1600

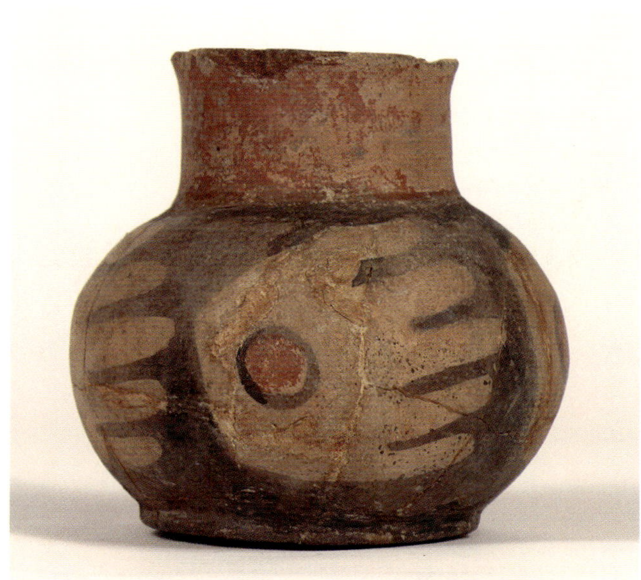

Figure 92. Negative Painted Bottle with Human Hand Motifs (OSHTL2006.003.64)
Ceramic; 15.2 x 30.5 cm
Barton Ranch, Crittenden County, Arkansas
Late Mississippi period, A.D. 1350–1600

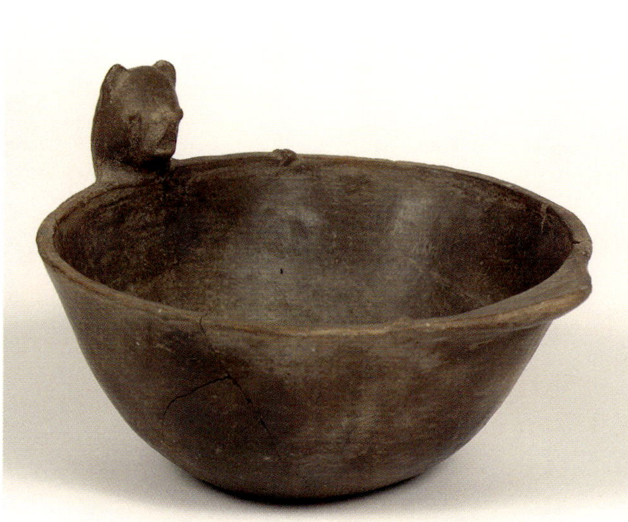

Figure 93. Bat Effigy Bowl (Bell Plain) (OSHTL2006.003.65)
Ceramic; 15.9 x 68.6 cm
Upper Nodena, Mississippi County, Arkansas
Late Mississippi period, A.D. 1350–1600

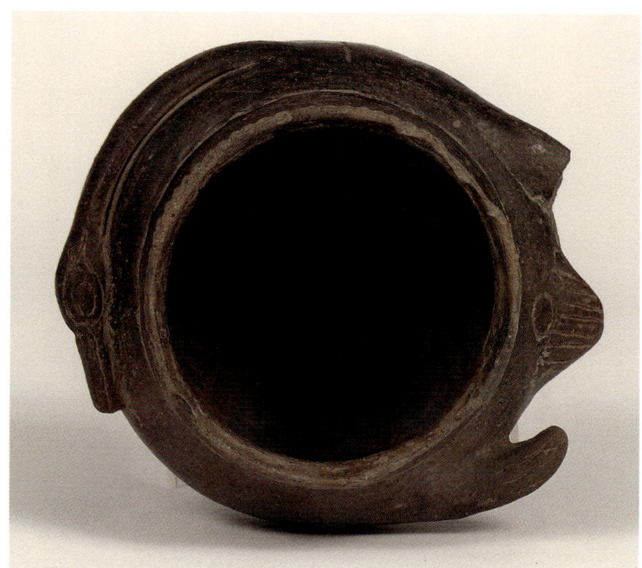

Figure 94. Goose or Swan Effigy Bowl (Bell Plain) (OSHTL2006.003.66)
Ceramic; 13.3 x 60.3 cm
Banks-Danner site, Crittenden County, Arkansas
Late Mississippi period, A.D. 1350–1600

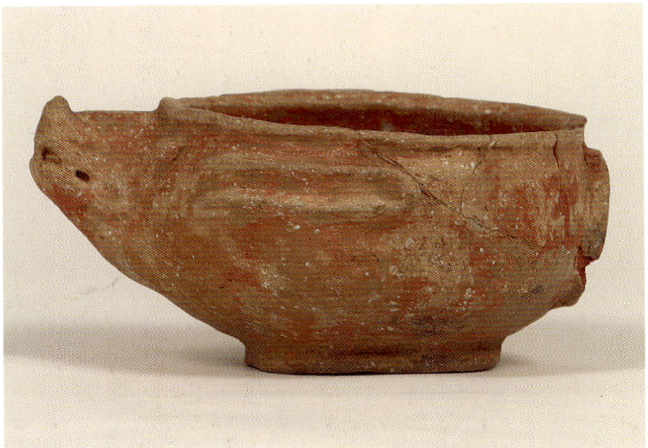

Figure 95a. Red Slipped (Old Town Red) Effigy Bowl (mythological beast?) (OSHTL2006.003.67)
Ceramic; 15.9 x 56.5 cm
Marked Tree (probably Hazel site), Poinsett County, Arkansas
Late Mississippi period, A.D. 1350–1600
Ceramic portrayals of the same creature are shown in Figures 37 and 72.

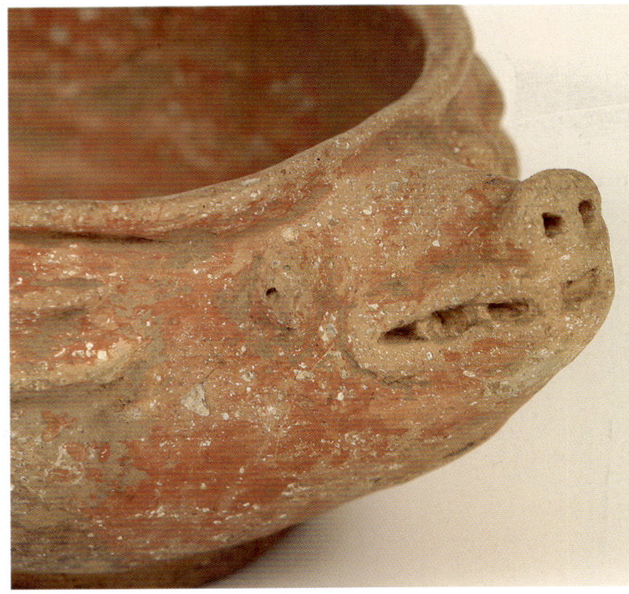

Figure 95b. Detail of Face (OSHTL2006.003.67)

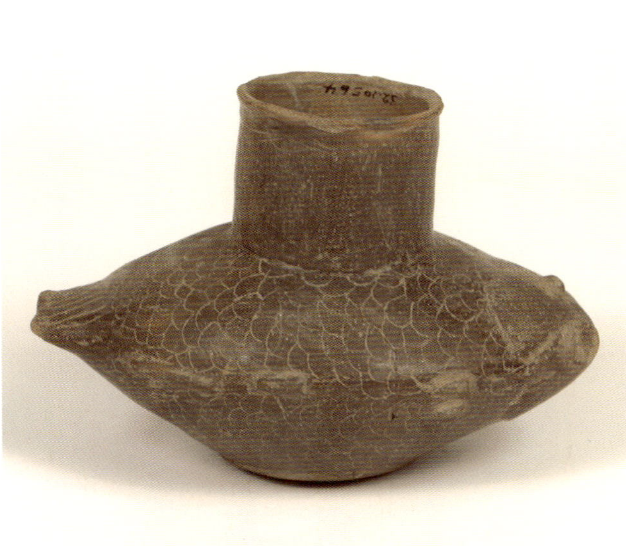

Figure 96. Bigmouth Buffalo Fish Effigy Bowl (Bell Plain) (OSHTL2006.003.68)
Ceramic; 17.8 x 27.8 cm
Upper Nodena, Mississippi County, Arkansas
Late Mississippi period, A.D. 1350–1600

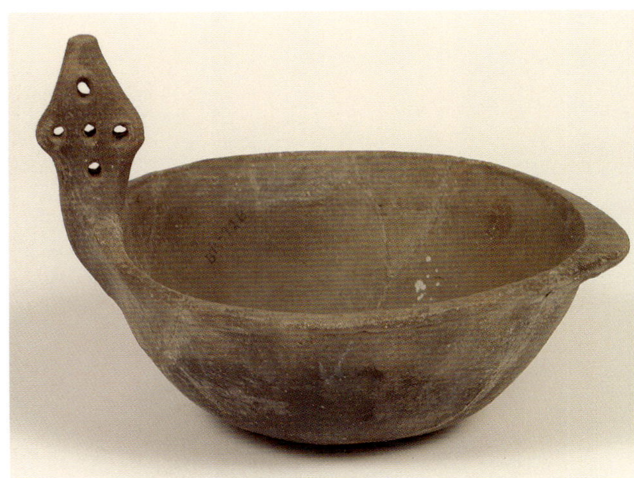

Figure 97. Bowl with Mace(?) Effigy Rim Rider (Bell Plain) (OSHTL2006.003.69)
Ceramic; 24.1 x 71.1 cm
Bradley Place, Crittenden County, Arkansas
Late Mississippi period, A.D. 1350–1600

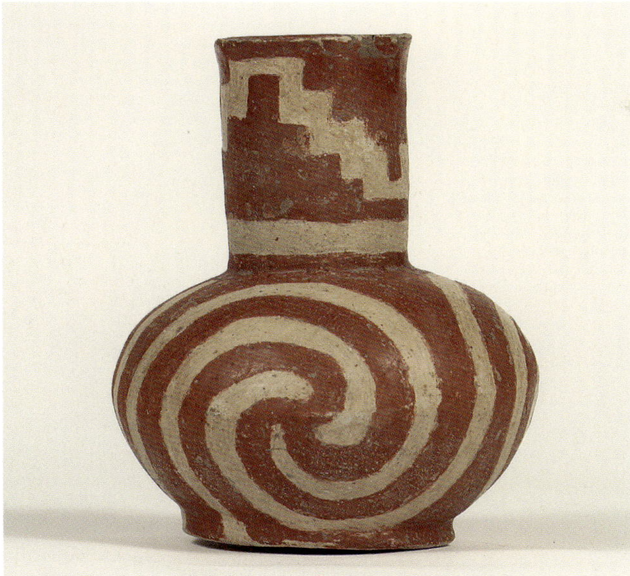

Figure 98. Red Slipped Bottle with Excised Spiral and Stairstep Designs (OSHTL2006.003.70)
Ceramic; 22.2 x 55.9 cm
Hazel site, Poinsett County, Arkansas
Late Mississippi period, A.D. 1350–1600

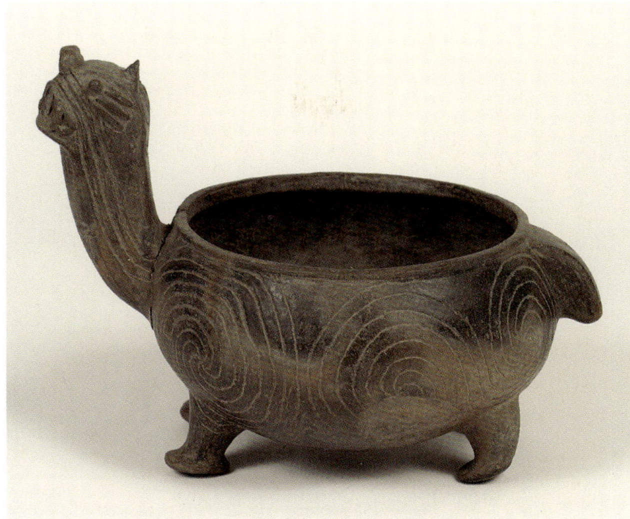

Figure 99. Zoomorphic Effigy Jar with Incised Spirals (Rhodes Incised) (OSHTL2006.003.71)
Ceramic; 22.9 x 71.1 cm
Beck Place, Crittenden County, Arkansas
Late Mississippi period, A.D. 1350–1600

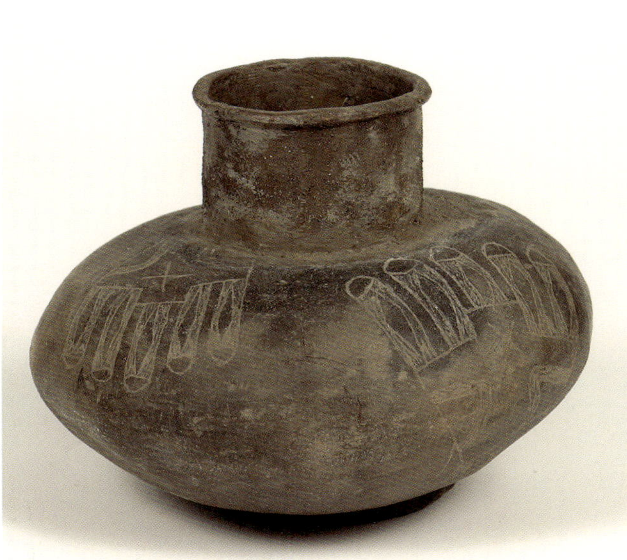

Figure 100. Bottle with Crudely Incised Hands (Bell Plain) (OSHTL2006.003.72)
Ceramic; 19.1 x 68.6 cm
Bob Rhodes Place, Crittenden County, Arkansas
Late Mississippi period, A.D. 1350–1600

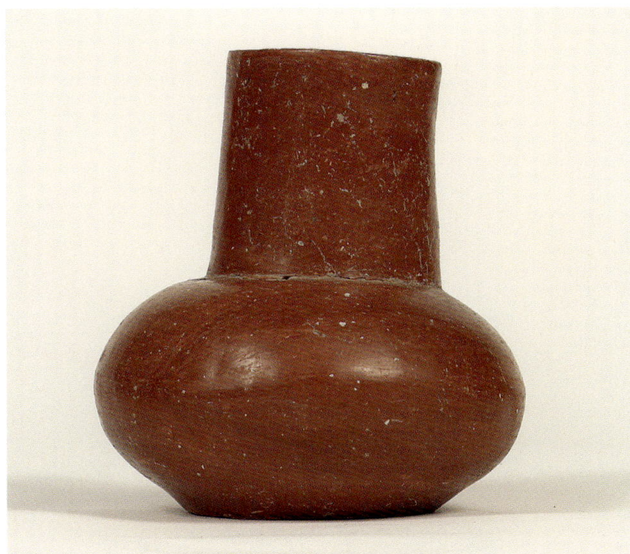

Figure 101. Red Slipped Bottle with Wide Neck (Old Town Red) (OSHTL2006.003.73)
Ceramic; 16.3 x 15.9 cm
Vernon Paul site, Cross County, Arkansas
Late Mississippi period, A.D. 1350–1600

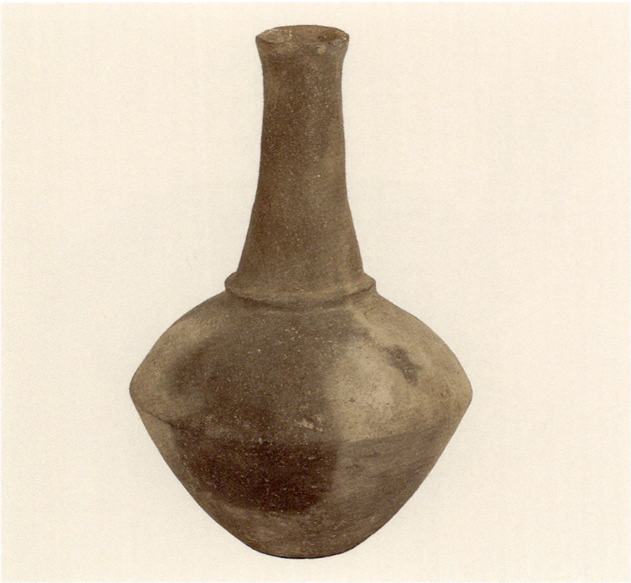

Figure 102. Carinated Bottle (Bell Plain) (OSHTL2006.003.74)
Ceramic; 27.3 x 53.3 cm
Hazel site, Poinsett County, Arkansas
Late Mississippi period, A.D. 1350–1600

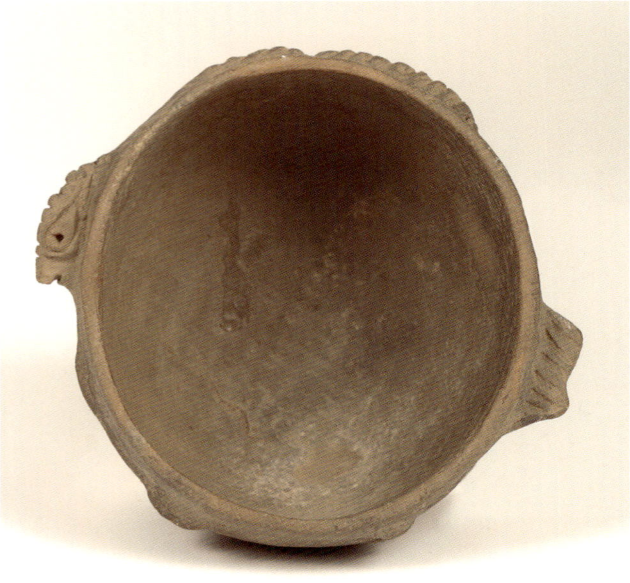

Figure 103. Effigy Bowl with Brook Lamprey Head and Fish Tail (Bell Plain) (OSHTL2006.003.75)
Ceramic; 16.5 x 54.6 cm
Bell Place, Mississippi County, Arkansas
Late Mississippi period, A.D. 1350–1600

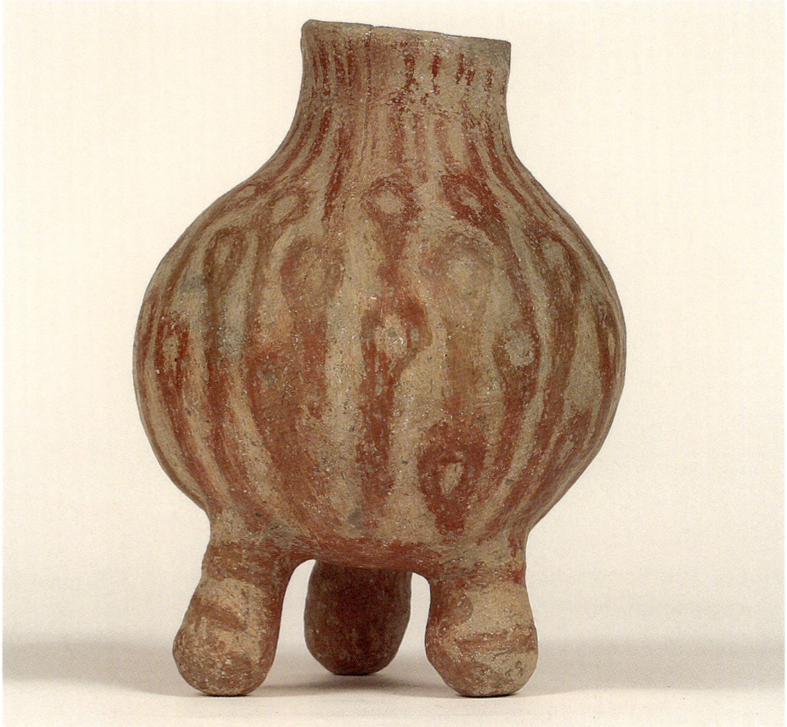

Figure 104. Red on Buff Tripod Bottle (Carson Red on Buff) (OSHTL2006.003.76)
Ceramic; 19.0 x 26.0 cm
Vernon Paul site, Cross County, Arkansas
Late Mississippi period, A.D. 1350–1600

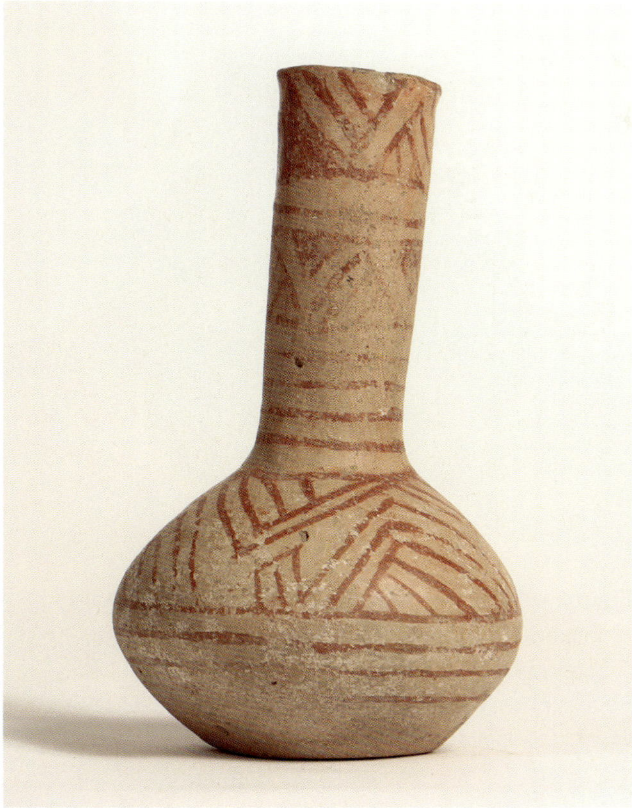

Figure 105. Red and Buff Slipped Bottle with Chevron Designs (OSHTL2006.003.77)
Ceramic; 20.3 x 38.7 cm
Hazel site, Poinsett County, Arkansas
Late Mississippi period, A.D. 1350–1600

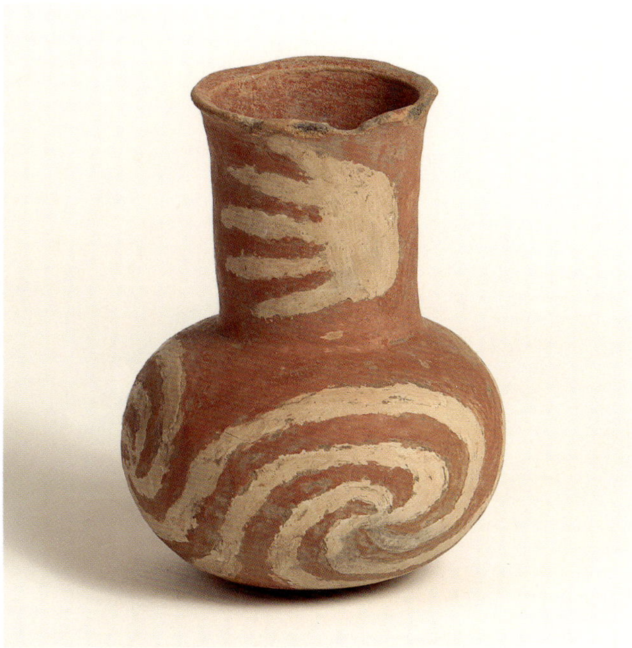

Figure 106. Red and White Slipped Bottle with Spirals and Hands (Nodena Red and White) (OSHTL2006.003.78)
Ceramic; 22.9 x 55.9 cm
Rhodes Place, Crittenden County, Arkansas
Late Mississippi period, A.D. 1350–1600

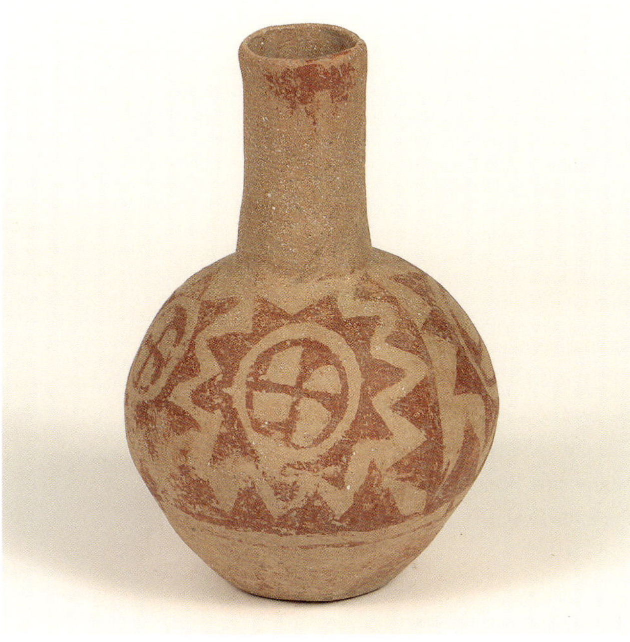

Figure 107. Red on Buff Bottle with Swastikas within Sun Bursts (Carson Red on Buff) (OSHTL2006.003.79)
Ceramic; 25.4 x 53.3 cm
Hazel site, Poinsett County, Arkansas
Late Mississippi period, A.D. 1350–1600

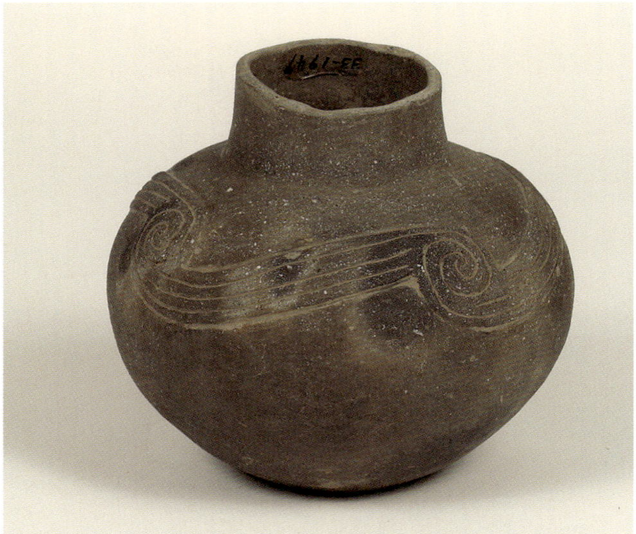

Figure 108. Incised Bottle with Curvilinear Scrolls (Mississippi Plain) (OSHTL2006.003.80)
Ceramic; 17.8 x 58.4 cm
Hazel site, Poinsett County, Arkansas
Late Mississippi period, A.D. 1350–1600

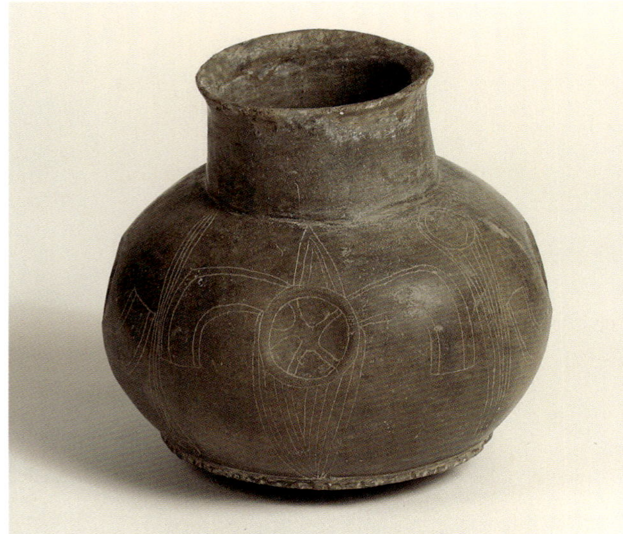

Figure 109. Engraved Bottle with Four Dimples (Walls Engraved) (OSHTL2006.003.81)
Ceramic; 17.8 x 50.8 cm
Rhodes Place, Crittenden County, Arkansas
Late Mississippi period, A.D. 1350–1600

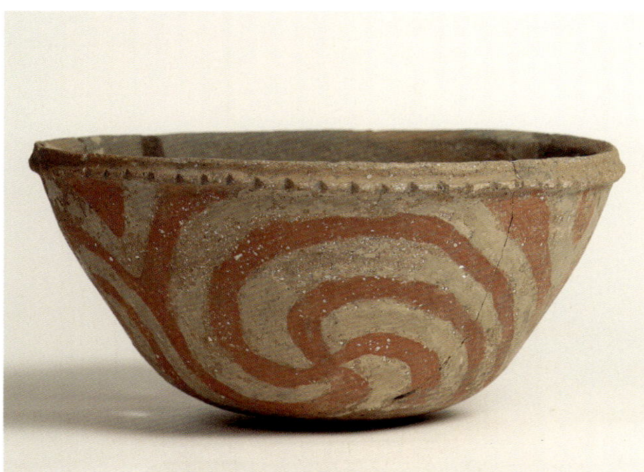

Figure 110. Red on Buff Bowl with Spirals (Carson Red on Buff) (OSHTL2006.003.82)
Ceramic; 28.6 x 88.9 cm
Hazel site, Poinsett County, Arkansas
Late Mississippi period, A.D. 1350–1600

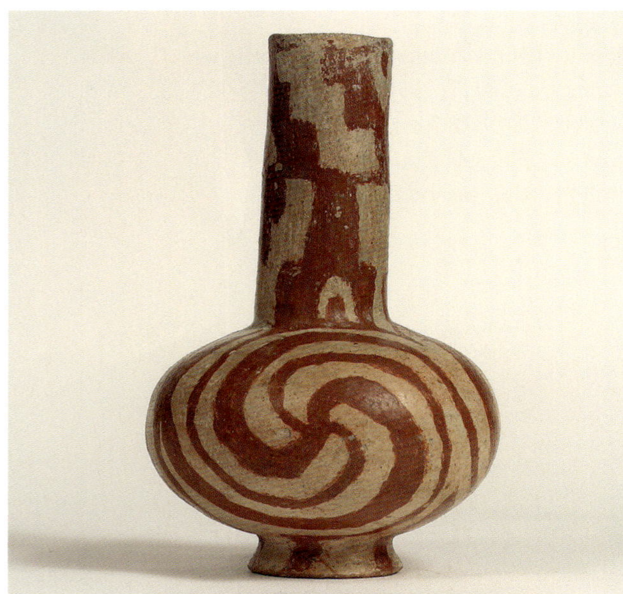

Figure 111. Red on Buff Bottle with Spirals and Stairstep Design (Carson Red on Buff) (OSHTL2006.003.83)
Ceramic; 30.5 x 63.5 cm
Hazel site, Poinsett County, Arkansas
Late Mississippi period, A.D. 1350–1600

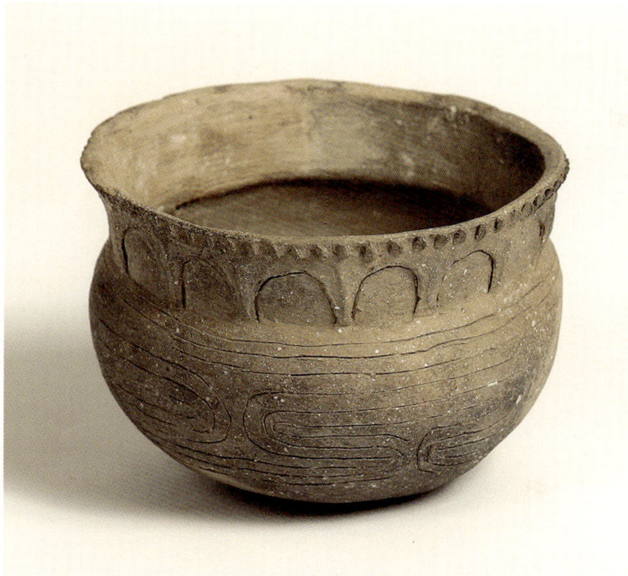

Figure 112. Incised Jar with Excised Symbolic Handles (Leland Incised, *var. Leflore*) (OSHTL2006.003.84)
Ceramic; 17.1 x 43.2 cm
Upper Nodena, Mississippi County, Arkansas
Late Mississippi period, A.D. 1350–1600

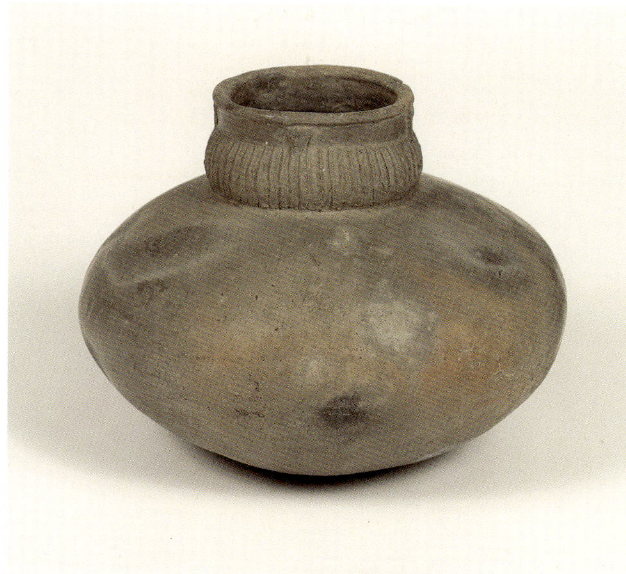

Figure 113. Compound ("Jar-Necked") Bottle (Bell Plain with Kent Incised on neck) (OSHTL2006.003.85)
Ceramic; 14.0 x 59.1 cm
Hazel site, Poinsett County, Arkansas
Late Mississippi period, A.D. 1350–1600

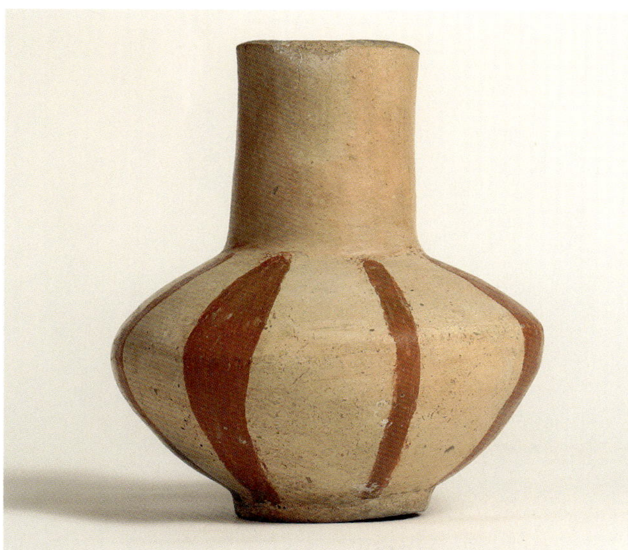

Figure 114. Red on Buff Bottle with Vertical Stripes (Carson Red on Buff) (OSHTL2006.003.86)
Ceramic; 22.9 x 63.5 cm
Upper Nodena, Mississippi County, Arkansas
Late Mississippi period, A.D. 1350–1600

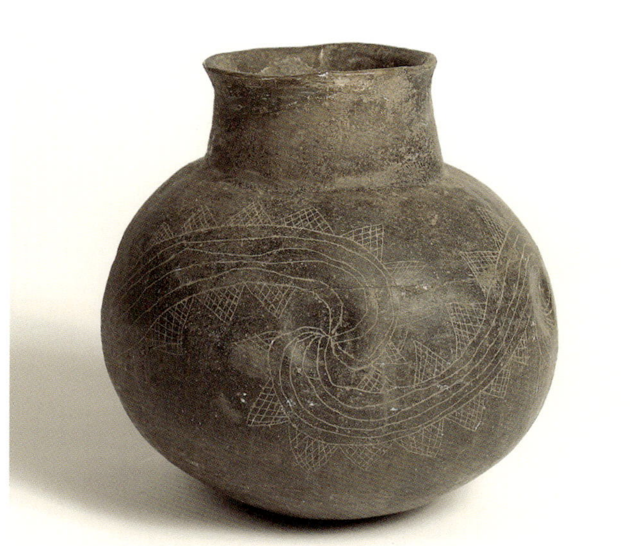

Figure 115. Bottle with Engraved Curvilinear Scroll and Four Dimples (Walls Engraved) (OSHTL2006.003.89)
Ceramic; 22.6 x 66.0 cm
Bell Place, Mississippi County, Arkansas
Late Mississippi period, A.D. 1350–1600

Figure 116. Red Slipped Head Pot with Incising (tattooing?) (Old Town Red) (OSHTL2006.003.91)
Ceramic; 13.3 x 50.8 cm
Lower Friend Place, Mississippi County, Arkansas
Late Mississippi period, A.D. 1350–1600

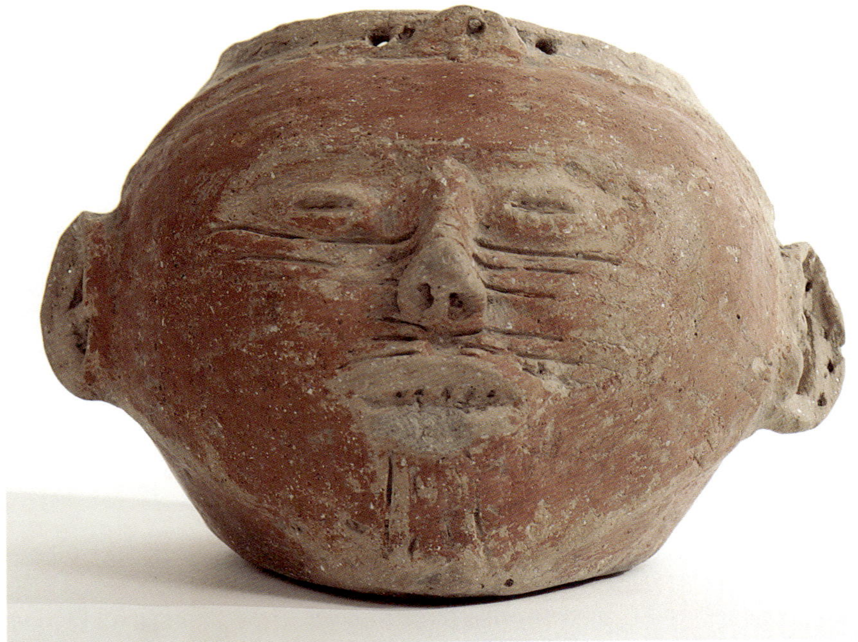

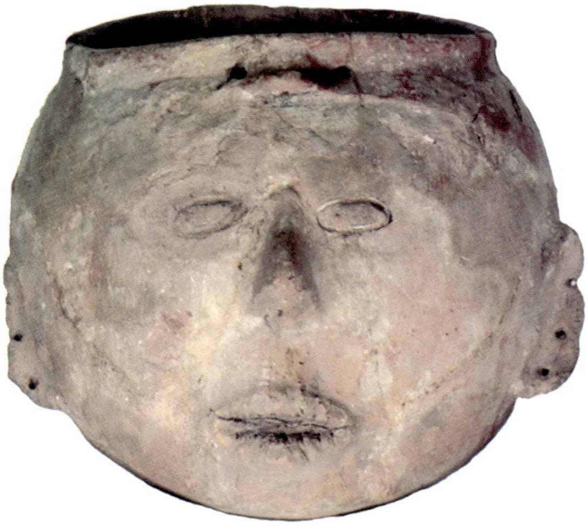

Figure 117. Red and Buff Head Pot (Carson Red and Buff) (OSHTL2006.003.92)
Ceramic; 15.0 x 38.1 cm
Bradley Place, Mississippi County, Arkansas
Late Mississippi period, A.D. 1350–1600
Partially restored.

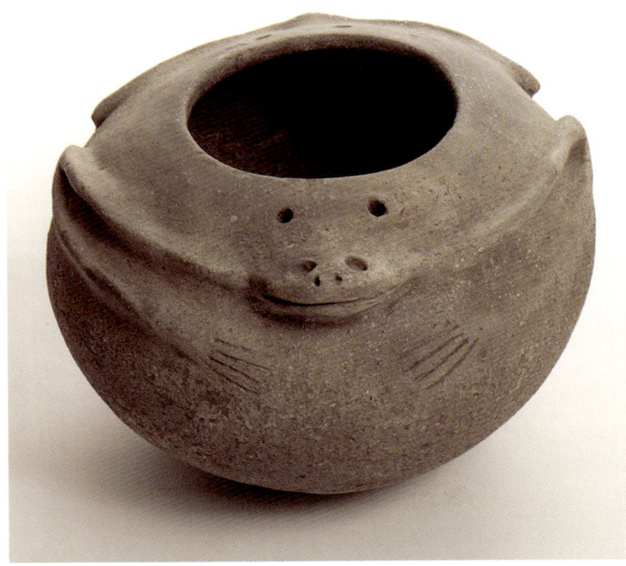

Figure 118. Frog Effigy Jar (Bell Plain) (OSHTL2006.003.93)
Ceramic; 22.9 x 73.7 cm
Near Earle, Crittenden County, Arkansas
Late Mississippi period, A.D. 1350–1600

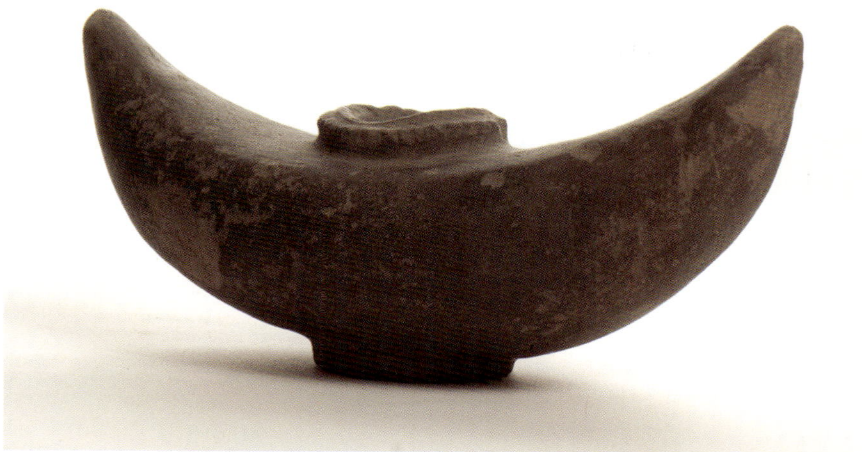

Figure 119. Horn or Boat Effigy Bottle (Bell Plain) (OSHTL2006.003.95)
Ceramic; 8.9 x 20.3 cm (neck removed prehistorically)
Bradley Place, Crittenden County, Arkansas
Late Mississippi period, A.D. 1350–1600

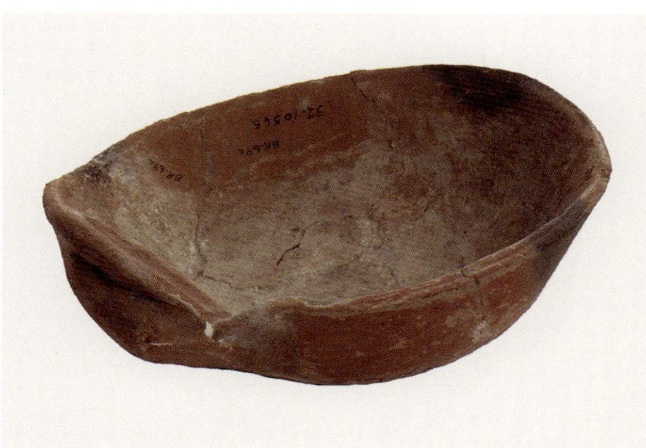

Figure 120. Red Slipped Mussel Shell Effigy Bowl (Old Town Red) (OSHTL2006.003.96)
Ceramic; 21.6 x 16.5 x 7.5 cm
Bradley Place, Crittenden County, Arkansas
Late Mississippi period, A.D. 1350–1600

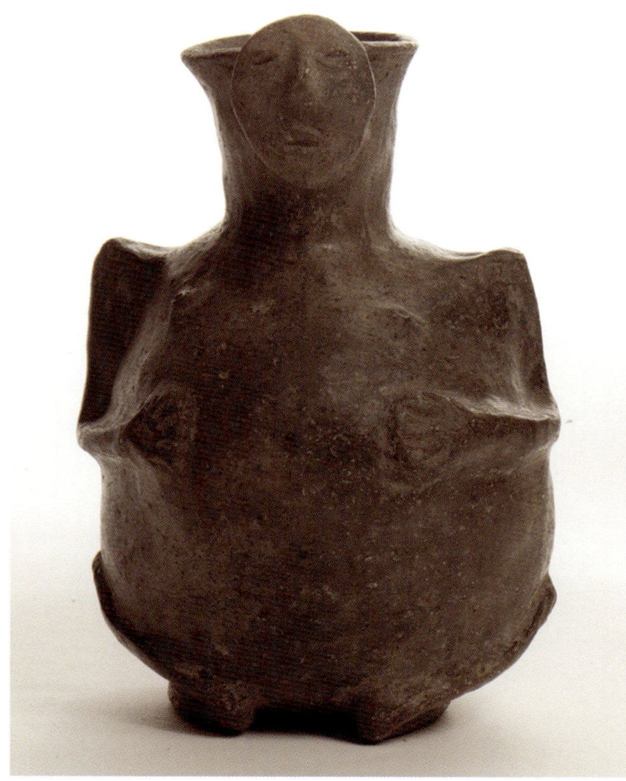

Figure 121. Human Effigy Bottle (Bell Plain) (OSHTL2006.003.98)
Ceramic; 17.8 x 44.5 cm
Near Earle, Crittenden County, Arkansas
Late Mississippi period, A.D. 1350–1600

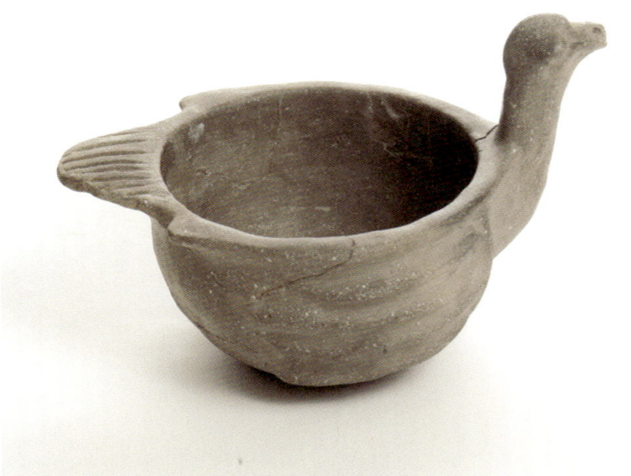

Figure 122. Bird Effigy Bowl (Mississippi Plain) (OSHTL2006.003.99)
Ceramic; 24.1 x 16.5 x 53.3 cm
Hazel site, Poinsett County, Arkansas
Late Mississippi period, A.D. 1350–1600

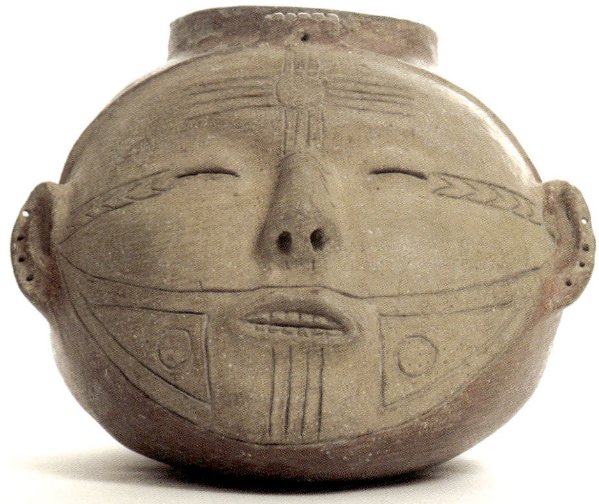

Figure 123. Red on Buff Head Pot with Incising (tattooing?) (Carson Red on Buff) (OSHTL2006.003.101)
Ceramic; 16.0 x 19.5 cm
Bradley Place, Crittenden County, Arkansas
Late Mississippi period, A.D. 1350–1600

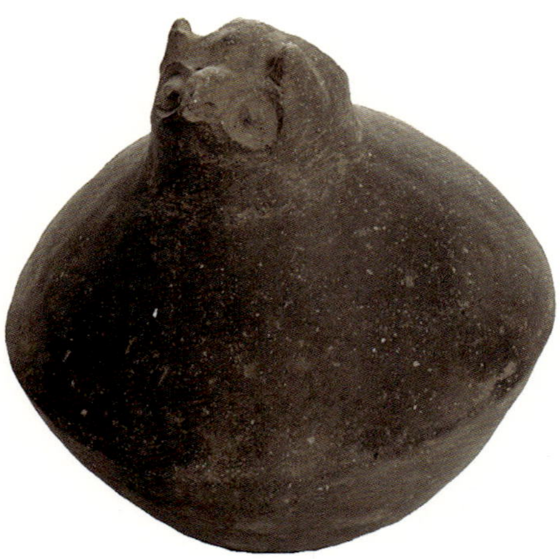

Figure 124. Owl Effigy Carinated Bottle (Mississippi Plain) (OSHTL2006.003.102)
Ceramic; 17.8 x 45.7 cm
Hazel site, Poinsett County, Arkansas
Late Mississippi period, A.D. 1350–1600

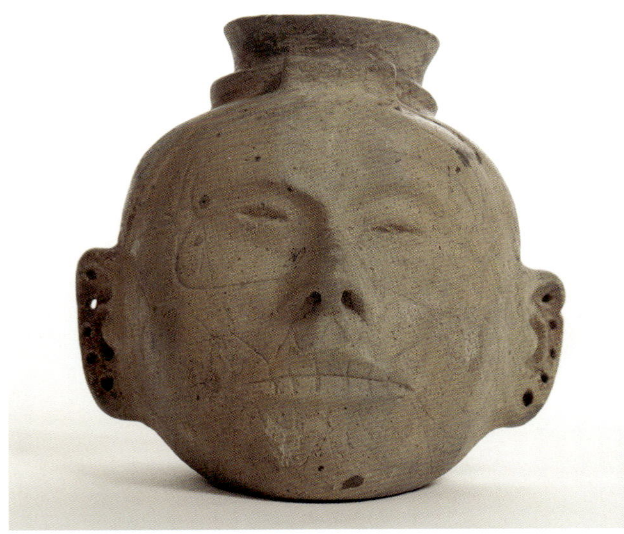

Figure 125. Red and White Head Pot with Incising (tattooing?) (Nodena Red and White) (OSHTL2006.003.104)
Ceramic; 15.1 x 18.1 cm
Shawnee Village site, Mississippi County, Arkansas
Late Mississippi period, A.D. 1350–1600

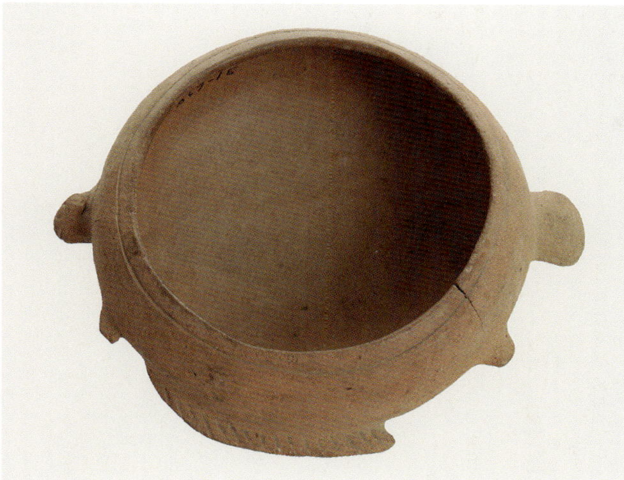

Figure 126. Minnow Effigy Bowl (Bell Plain) (OSHTL2006.003.106)
Ceramic; 17.8 x 55.9 cm
Chapman Dewey farm, Mississippi County, Arkansas
Late Mississippi period, A.D. 1350–1600

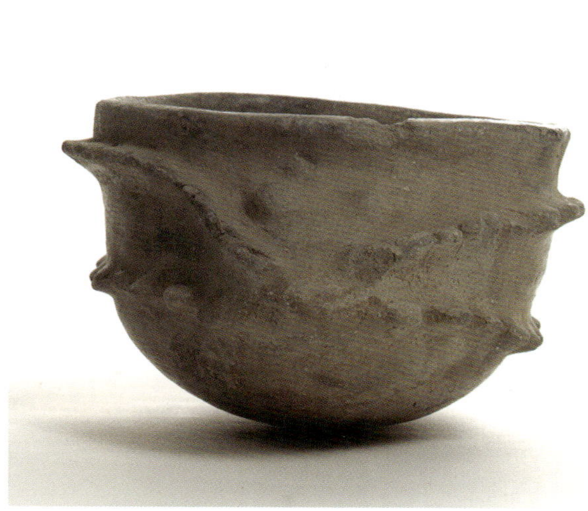

Figure 127. Sturgeon Effigy Bowl (Mississippi Plain) (OSHTL2006.003.107)
Ceramic; 6.6 x 11.4 cm
Neeley's Ferry or Togo site, Cross County, Arkansas
Late Mississippi period, A.D. 1350–1600
The modeled nodes on this vessel probably represent the rows of bony plates characteristic of freshwater sturgeon, which were common historically in the Mississippi River.

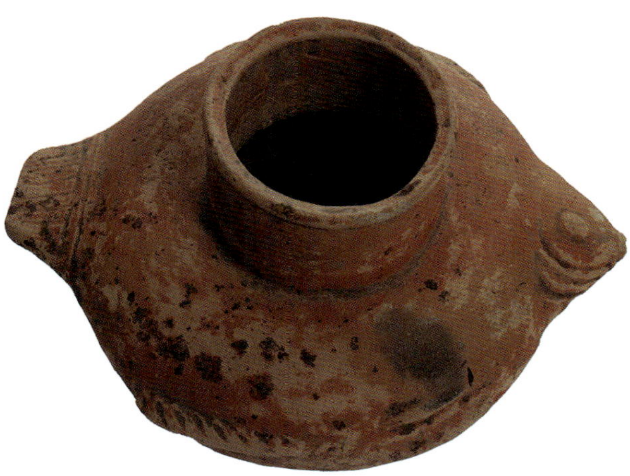

Figure 128. Red Slipped Sunfish Effigy Bottle (Old Town Red) (OSHTL2006.003.108)
Ceramic; 12.7 x 58.4 cm
Little Warner (near Shawnee Village), Mississippi County, Arkansas
Late Mississippi period, A.D. 1350–1600

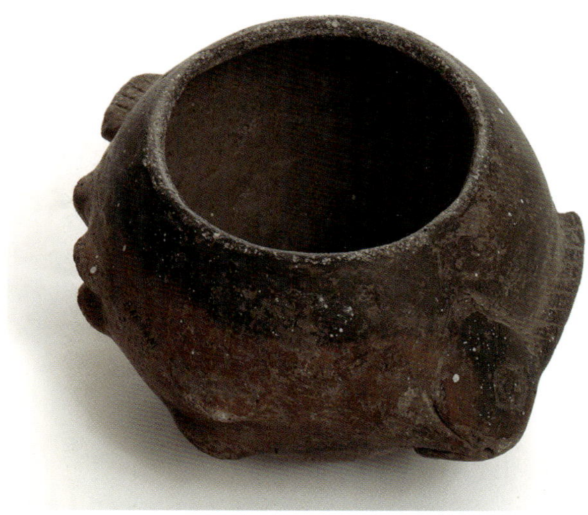

Figure 129. Fish Effigy (Drum) Bowl (Bell Plain) (OSHTL2006.003.110)
Ceramic; 3.8 x 6.0 cm
Near Osceola, Mississippi County, Arkansas
Late Mississippi period, A.D. 1350–1600

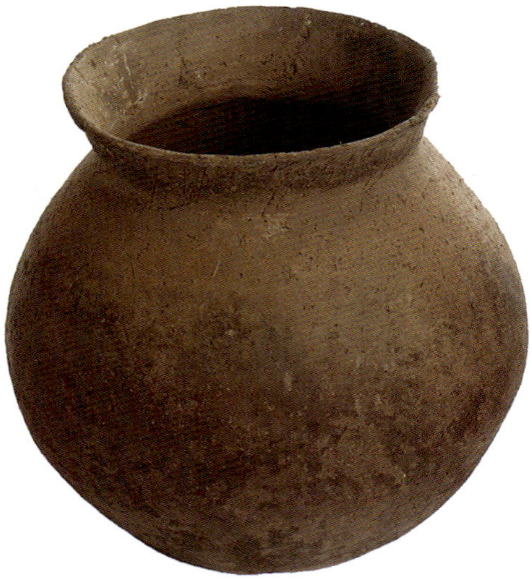

Figure 130. Jar with Outflaring Incised Rim (Mississippi Plain) (OSHTL2006.003.117)
Ceramic; 26.7 x 40.6 cm
Big Piney Creek, Poinsett County, Arkansas
Late Mississippi period, A.D. 1350–1600

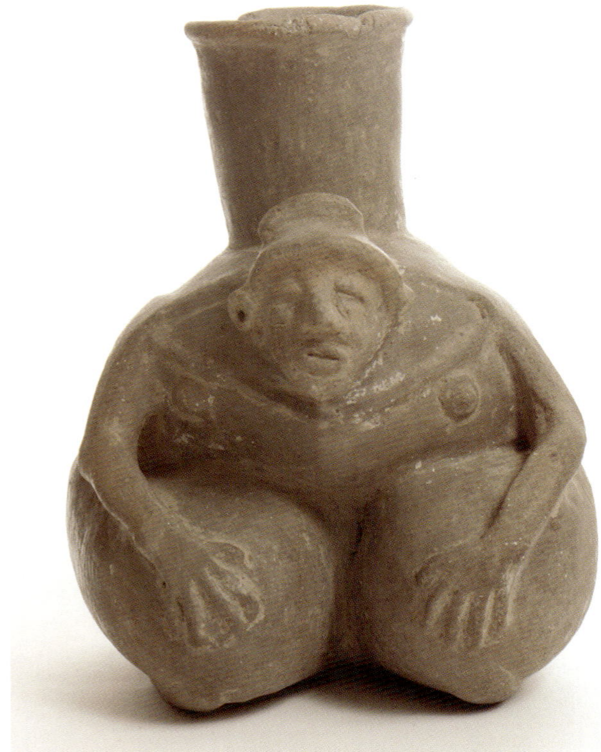

Figure 131. Kneeling Female Effigy Bottle (Bell Plain) (OSHTL2006.003.125)
Ceramic; 21.6 x 58.4 cm
Bradley Place, Crittenden County, Arkansas
Late Mississippi period, A.D. 1350–1600

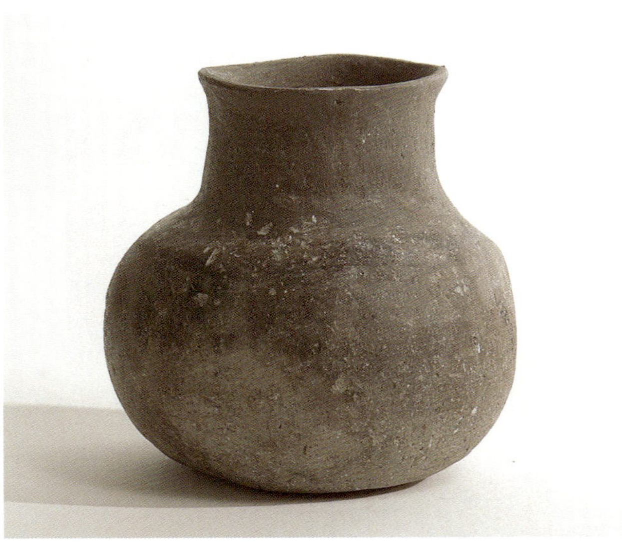

Figure 132. Miniature Bottle (Mississippi Plain) (OSHTL2006.003.131)
Ceramic; 9.4 x 9.4 cm
Vernon Paul site, Cross County, Arkansas
Late Mississippi period, A.D. 1350–1600

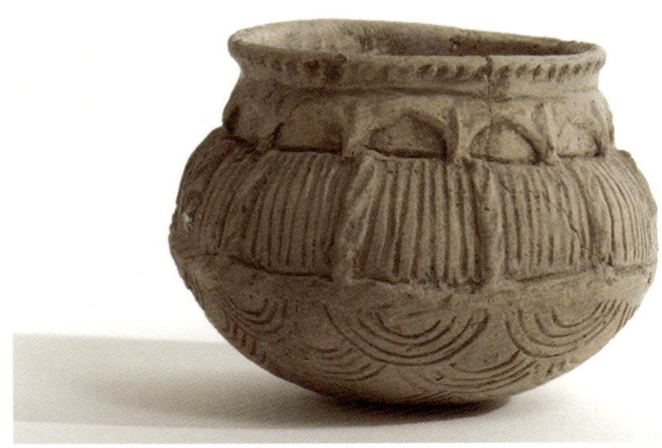

Figure 133. Incised Jar with Excised Symbolic Handles (Kent Incised and Ranch Incised) (OSHTL2006.003.135)
Ceramic; 7.6 x 8.3 cm
Higginbottom Place at Shawnee Village, Mississippi County, Arkansas
Late Mississippi period, A.D. 1350–1600

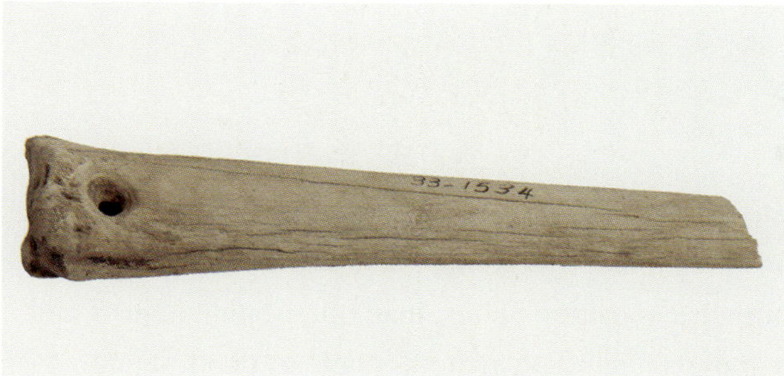

Figure 134. Bone Awl (OSHTL2006.003.148)
Animal bone; 12.7 x 2.5 cm
Hazel site, Poinsett County, Arkansas
Late Mississippi period, A.D. 1350–1600

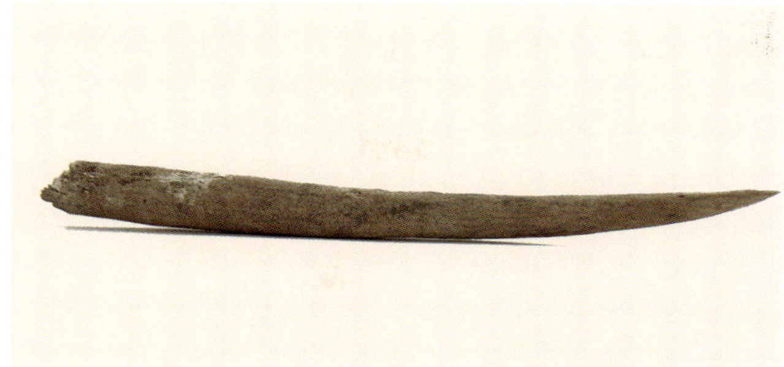

Figure 135. Piercing Tool (OSHTL2006.003.149)
Deer horn; 27.3 x 2.5 cm
Hazel site, Poinsett County, Arkansas
Late Mississippi period, A.D. 1350–1600

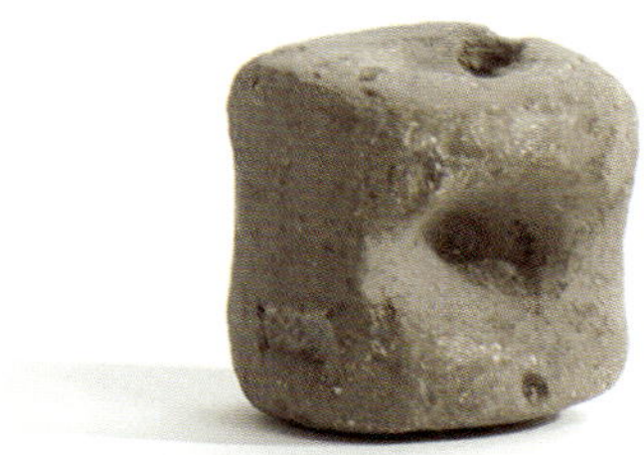

Figure 136. Astragalus Die Replica (OSHTL2006.003.150)
Ceramic; 3.2 x 3.2 cm
Bradley Place, Crittenden County, Arkansas
Late Mississippi period, A.D. 1350–1600
Compare to objects in figure 137.

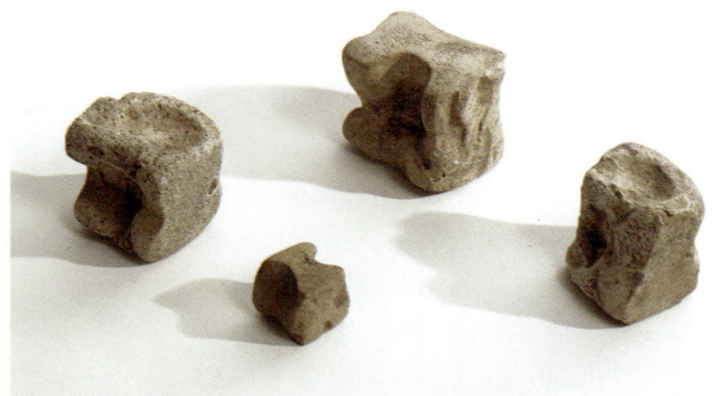

Figure 137. Ground Astragali "Dice" (*left to right:* OSHTL2006.003.154, 151, 152, 153)
Astragali (ankle bone) of deer, elk, and bison; 5.1 x 5.1 cm (largest example)
Bradley Place, Crittenden County, Arkansas
Late Mississippi period, A.D. 1350–1600
Often buried with children, these and similar objects probably were gaming pieces.

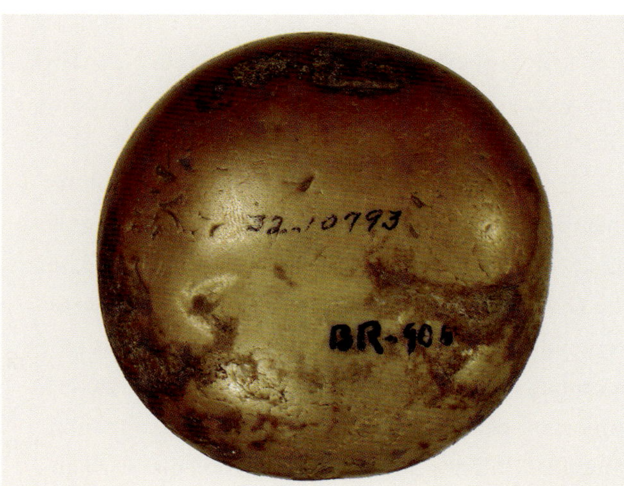

◄**Figure 138**. Discoidal (OSHTL2006.003.155)
Unidentified stone; 7.9 x 7.6 cm
Bradley Place, Crittenden County, Arkansas
Late Mississippi period, A.D. 1350–1600

■ *Ozark Bluff Shelters*

Archaeologists study the material remains of past peoples, but over a period of hundreds or thousands of years, a great deal of material culture—especially items made from organic materials—will decompose under normal conditions. Thus, at the vast majority of archaeological sites objects of wood, bark, vegetable fibers, skins, furs, and feathers have long since vanished. The only items remaining are those that happened to be made of durable materials, such as stone, fired clay, and perhaps bone. Only rarely do archaeologists find items such as clothing, footwear, baskets, nets, and cordage because these will be preserved only under certain rare conditions, so the discovery of a prehistoric archaeological site at which these materials are preserved is of enormous importance. A number of such sites—bluff shelters and caves—have been found throughout the Arkansas and Missouri Ozarks.

A bluff shelter is essentially an overhang along a cliff face. Overhangs are formed by different rates of weathering and erosion at the level of less resistant zones of rock. Deposits build up in bluff shelters as a result of rock falls (due to weathering) and wind-blown sediments. In addition to covering archaeological deposits and helping to preserve them, the wind-blown sediments contain pollen from plants, thus allowing reconstructions of the environment around a shelter over a long period of time.

The soils and cultural deposit within some of these shelters are very dry. One obvious reason is that the overhangs normally protect the shelters from the rain except for instances where moisture can seep into the shelter. Further, the upper levels of many of the deposits within bluff shelters are high enough that they are not affected by groundwater. In shelters where both of these conditions are found, the upper levels of the deposits have remained exceedingly dry, probably from the time of their deposition. Thus, many perishable objects and materials, including artifacts made of plant fibers, wood, cane, or animal hide, are preserved in some shelters.

People have used the sheltered areas along the faces of cliffs for thousands of years in North America (and around the world) because of the same qualities that make these localities unique archaeological sites. These "bluff shelters" offer protection from the weather, making them attractive places to live and work. The dry conditions also made shelters desirable locations for storing food and other materials, as well as places to bury the dead. The archaeological remains found in the Ozark bluff shelters do not represent a single ethnic group or a single time period. Rather, Native Americans used the various shelters over a period spanning at least 10,000 years.

Ozark bluff shelters and their remarkable contents first came to the attention of pioneer archaeologists and museum directors in the early 1900s, when the Phillips Academy of Andover, Massachusetts, and the Smithsonian Institution sponsored excavations in the region.[12] In the early 1920s, Mark R. Harrington, an archaeologist with the Heye Foundation in New York City, excavated in several bluff shelters in the Arkansas Ozarks.[13]

Sam Dellinger's interest was drawn to the bluff shelters due for several reasons. Foremost among these likely was the notion, commonly held at the time, that the archaeological remains in the bluff shelters were very old and primitive, leading some researchers to speculate that the bluff shelter material may "have an important bearing on determining the age of man in America."[14] Since Dellinger was a zoologist with an interest in evolution, it was natural that he would select the bluff shelters for archaeological investigation.

By his own account, Dellinger became interested in the "Ozark Bluff Dwellers" while pursuing his graduate studies at Columbia University in New York City, perhaps during his leave of absence during the 1924–25 academic year.[15] It seems likely that at this time he viewed some of the bluff shelter artifacts excavated a few years earlier by Mark Harrington of the New York-based Heye Foundation. Several years later, Dellinger would accuse the Heye Foundation of "robbing" some of the bluff shelters he was studying.[16]

In 1925 his geology colleague Carey Croneis conducted excavations at several caves in Madison and Newton Counties while Dellinger was completing his graduate studies at Columbia University.[17] Less than a year later, the Oklahoma Historical Society sponsored excavations at bluff shelters and caves in Boone County, Arkansas,[18] much to Dellinger's displeasure.[19] Oddly enough, Dellinger seems to have largely ignored the 1931 excavations by the Smithsonian Institutions in bluff shelters along the Buffalo River.[20]

In 1931, the first sites that the University of Arkansas Museum investigated using the Carnegie Corporation grant funds were some bluff shelters in the headwaters of the Buffalo River, such as Cob Cave, where well-preserved woven bags, cordage, baskets, and cultivated plants were found. The excavators also recorded important pictographs and petroglyphs at Cob Cave, Indian Rock House, and other shelters. Aware of the importance of these finds, Dellinger presented a paper on the first bluff shelter finds at the annual meeting of the American Association for the Advancement of Science in New Orleans over the 1931 Christmas holidays.[21]

In all, Dellinger's field crews excavated in over 80 bluff shelters in the Ozarks from 1931 through 1934. The majority of these are located along the main branch of the upper White River. Others are located on the Kings River, the Buffalo River, and other tributaries of the White, and a few were excavated on small tributaries of the Arkansas River in the southwestern portion of the Arkansas Ozarks. The same dry conditions that contributed to the preservation of so many perishables and the fine silty soils presented a potential health hazard, so the excavators wore respirators during the excavations.[22]

Wayne Henbest and Charles Finger Jr. were the students who supervised most of the bluff shelter surveys and excavations, with James Durham and Thomas Millard also having brief supervisory roles. Two other students, James Gore and Eugene Cypert Jr., also assisted with the bluff shelter investigations, but seem not to have served as supervisors.[23] As with the excavations in northeast Arkansas, the field supervisors hired local men to assist with the excavations, typically paying them 15 cents per hour.[24] The local citizens were friendly and helpful.

Although he published several articles on the Ozark bluff shelters, Dellinger never published a comprehensive monograph on the 1930s excavations conducted under his direction. Dellinger was extremely disappointed by the publication in 1960 of Mark Harrington's *The Ozark Bluff Dwellers*, which covered the same area and some of the same sites where Dellinger's crews worked.[25] Apparently Dellinger felt that he would not be able to contribute anything beyond Harrington's volume.[26] In fact, this was not the case at all, as shown by Sandra Scholtz's outstanding *Prehistoric Plies*, which presents a detailed analysis of many of the perishable artifacts from University of Arkansas Museum excavations, as well as a discussion of the techniques used in their manufacture.[27]

Another important study of the museum's bluff shelter collections contributed important new information about early Native American agriculture. Many people are aware that, at the time of their initial encounters with Europeans, many Native American societies cultivated corn, beans, and squash. Archaeologist Gayle Fritz carefully examined a large number of seeds found in woven fiber bags within a crevice at the Marble Bluff shelter in Searcy County, Arkansas, in 1934. The seeds included sunflower and gourd/squash (*Cucurbita pepo*), as well as those of plants that today we regard as weeds—lambs quarters (*Chenopodium berlandieri* ssp. *Jonesianum*) and marsh elder (*Iva annua* var. *macrocarpa*). Most of the sunflower, squash/gourd, and marsh elder seeds were considerably larger than those seen in the wild, and the seed coats of the lambs quarters seeds were unusually thin. These characteristics indicate that Native Americans had domesticated these plants. Remarkably, radiocarbon dates obtained from some of the seeds indicate that plant domestication was well established in the Arkansas Ozarks around 3,000 years ago.[28]

The actual age of most of the bluff shelter perishables is unknown. The seeds from Marble Bluff are the oldest material that has been radiocarbon dated. Most other dated specimens are of late prehistoric age (A.D. 900–1600), but this may not be representative of the collection as a whole.

As is the case for virtually all archaeological excavations conducted in the early 1930s in the United States, the field records from Dellinger's work in the bluff shelters fall considerably short of today's standards. Nonetheless, the field crews excavated an extraordinary amount of well-preserved perishable artifacts. These have been well cared for over the years and remain some of the most important collections curated by the University of Arkansas Museum.

THE COLLECTIONS

The museum's collections include over 1,000 specimens of cordage, basketry, fabric, sandals, and related items from bluff shelters in the Ozark Mountains. Numerically, the vast majority (n = 756) are individual pieces of cordage, including plied and braided. Other perishables include interlaced basketry and fabric (n = 115), twined basketry and fabric (n = 121), coiled basketry (n = 29), netting (n = 7), and footgear (n = 11).[29]

With grant support from the Arkansas Natural and Cultural Resources Council, the Arkansas Archeological Survey and the University of Arkansas Museum Collections Facility staff have begun a long-term project to inventory all of the bluff shelter material collected under Dellinger's supervision and to bring curation up to modern standards.

Of course, perishables are not the only artifacts found in the shelters. The museum's collections also include many stone tools, bone tools, pottery, as well as animal bones. Dellinger's crews also excavated some human burials in the shelters, as well as a few dog burials.

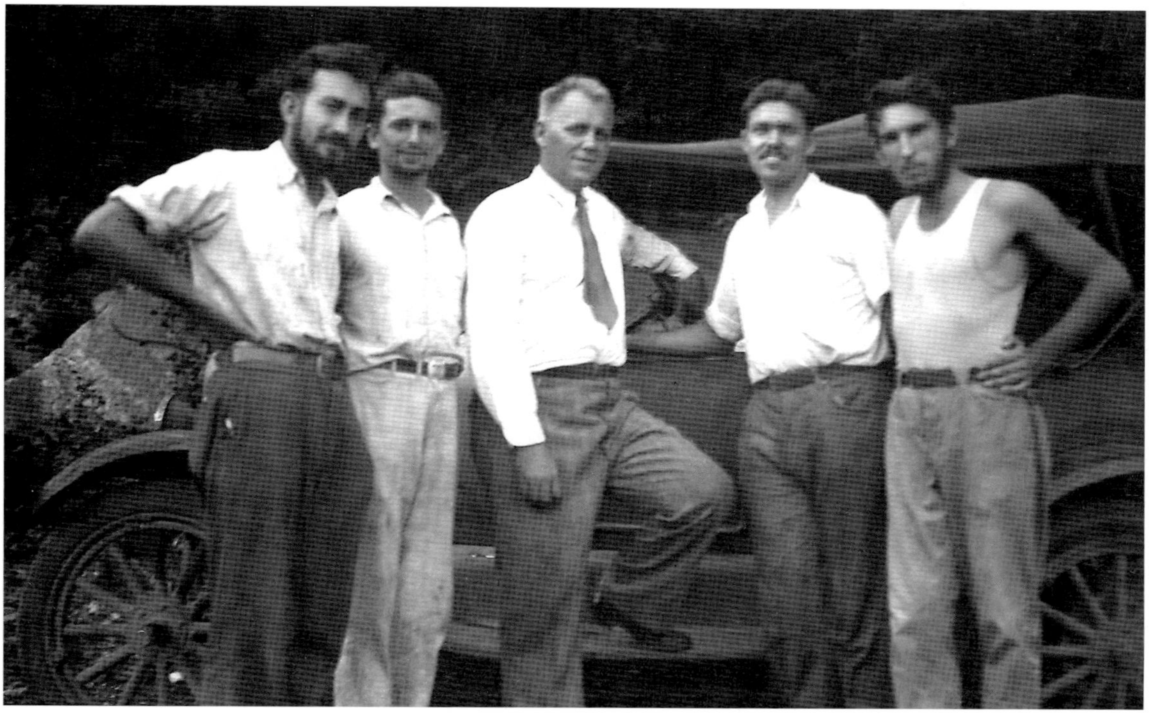

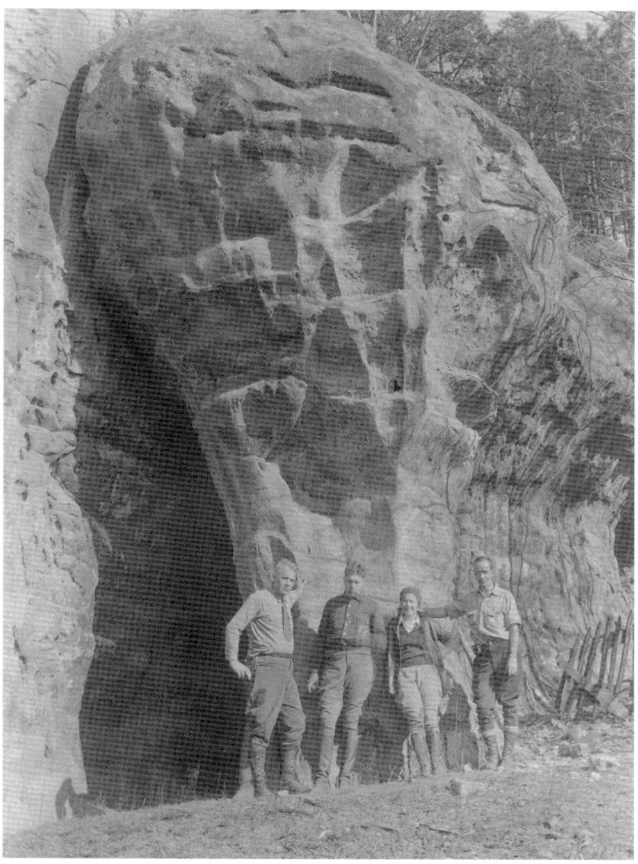

Figure 139. Dellinger with four of his field assistants at Cob Cave, 1931. *Left to right:* James Durham, James Gore, Dellinger, Thomas Millard, Eugene Cypert Jr.

Figure 140. Dellinger at Edgemont Cave, circa 1931. *Left to right:* Dellinger, Thomas Millard, and two unknown individuals.

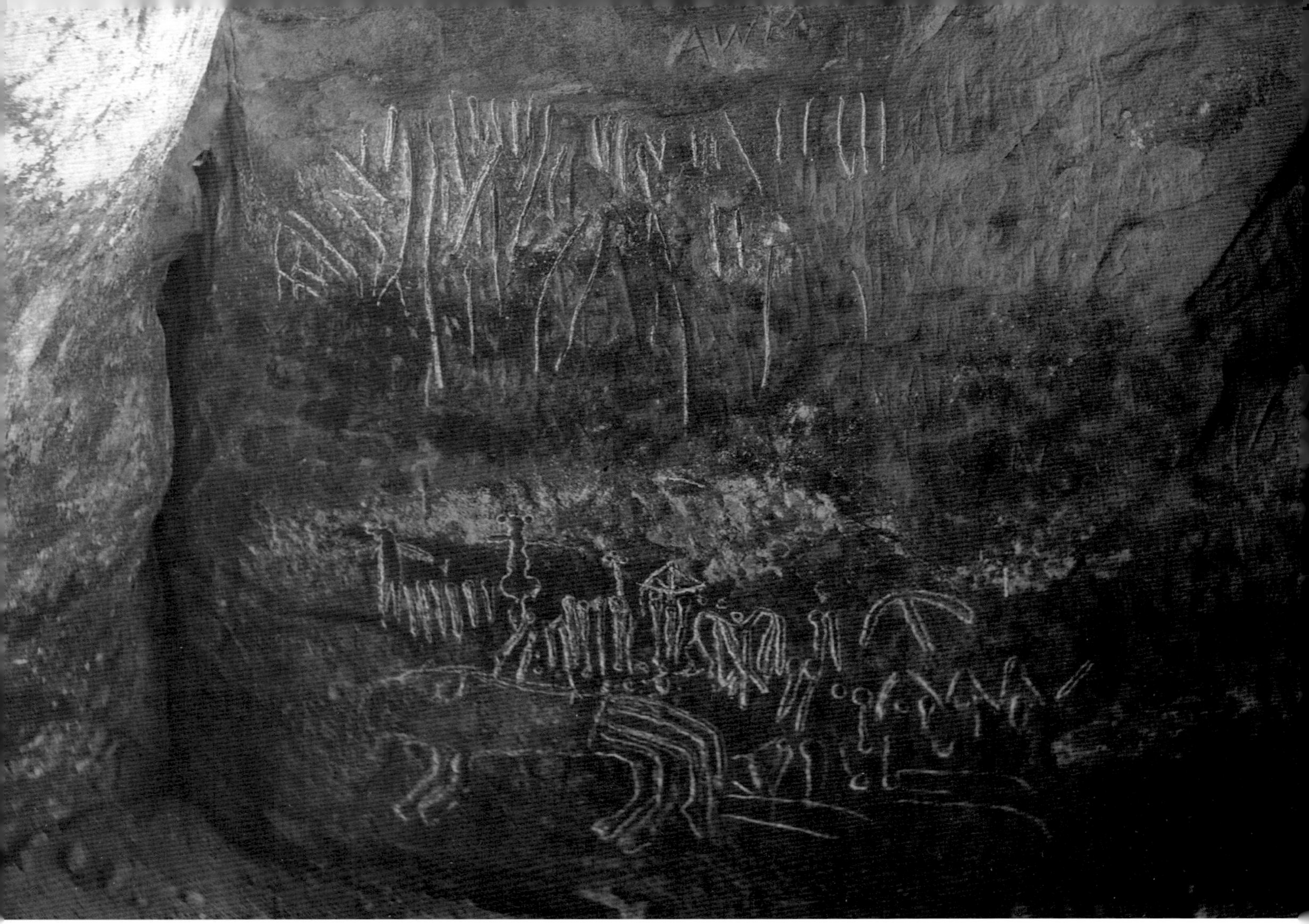

Figure 141. Rock art at Edgemont Cave.

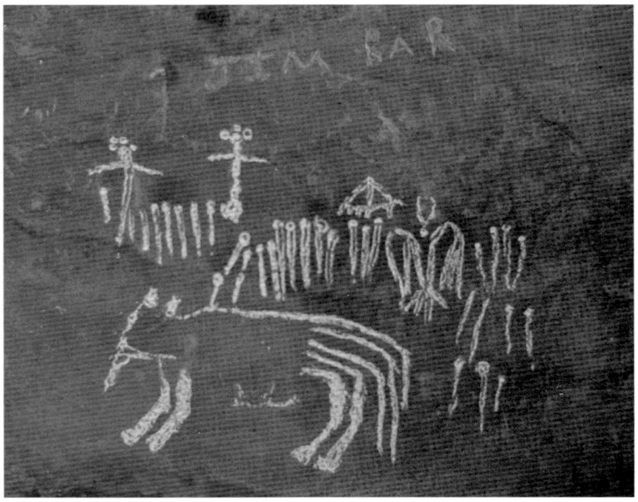

Figure 142. Detail of Edgemont Cave rock art. "Chalking" is no longer considered to be an appropriate aid to photographing rock art. Note the more recent markings above the prehistoric rock art panel.

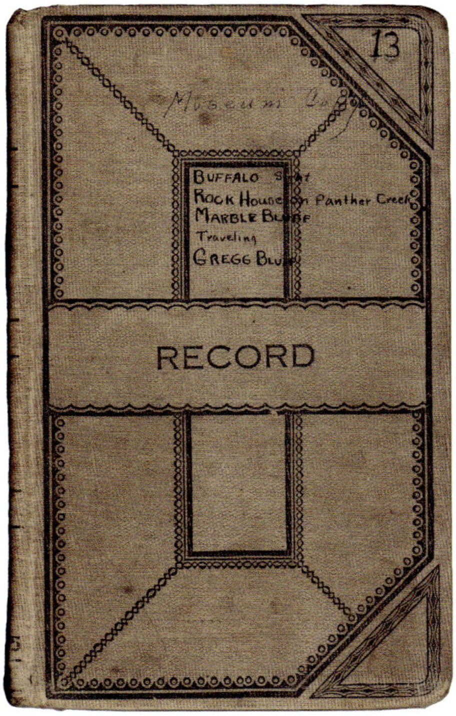

Figure 143. One of the field notebooks used during the museum's excavations at bluff shelters.

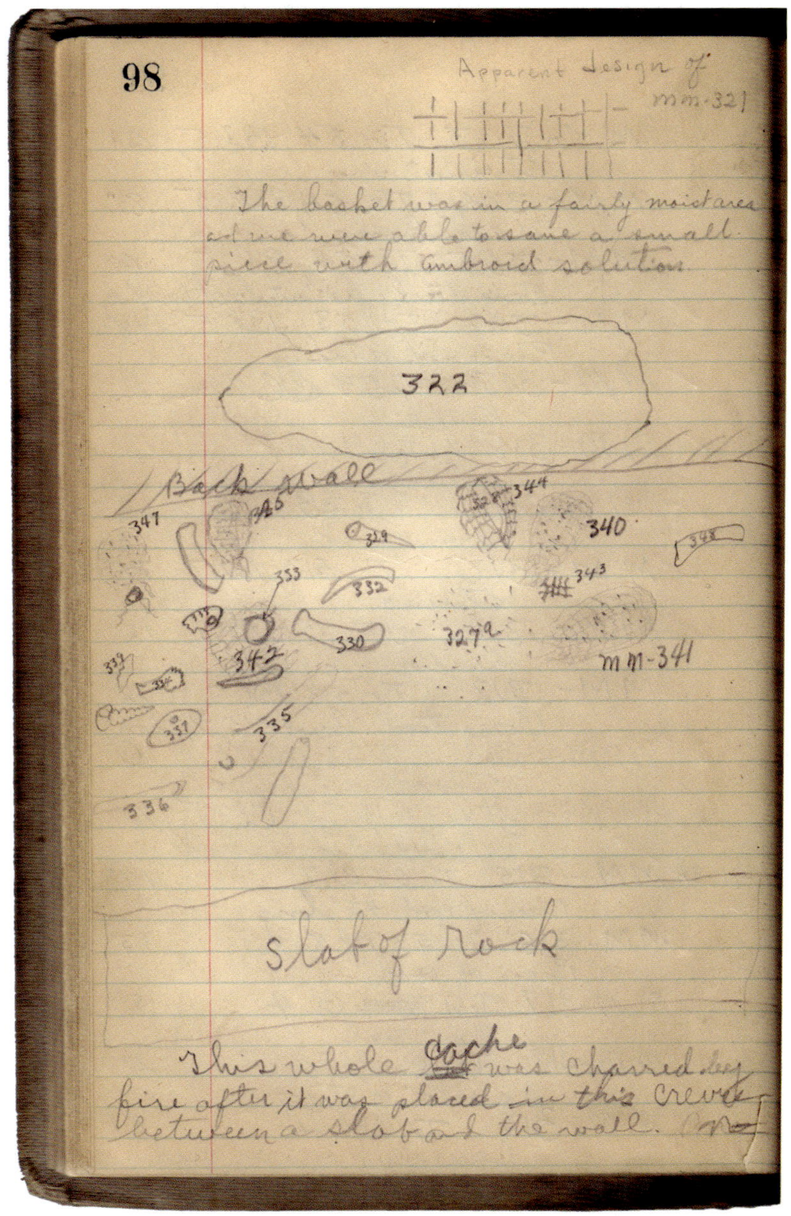

Figure 144. Page from Marble Bluff field notebook with Wayne Henbest's sketch of a "cache" of woven fiber bags that contained native cultigens (goosefoot, marshelder, sunflower, squash/gourd).

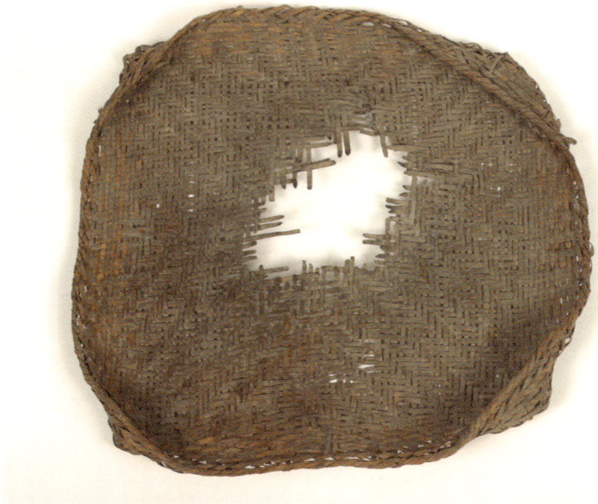

Figure 145. Patterned Float Weave Basket (OSHTL2006.003.11)
Split cane; 54.0 x 52.0 x 6.0 cm
Cob Cave, Newton County, Arkansas
Probably Mississippi period, circa A.D. 900–1600

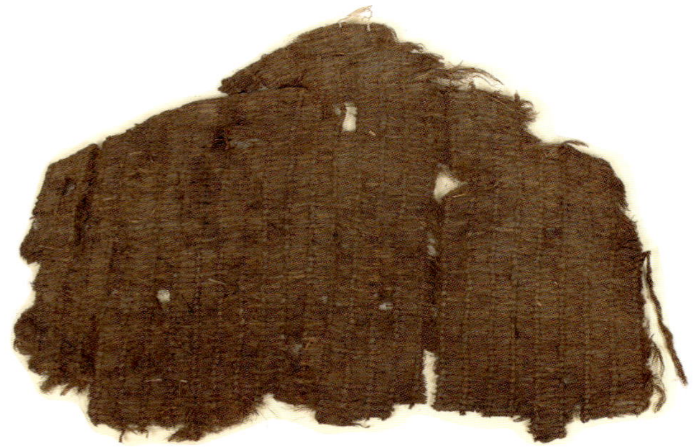

Figure 146. Fragment of Twined Fabric (OSHTL2006.003.13)
Hard plant fibers (species unidentified); 56.5 x 37.0 cm
Eden Bluff site, Benton County, Arkansas
Probably Woodland or Mississippi period, circa A.D. 1–1600

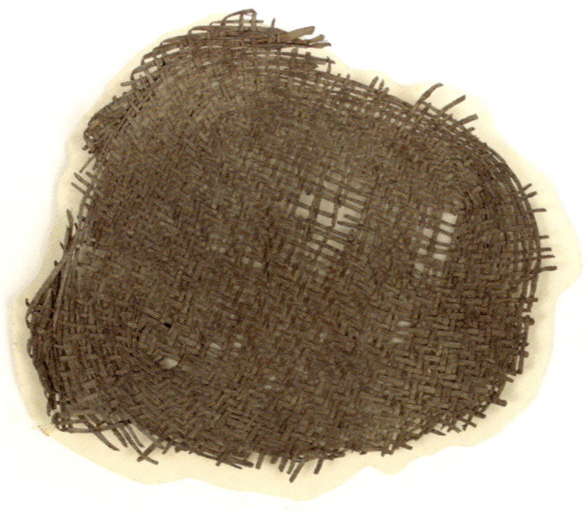

Figure 147. Fragment of Even Regular Twill Basket (OSHTL2006.003.14)
Bark (species unidentified); 38.0 x 40.5 cm
Eden Bluff site, Benton County, Arkansas
Probably Woodland or Mississippi period, circa A.D. 1–1600

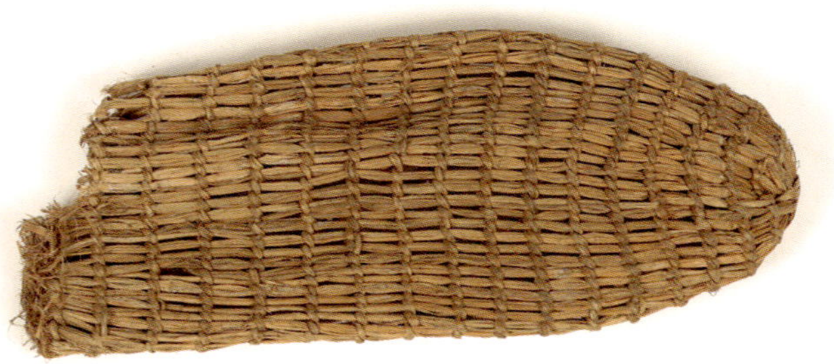

Figure 148. Twined Fabric Bag (OSHTL2006.003.15)
Plant fibers (species unidentified); 25.5 x 9.0 cm
Arch Vaughn Shelter, Madison County, Arkansas
Probably Late Woodland or Mississippi period, circa A.D. 400–1600

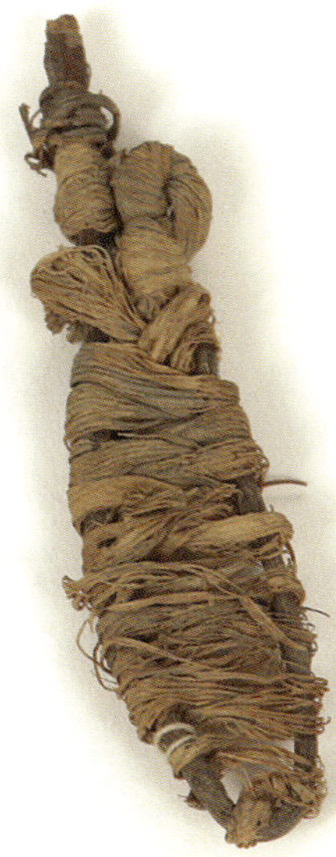

Figure 149. Grass Ornament (OSHTL2006.003.16)
Grass woven around a curved stick; 10.0 x 2.0 cm
Cob Cave, Newton County, Arkansas
Probably Mississippi period, circa A.D. 900–1600

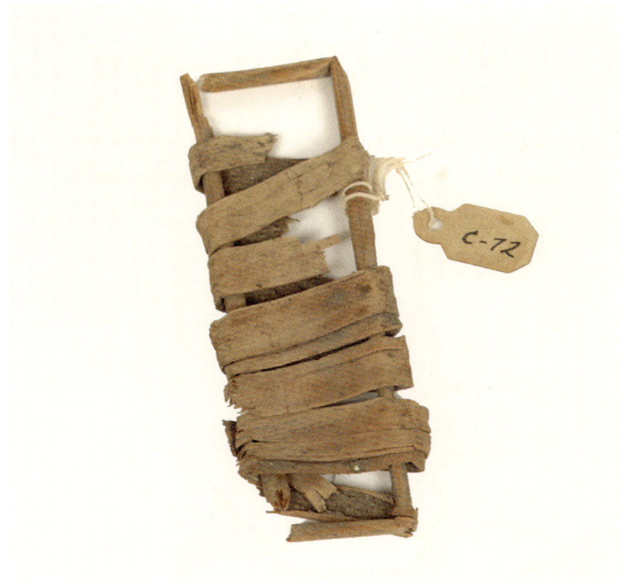

Figure 150. Grass Ornament (OSHTL2006.003.17)
Grass on rectangular stick frame; 10.5 x 3.2 cm
Cob Cave, Newton County, Arkansas
Probably Mississippi period, circa A.D. 900–1600

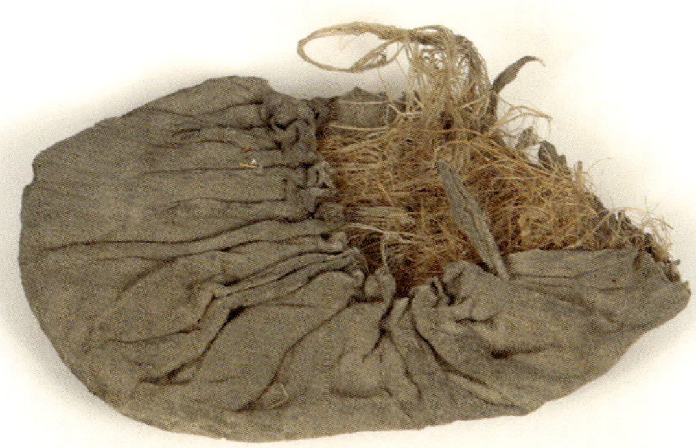

Figure 151. Baby's Moccasin (OSHTL2006.003.18)
Buckskin lined with fibers of Indian hemp (*Apocynum cannabinum*); 9.5 x 6.5 cm
Cob Cave, Newton County, Arkansas
Probably Mississippi period, circa A.D. 900–1600

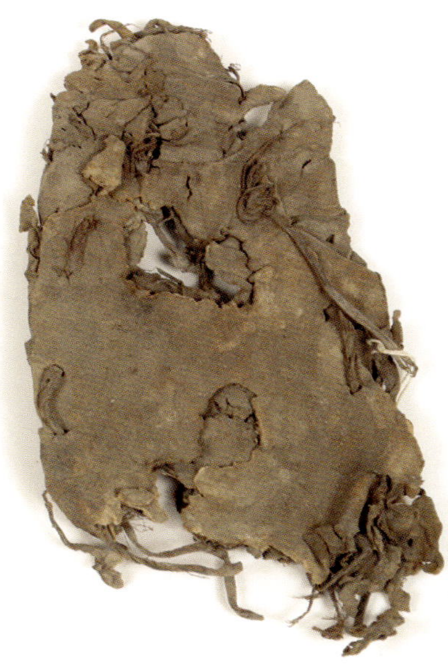

Figure 152. Buckskin Moccasin (OSHTL2006.003.19)
Buckskin lined with twined fibers; 21.5 x 11.5 cm
Eden Bluff, Benton County, Arkansas
Probably Woodland or Mississippi period, circa A.D. 1–1600

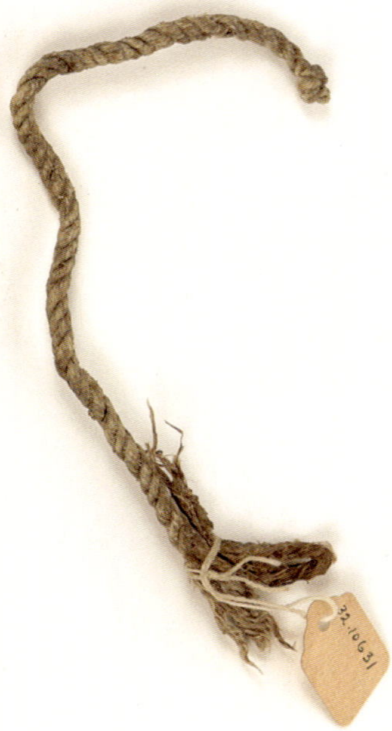

Figure 153. Plied Cordage (OSHTL2006.003.20)
Bark fibers (species unidentified); length, 18.3 cm
Eden Bluff, Benton County, Arkansas
Probably Woodland or Mississippi period, circa A.D. 1–1600

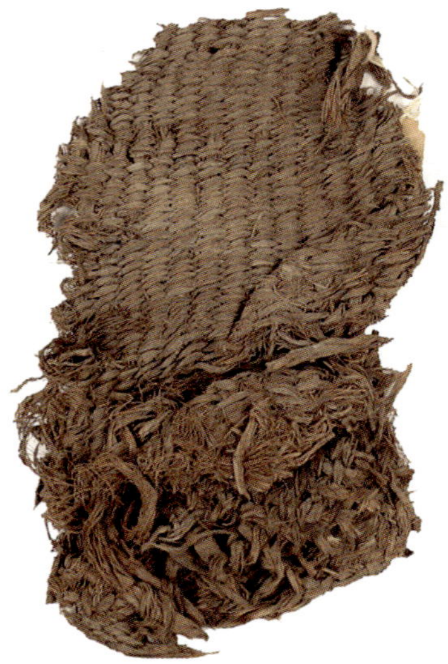

Figure 154. Fragment of Basketry (OSHTL2006.003.22)
Material unidentified; 19.1 x 8.9 cm
Eden Bluff, Benton County, Arkansas
Probably Woodland or Mississippi period, circa A.D. 1–1600

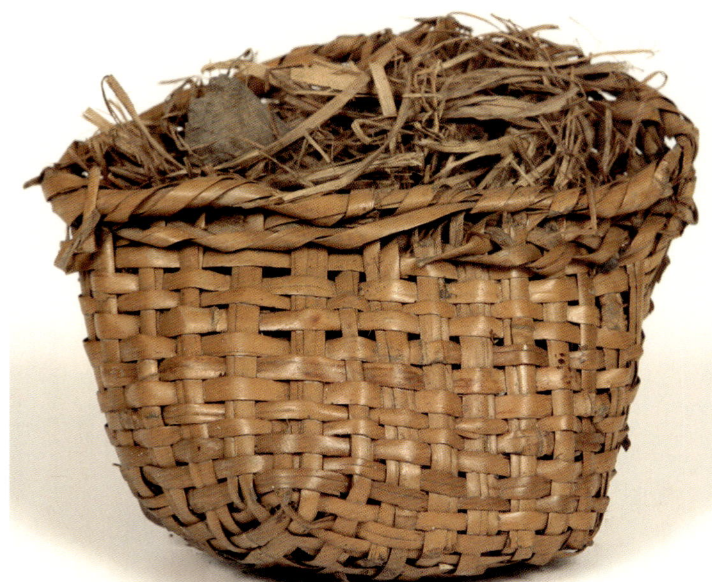

Figure 155. Basket with Complicated Float Weave in Base (OSHTL2006.003.49)
Cane strips; 8.8 x 12.1 cm
Montgomery Farm Shelter, Barry County, Missouri
Probably Mississippi period, A.D. 900–1600

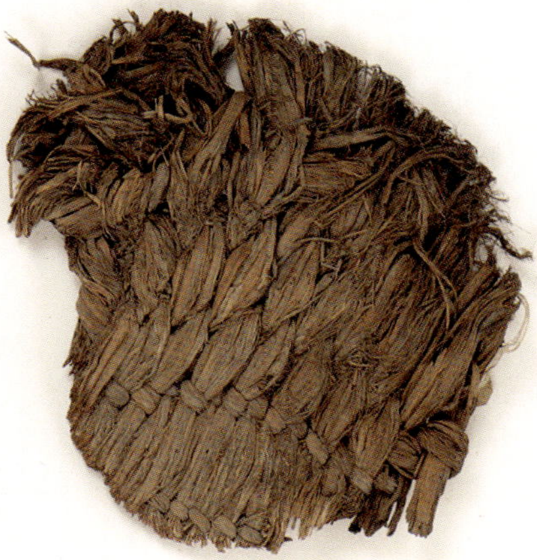

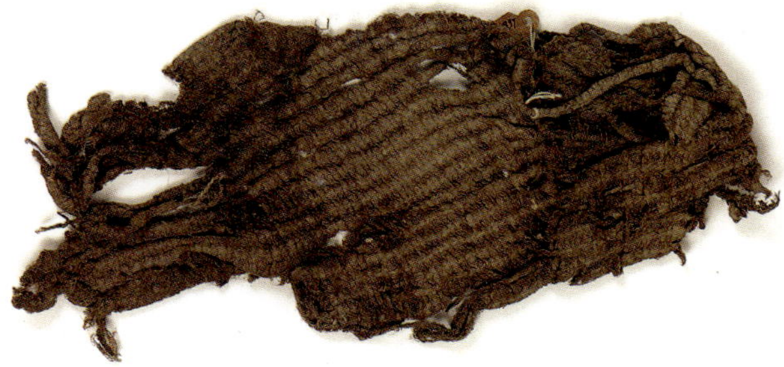

Figure 157. Twined Fabric (OSHTL2006.003.137)
Indian hemp; 20.0 x 6.4 cm
Cob Cave, Newton County, Arkansas
Probably Late Mississippi period, A.D. 1350–1600

Figure 156. Interlaced and Twined Fiber Sandal Fragment (OSHTL2006.003.136)
Unidentified fiber; 17.8 x 17.8 cm
Cob Cave, Newton County, Arkansas
Probably Late Mississippi period, A.D. 1350–1600

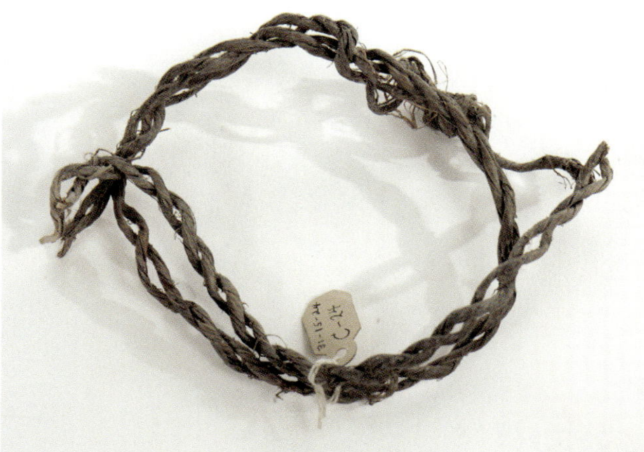

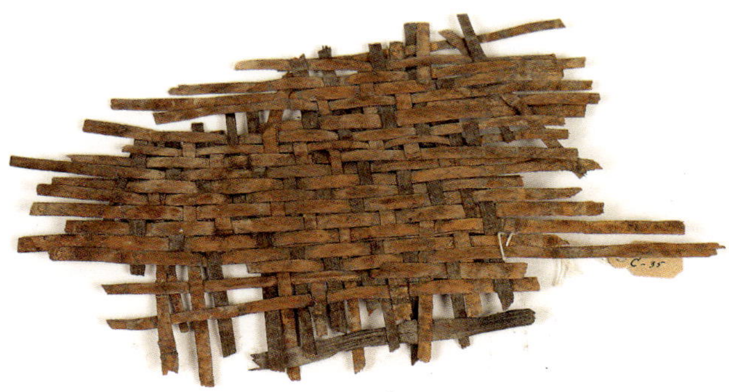

Figure 159. Float Weave Basketry Fragment (OSHTL2006.003.139)
Probably cane splints; 10.5 x 4.5 cm
Cob Cave, Newton County, Arkansas
Probably Late Mississippi period, A.D. 1350–1600

Figure 158. Two Pieces of Cordage (OSHTL2006.003.138)
Bark (species unidentified); apx. 40 cm long
Cob Cave, Newton County, Arkansas
Probably Late Mississippi period, A.D. 1350–1600

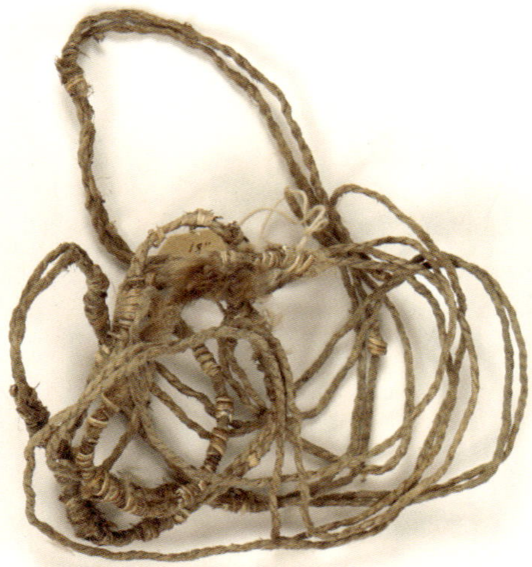

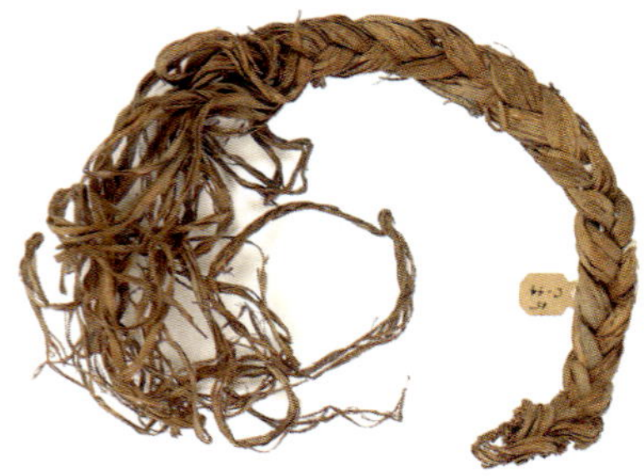

Figure 161. 3-element Braided Rope (OSHTL2006.003.141)
Unidentified hard fibers (grass?); 35.6 cm long
Cob Cave, Newton County, Arkansas
Probably Late Mississippi period, A.D. 1350–1600

Figure 160. Plied Cordage (OSHTL2006.003.140)
Feathers wrapped over bast fibers; apx. 173 cm long
Cob Cave, Newton County, Arkansas
Probably Late Mississippi period, A.D. 1350–1600

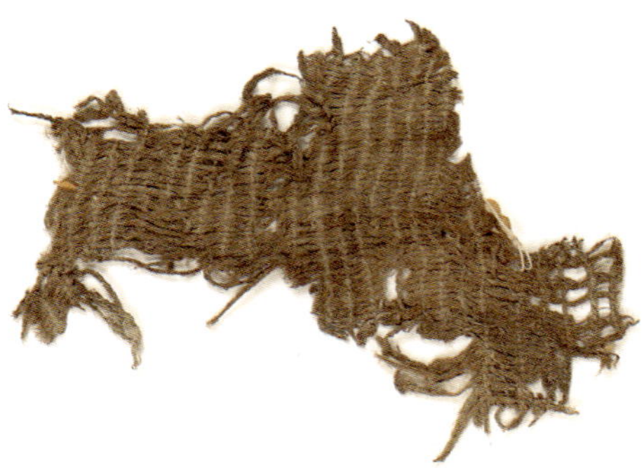

Figure 162. Twined Fabric Fragment (OSHTL2006.003.146)
Indian hemp; 33.0 x 7.6 cm
Cob Cave, Newton County, Arkansas
Probably Mississippi period, A.D. 900–1600

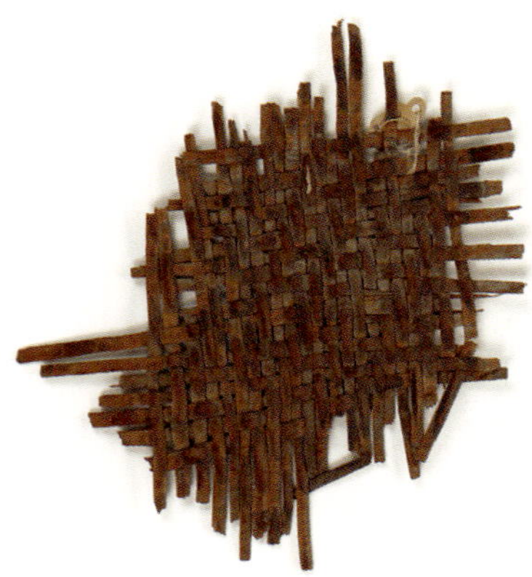

Figure 163. Float Weave Basketry Fragment (OSHTL2006.003.147)
Switch cane (*Arundinaria tecta*); 17.8 x 17.8 cm
Cob Cave, Newton County, Arkansas
Probably Mississippi period, A.D. 900–1600

Central Arkansas River Valley

As we have seen, throughout his career at the University of Arkansas, Samuel Dellinger was very outspoken about keeping archaeological material from Arkansas within the state.[30] Events in the central Arkansas River valley shortly after he began working at the university probably helped to shape Dellinger's attitude.

Commercial "pothunters" began working in the central Arkansas River valley, particularly the vicinity of Dardanelle, in 1923. These individuals excavated and purchased pottery vessels and sold the objects to private collectors and museums in the United States and Europe. In January 1924, the archaeologist Mark R. Harrington (representing the Heye Foundation Museum of the American Indian in New York City) came to Arkansas after learning of the situation and soon thereafter published a description of the situation he found:

> Somehow the poor "renters"—the tenant farmers—of the neighborhood had discovered the art of probing with a steel rod in the plowed fields for these unmarked graves, had learned that they frequently contained pottery, and had found that this pottery could be sold. A miniature gold-rush resulted, and before long nearly everyone in Carden Bottoms, from small boys of eight upwards, had become a "pot-digger."
>
> As we approached the ridges the little groups of diggers made a weird picture as they toiled in the mud, unmindful of drizzling rain and flurries of snow. Crops had been poor last year, money was scarce, and so they were improving every moment of daylight. But it was sickening to an archaeologist to see the skeletons chopped to pieces with hoes and dragged ruthlessly forth to be crushed under foot by the vandals—who were interested only in finding something to sell, caring nothing for the history of a vanished people. Of course, no record was kept of the burials, information that might have resulted from careful work has been lost forever. Unskilled hands probably ruined a large part of the pottery while trying to remove it from the graves, and untrained eyes have doubtless overlooked a great proportion of the smaller articles laid away with the dead.[31]

The local press noticed Harrington's visit:

> M. R. Harrington, of New York City, representing the Heye Foundation, Museum of the American Indian, spent several days here the past week inspecting the superb collection of Indian relics owned by our local collector, G. E. Pilquist. He purchased a collection of choice pieces from Mr. Pilquist. Mr. Harrington, himself part Indian, is one of the greatest living authorities on Indian customs and relics. He speaks five Indian languages. He also purchased choice relics from Overton and Bailey, of Atkins and Carden Bottom. According to Mr. Harrington, Arkansas is the richest State in the Union in Indian relics.[32]

Harrington purchased no more than 57 vessels.[33]

The Carden Bottom, east of Russellville and near the mouth of the Petit Jean River, is the best-known, but was by no means the only, locality of extensive pothunting in the Arkansas River valley. An excerpt from the *Dardanelle Post-Dispatch* provides a local perspective on the activities:

> The old Indian burying ground on the river below Fowler is now the center of activity in our community. Many can be seen here each day with probing rod and spade prospecting for Indian relics. Many beautiful pieces have been found. Tradition tells us that the property of each Indian was placed in his grave. So we find pipes, beads, arrows, bowls and water bottles in their graves. The water bottles are made in many forms. Some are in the shape of gourds, others are made in the form of terrapins, frogs and the human head. The water bottle seems to have been the Indian's most prized piece for on them he displayed most of his art and skill. Some are very beautiful and very valuable. Buyers come from distant

> places to purchase these old relics. It is very fascinating to some to dig for this pottery, while others find it profitable also, there frequently being as much as $50.00 worth of relics in one grave.[34]

Unfortunately, Harrington's purchase of artifacts in the area could only have served to exacerbate the situation. The initial peak of pothunting in Carden Bottom and other localities along the Arkansas River, as well as along the Petit Jean River, occurred while Dellinger was completing his graduate studies at Columbia University in New York City. It seems likely that he learned about the situation via letters and newspaper accounts from home, and it is quite possible that he viewed some of Harrington's collection at the Heye Foundation Museum of the American Indian.

While despoiling human graves in order to remove artifacts placed with the dead is quite shocking by today's standards, it is important to consider the context of the activities. In the first decades of the 1900s, most of the families living along the Arkansas River in the Carden Bottom area were tenant farmers or sharecroppers who grew cotton on tracts of 40 acres or less. In short, they were very poor. The collapse of cotton prices after 1920 drove many families into considerable debt. This dismal state of affairs was compounded in the 1920s, when a series of floods devastated the area. In addition to washing away crops and fields, the high water exposed a number of Native American graves and pottery vessels placed with the dead.[35] It is not clear precisely when rampant pothunting began; the accounts cited above suggest that one peak of activity occurred in late 1923 and early 1924, following several floods.[36] Thus, the widespread, uncontrolled digging of human graves was a product of both opportunity and economics. Another major flood, in 1927, apparently prompted another peak in digging, and the practice continued into the 1930s.[37]

The numbers of funerary objects collected during this time and their disposition is largely unknown. In 1933, artifact dealer G. E. Pilquist claimed to have handled over 12,000 pottery vessels from Carden Bottom alone. Archaeologist Mark R. Harrington reported "wagon loads" and "a small barn full" of vessels.[38] Even if Pilquist was greatly exaggerating, it is clear that a great many pottery vessels were removed from graves in this area during the 1920s and 1930s, but there are no records of who acquired the bulk of this pottery. Harrington purchased only 57 vessels for the Museum of the American Indian, while the Lemley collection at the Gilcrease Museum (Tulsa, Oklahoma) includes 117 vessels. The University of Arkansas Museum curates the largest known collection of vessels from the region, numbering 267 specimens.[39]

From newspaper accounts and anecdotal evidence, it is clear that the Arkansas and Petit Jean River valleys between Russellville and Little Rock supported a substantial population of Native Americans between approximately A.D. 1500 and 1700. Unfortunately, the size and nature of this occupation likely will remain unknown because of the scale and intensity of pothunting and the lack of professional archaeological investigations. Virtually our only source of information about the people who once lived in the region comes from collections of ceramic vessels and a few non-ceramic items curated by various museums. One of the larger collections is housed by the University of Arkansas Museum, thanks to the efforts of Samuel Dellinger, who raised sufficient money to purchase a number of pottery vessels from local relic dealers such as J. W. Bailey.[40]

Undoubtedly Dellinger was aware of the ethical dilemma he faced in the Arkansas River valley. An enormous number of important archaeological specimens were being ripped from the ground without proper recording. These artifacts represented an important archaeological legacy of the state of Arkansas, yet many were being sold to out-of-state museums and private collectors. Clearly Dellinger wanted to preserve as many of the artifacts as possible for the University of Arkansas Museum, but by purchasing specimens from the relic dealers, Dellinger was increasing "demand" for artifacts and therefore in effect encouraging the uncontrolled digging. Yet, had he not acted as he did, it is likely that most of the Arkansas River valley artifacts curated by the museum would not be available for study and appreciation today.

In 1932, Dellinger's students supervised the excavation of 57 human burials at a site they referred to as "Natural Steps," located several miles west of Pinnacle Mountain near Little Rock. Funerary objects found with the burials included 122 ceramic vessels, stone and bone tools, shell beads, and copper ornaments.[41] The pottery vessels are stylistically similar to those found in the vicinity of Dardanelle and are some of the only late-prehistoric vessels from the central Arkansas River valley with certain provenience.

THE COLLECTIONS

Most of the University of Arkansas Museum's collections from the region date between approximately A.D. 1350 and 1700. The first date is based on the form and decoration of the pottery vessels in the collections, while the latter date is based on the discovery of a few European beads and metal (brass) objects, as well as crossdating of Caddo vessels.

The collections consist primarily of pottery vessels. Numbering nearly 270 complete specimens, this is the largest museum collection of ceramic vessels from this region.[42] Many other kinds of objects probably were placed with the dead, such as stone and bone tools, but the early relic hunters were interested primarily in pottery. The ceramic vessels from the region are distinctive; they differ markedly from vessels produced in northeast Arkansas that date to the same time period. As noted in the individual artifact descriptions, some of the vessels in the museum's collection clearly were made in southern or southwest Arkansas; they are not local imitations of pottery from these areas. Several other vessels are stylistically similar (both in shape and surface decoration) to pottery characteristic of sites farther downstream along the Arkansas River.

Especially characteristic of the central Arkansas River collections are large bowls with red-painted rims and geometric designs on the interiors of vessels; these have no counterparts in the painted pottery from northeast Arkansas or in the traditional Caddo area. Bottles typically have necks that resemble an hourglass and often feature interlocking red and white swirls. Carinated bowls (bowls having a keel-defined ridge where two portions of the body join), including examples made by late-prehistoric Caddo potters, also occur.

...WANTED TO BUY...

I will Buy and Pay Cash for

All Types of Indian Relics

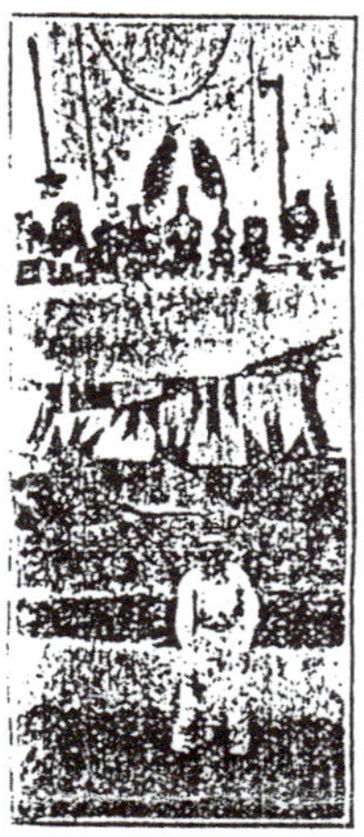

SUCH AS ARROWHEADS, SPEARS, TOMAHAWKS, GROOVED AXES AND CELTS, BEADS, BOAT STONES, POTTERY VESSELS, STONE ORNAMENTS, STONE AND FLINT HOES, SPADES, PLUMMETS OR PLUMB BOBS OF STONE OR IRON ORE, FLINT KNIVES, PIPES, OR ANY UNUSUAL OR FINE RELICS OF THE INDIANS.

Send any of the above Relics to me by Parcel Post or Express, well packed. Check will be sent same day as shipment is received for full value. I want shippers from each County. I pay Cash. Twelve years in the business. If you have any Good Indian Relics it will pay you to get in touch with the address below.

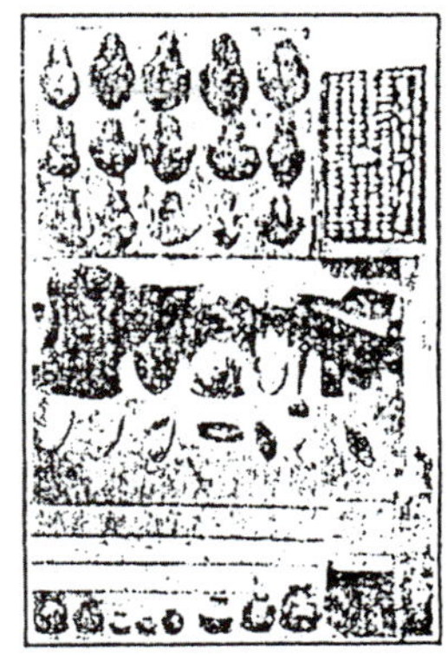

H T. DANIEL

Box 698. DARDANELLE, ARK.

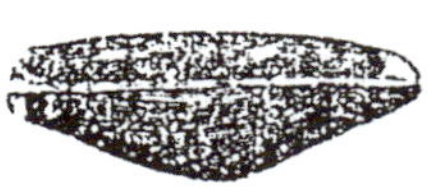

BOAT STONE.

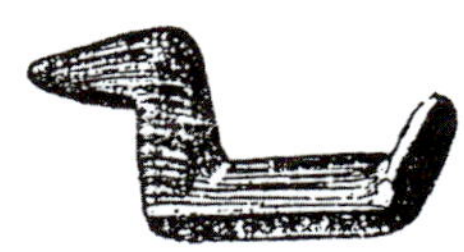

BIRD STONE.

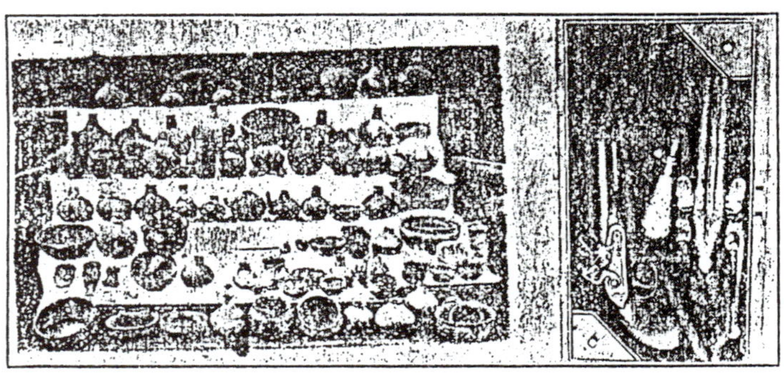

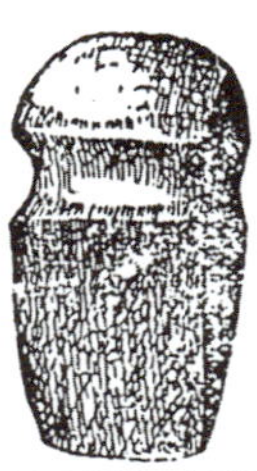

GROOVED AXE.

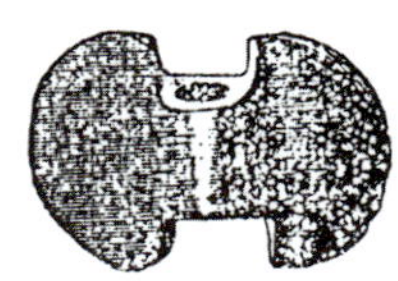

BANNER STONE.

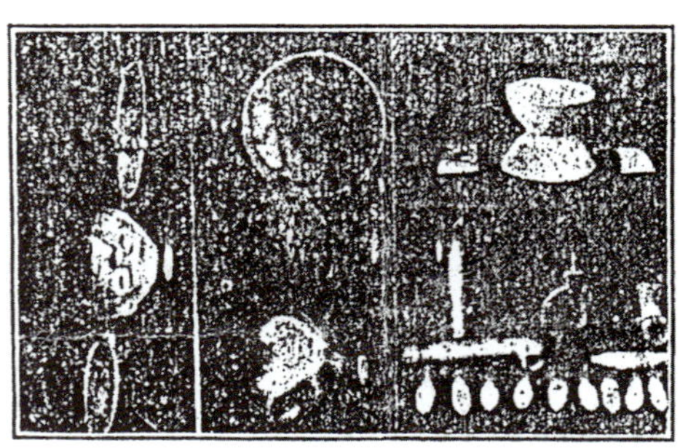

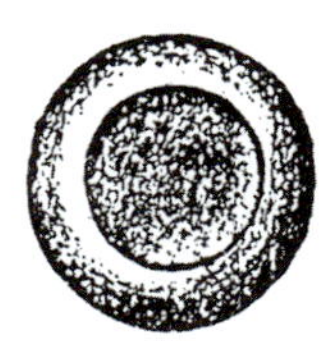

DISCOIDAL.

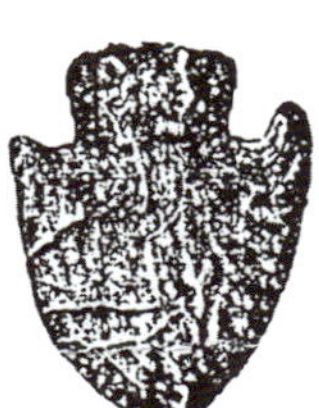

ARROWHEAD.

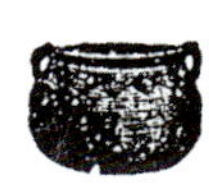

POTTERY.

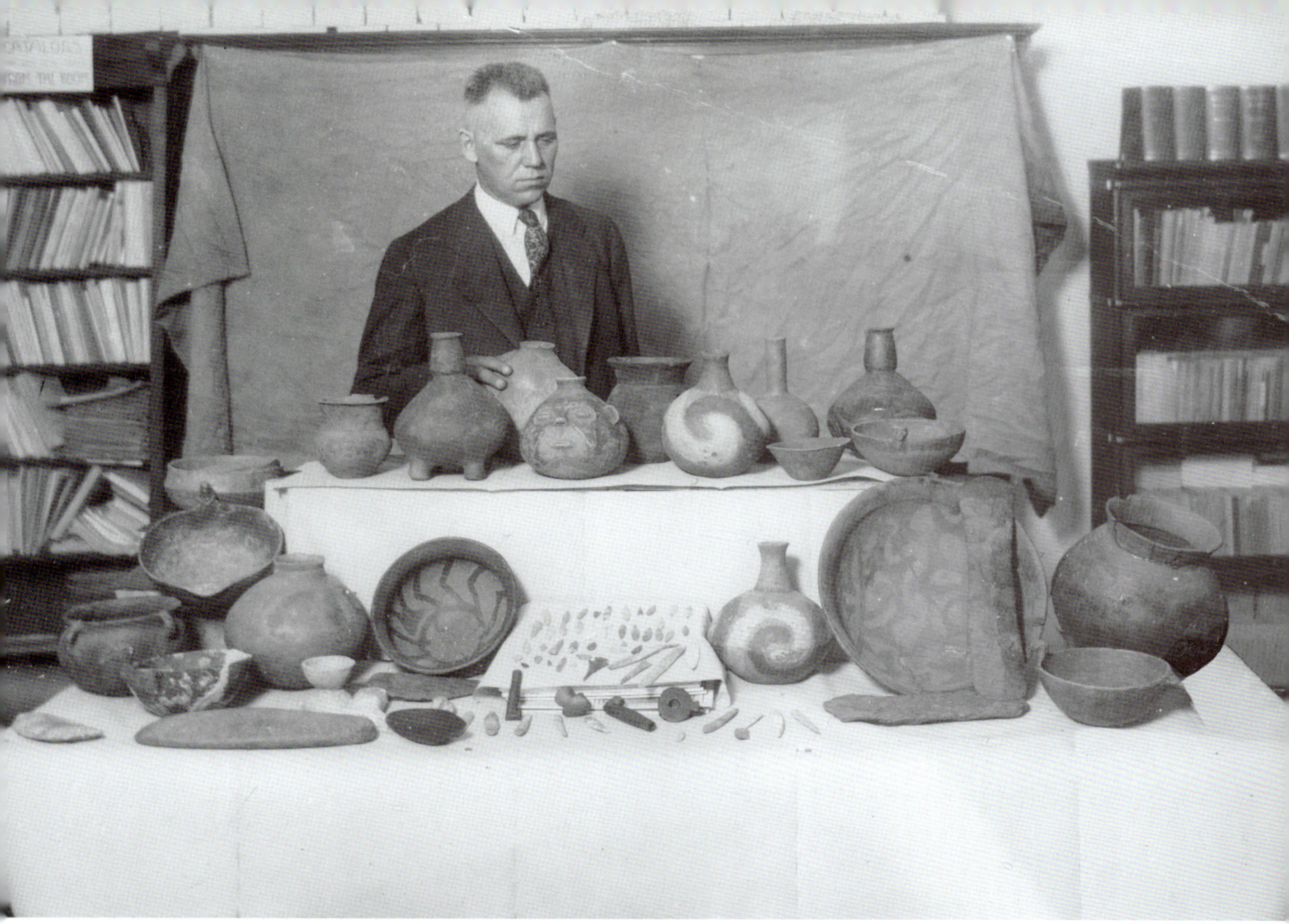

Figure 165. Dellinger in the museum circa 1928 with a number of pottery vessels and other objects from the central Arkansas River valley (some from the Fields Chapel site).

◀**Figure 164**. Handbill for H.T. Daniels, a well-known dealer in prehistoric Native American artifacts. Circa 1925. The town of Dardanelle, mentioned as Daniels's address, is located south of Russellville in the Arkansas River valley.

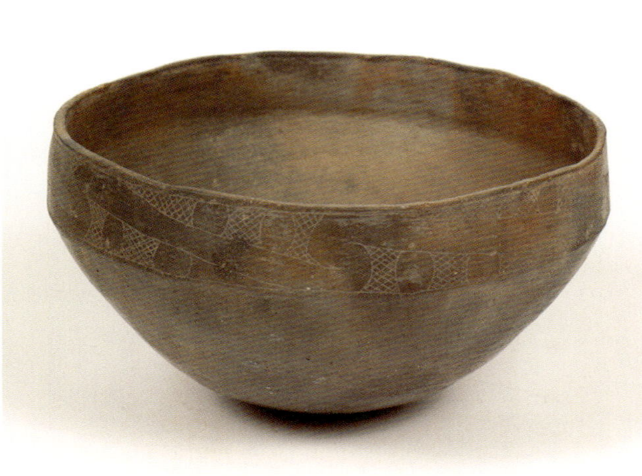

Figure 166. Incised Bowl (Hodges Engraved) (OSHTL2006.003.23)
Ceramic; 12.7 x 25.4 cm
Carden Bottom, Yell County, Arkansas
Late Caddo period, A.D. 1500–1700
This vessel was produced in the middle Ouachita River basin.

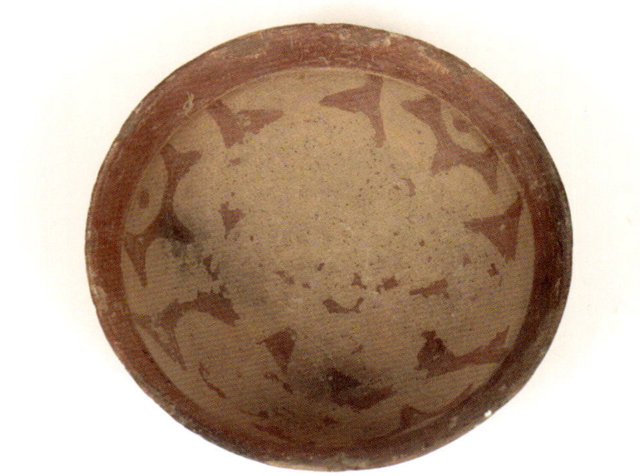

Figure 167. Red on Buff Bowl (OSHTL2006.003.24)
Ceramic; 10.2 x 24.1 cm
Carden Bottom, Yell County, Arkansas
Late Mississippi period, A.D. 1350–1600

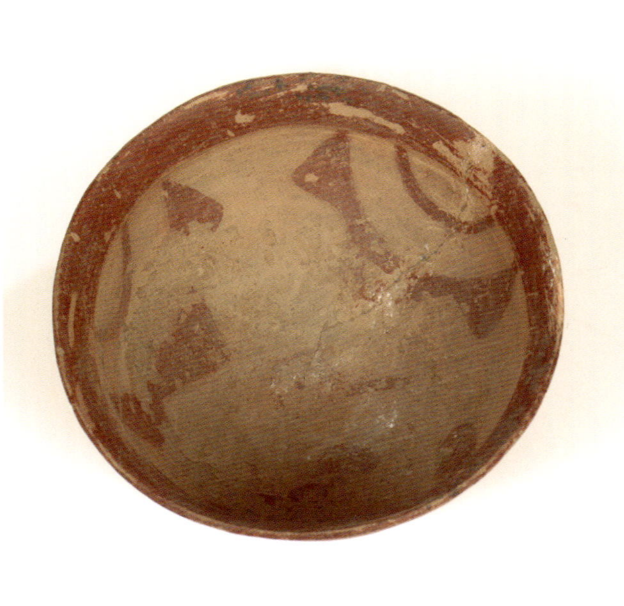

Figure 168. Red on Buff Bowl (OSHTL2006.003.25)
Ceramic; 7.6 x 24.8 cm
Carden Bottom, Yell County, Arkansas
Late Mississippi period, A.D. 1350–1600

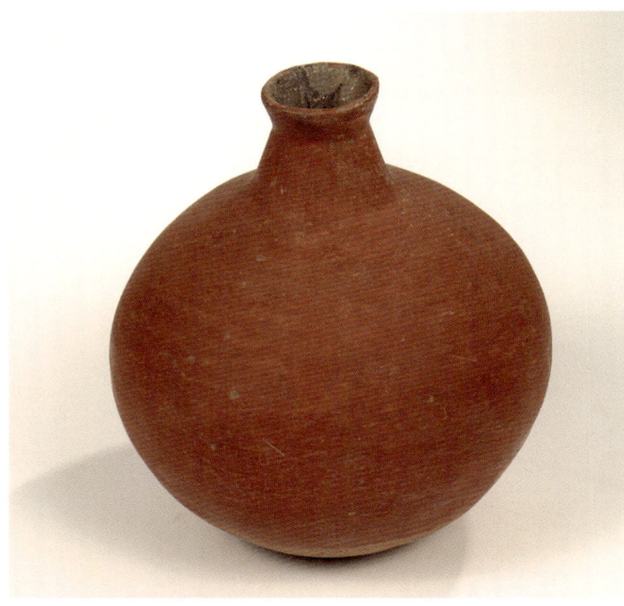

Figure 169. Red Slipped Bottle (OSHTL2006.003.26)
Ceramic (restored); 17.5 x 19.3 cm
Carden Bottom, Yell County, Arkansas
Late Mississippi period, A.D. 1350–1600

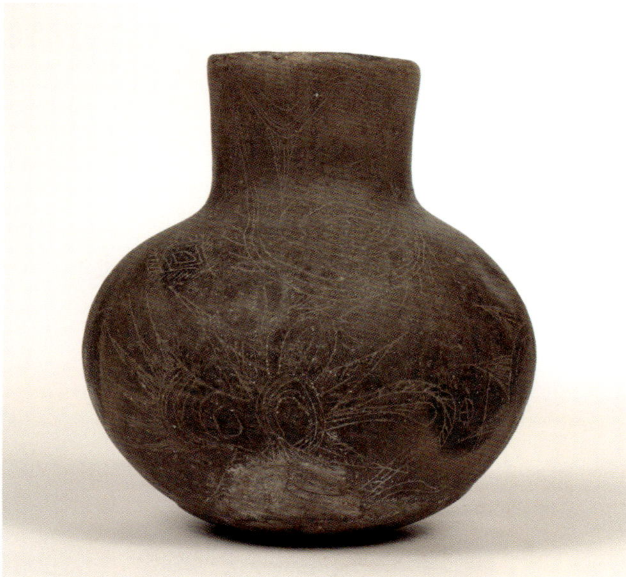

Figure 170. Incised Bottle (OSHTL2006.003.27)
Ceramic; 23.0 x 25.6 cm
Near Dardanelle, Yell County, Arkansas
Late Mississippi period, A.D. 1350–1600

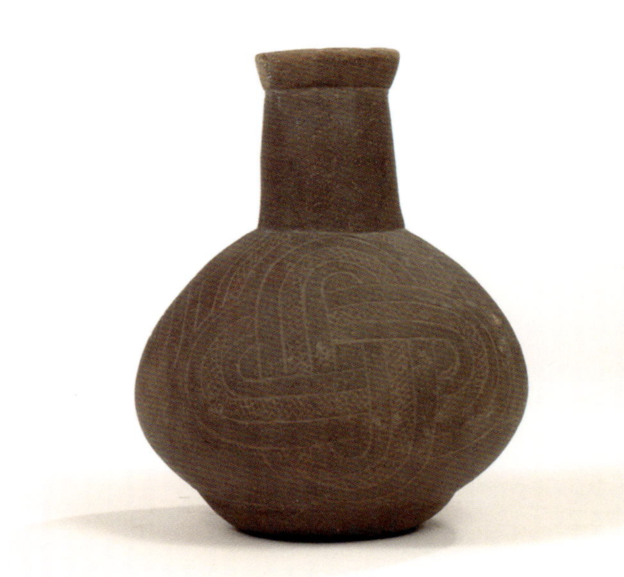

Figure 171. Incised Bottle (Hudson Engraved) (OSHTL2006.003.28)
Ceramic; 19.1 x 49.5 cm
Carden Bottom, Yell County, Arkansas
Late Caddo period, A.D. 1500–1700
This vessel was produced in the Arkansas River valley.

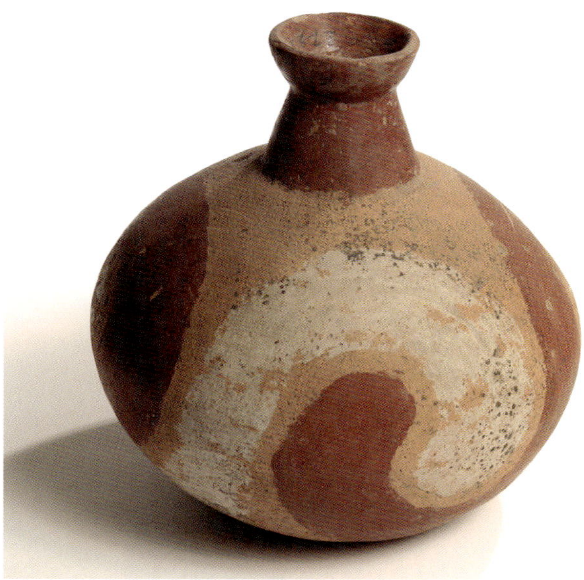

Figure 172. Bottle with Red and White Spiral Design (OSHTL2006.003.29)
Ceramic; 20.3 x 63.5 cm
Carden Bottom, Yell County, Arkansas
Late Mississippi period, A.D. 1350–1600

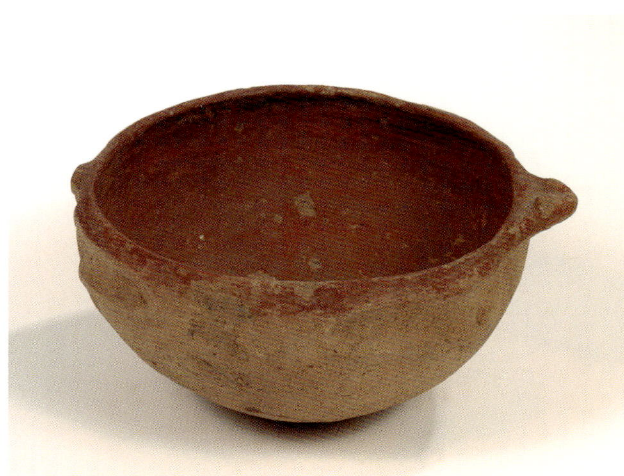

Figure 173. Frog Effigy Bowl (OSHTL2006.003.30)
Ceramic; 16.5 x 55.9 cm
Carden Bottom, Yell County, Arkansas
Late Mississippi period, A.D. 1350–1600

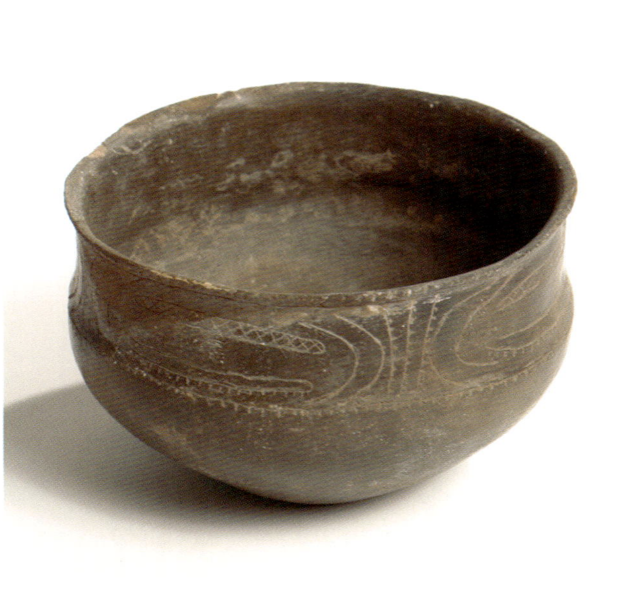

Figure 174. Engraved Bowl (cf. Natchitoches Engraved) (OSHTL2006.003.31)
Ceramic; 18.4 x 58.4 cm
Carden Bottom, Yell County, Arkansas
Late Caddo period, A.D. 1500–1700
The vessel shape and decorative modes suggest a southwest Arkansas origin.

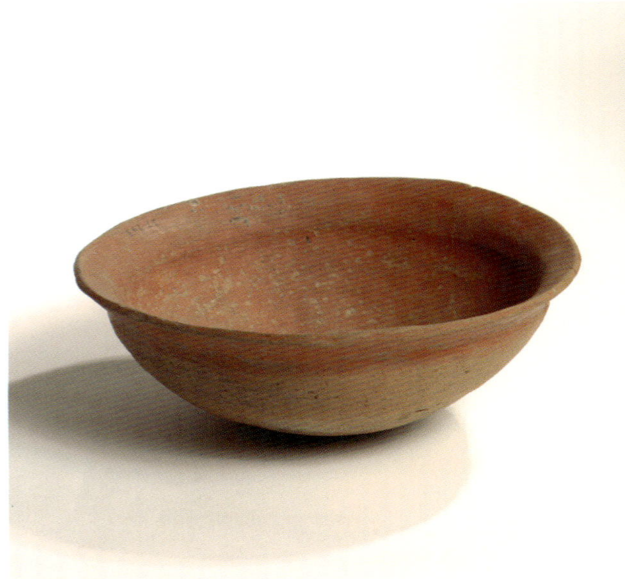

Figure 175. Red on Buff Bowl (OSHTL2006.003.32)
Ceramic; 22.9 x 63.5 cm
Carden Bottom, Yell County, Arkansas
Late Mississippi period, A.D. 1350–1600

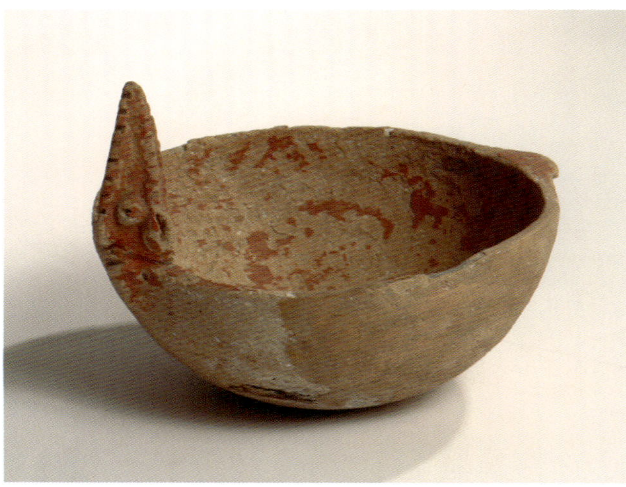

Figure 176a. Red Slipped "Corn God" Effigy Bowl (OSHTL2006.003.33)
Ceramic; 17.8 x 55.9 cm (some restoration)
Carden Bottom, Yell County, Arkansas
Late Mississippi period, A.D. 1350–1600

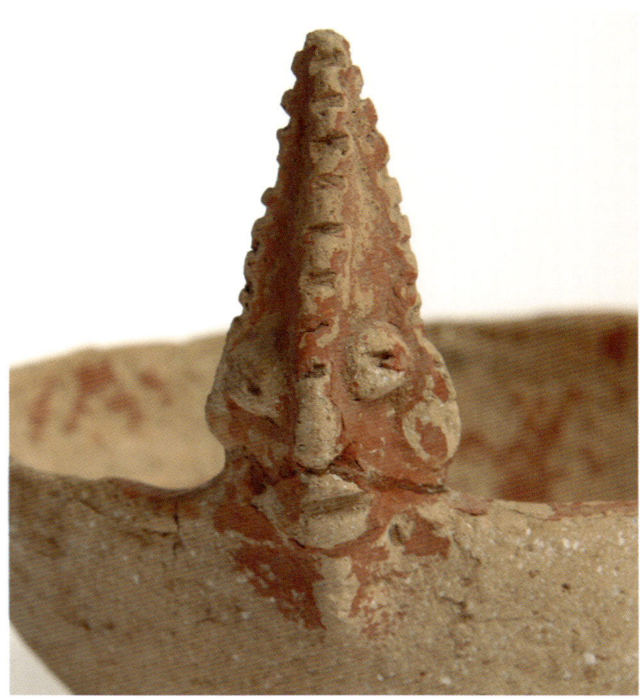

Figure 176b. Detail of head (OSHTL2006.003.33)

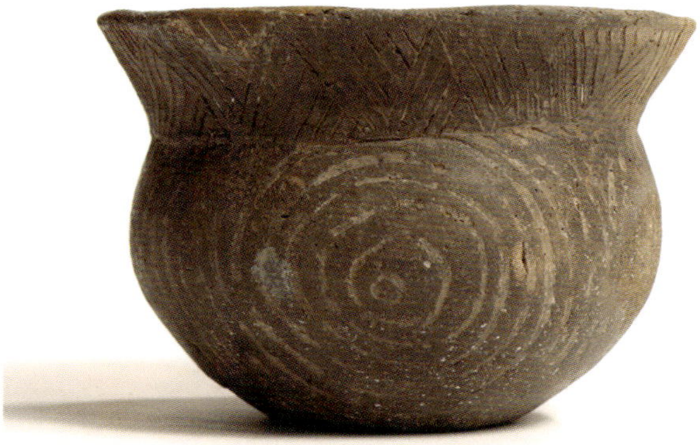

Figure 177. Incised Jar with Flared Rim (Foster Trailed Incised) (OSHTL2006.003.35)
Ceramic; 12.7 x 33.0 cm (reconstructed)
Carden Bottom, Yell County, Arkansas
Late Caddo period, A.D. 1500–1700

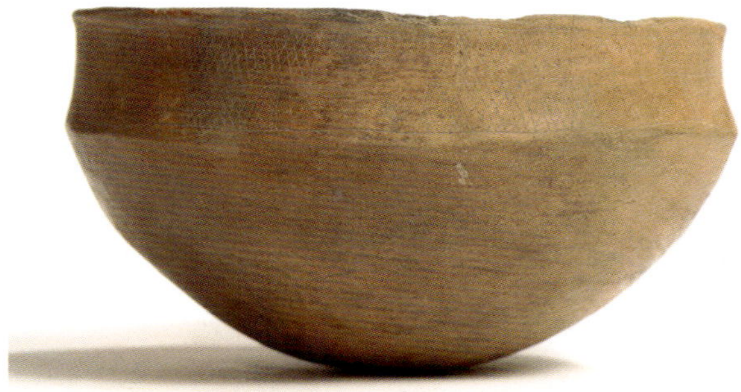

Figure 178. Red Slipped Incised Bowl (OSHTL2006.003.36)
Ceramic; 17.8 x 48.3 cm (a portion of a second bowl rests within)
Carden Bottom, Yell County, Arkansas
Late Mississippi period, A.D. 1350–1600

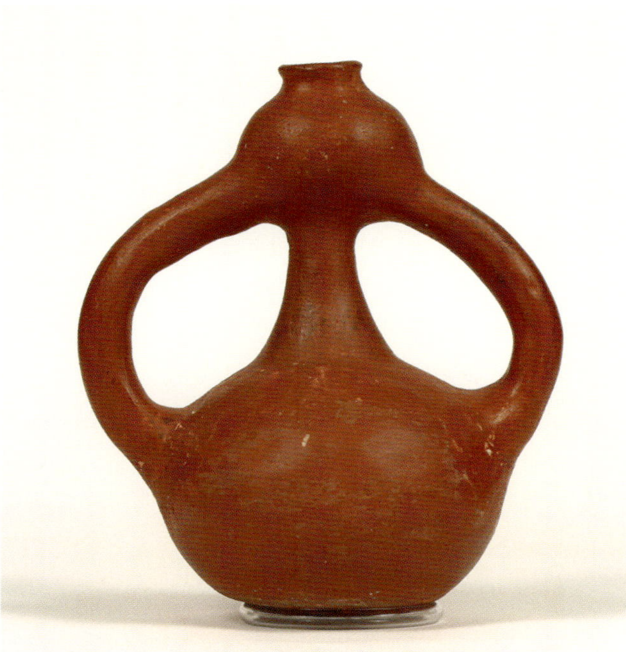

Figure 179. Red Slipped Stirrup Neck Bottle (OSHTL2006.003.46)
Ceramic; 25.4 x 53.3 cm (restored)
Owen Place, Perry County, Arkansas
Late Mississippi period, A.D. 1350–1600

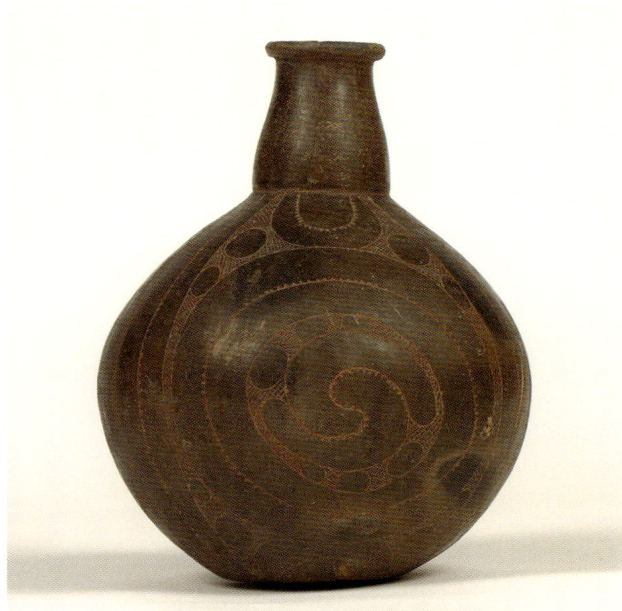

Figure 180. Engraved Bottle (Hodges Engraved, *var. Hodges*) (OSHTL2006.003.47)
Ceramic (red pigment in engraved decoration); 7.0 x 19.9 cm
Field's Chapel, Yell County, Arkansas
Late Caddo period, A.D. 1400–1700
This vessel was produced in the middle Ouachita River basin.

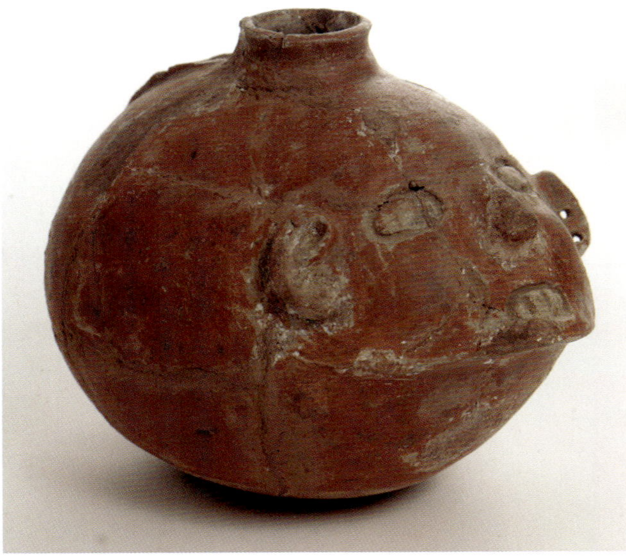

Figure 181. Red Slipped Head Pot (OSHTL2006.003.100)
Ceramic; 24.1 x 58.4 cm
Kinkead-Mainard site, Pulaski County, Arkansas
Late Mississippi period, A.D. 1350–1600

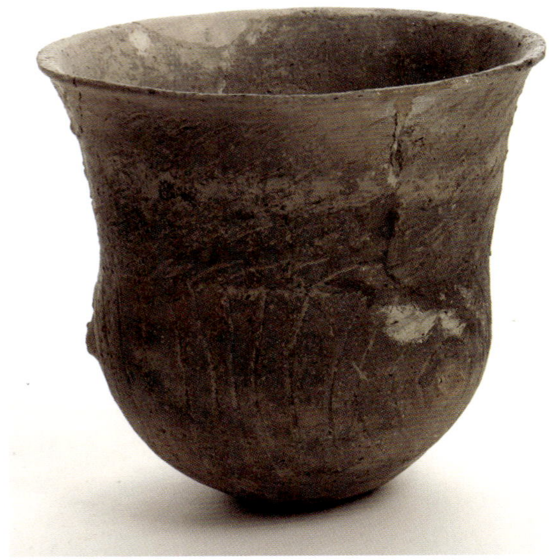

Figure 182. Trailed and Incised Jar (Foster Trailed Incised, *var. Foster*) (OSHTL2006.003.123)
Ceramic; 17.8 x 35.6 cm
Carden Bottom, Yell County, Arkansas
Late Caddo period, A.D. 1500–1700
This vessel was made in southwest Arkansas.

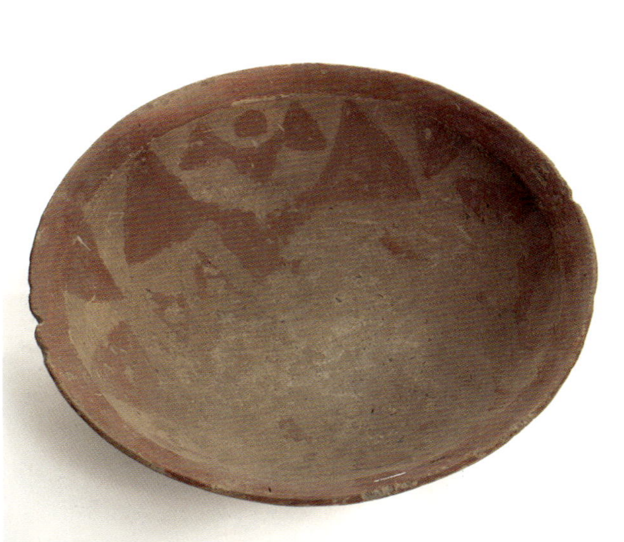

Figure 183. Red on Buff Bowl (OSHTL2006.003.126)
Ceramic; 36.3 x 19.0 cm
Carden Bottom, Yell County, Arkansas
Late Mississippi period, A.D. 1350–1600

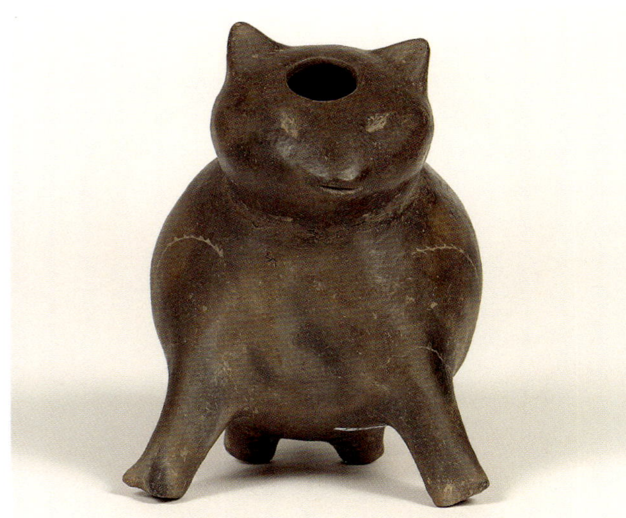

Figure 184. Engraved Four-legged Animal Effigy Bottle (OSHTL2006.003.128)
Ceramic; 21.0 x 13.0 cm
Near Shoal Creek, Logan County, Arkansas
Late Mississippi period, A.D. 1350–1600

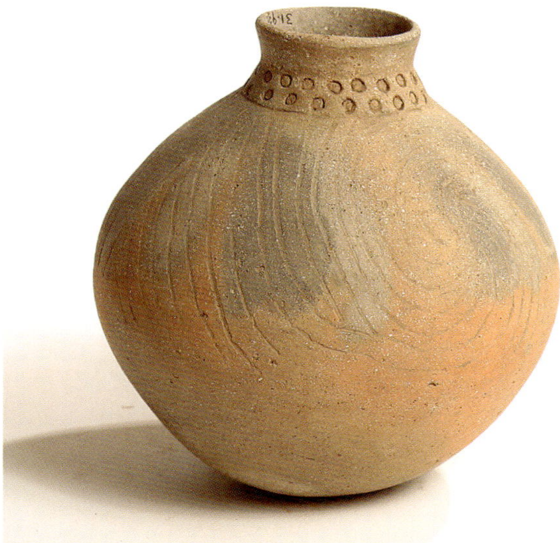

Figure 185. Incised Bottle with Swirls (OSHTL2006.003.142)
Ceramic; 15.8 x 14.9 cm
Carden Bottom, Yell County, Arkansas
Late Mississippi period, A.D. 1350–1600
This vessel was produced in the Arkansas River valley.

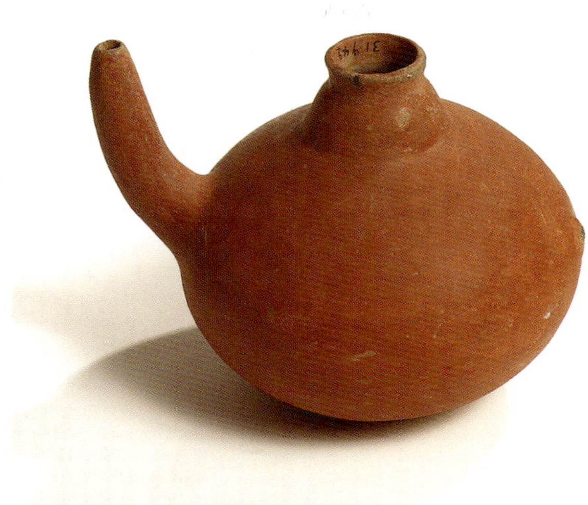

Figure 186. Red Slipped "Teapot" (OSHTL2006.003.143)
Ceramic; 14.5 x 16.1 cm
Carden Bottom, Yell County, Arkansas
Late Mississippi period, A.D. 1350–1600

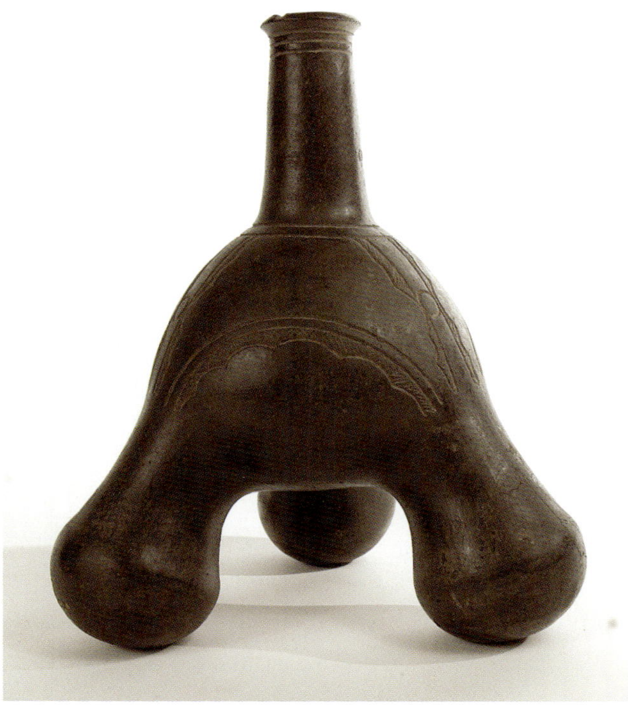

Figure 187. Incised Tripod Bottle (OSHTL2006.003.144)
Ceramic; 27.9 x 48.3 cm
Field's Chapel, Yell County, Arkansas
Middle to Late Caddo period, A.D. 1300–1700
This vessel was produced in the Ouachita River basin.

The Spiro Mound Group

Located just west of Fort Smith, Arkansas, the Spiro Mound Group is one of the most famous archaeological sites in North America because an unprecedented number of truly remarkable artifacts, dating between about A.D. 1100 and 1450, have been found there.[43] Unfortunately, most of these were found when the site, and the largest mound in particular, was looted in the early 1930s. The magnitude of the discoveries was captured, if a bit overstated, by a December 1935 story in the *Kansas City Star* bearing the headline "A 'King Tut' Tomb in the Arkansas Valley":

> The mound group is located within the Arkansas River valley in eastern Oklahoma, about nine miles southwest of Fort Smith, Arkansas, and northeast of the town of Spiro. This archaeological site, which includes 11 constructed earthen mounds within an area of about 80 acres, is now an archaeological park managed by the State of Oklahoma. The largest earthwork at the site is a group of four overlapping conical burial mounds known as the Craig Mound, the highest portion of which was at least 33 feet tall.[44]

Uncontrolled digging at the Spiro site began in the summer of 1933, but the actual mining of the site for relics began in November 1933 and continued for two years by a group of six men calling themselves the "Pocola Mining Co." These individuals leased the Craig property portion of the site on which the largest mound stood. At the time it was called the Great Temple mound at Fort Coffee, but following the University of Oklahoma's site-naming practice it became known as the Craig Mound. The looters tunneled into the earthwork and ransacked the contents of the central burial feature, which was protected by a natural dome. They finished their lease by setting off a charge of dynamite that effectively sealed their main access tunnel. Professional excavations began soon thereafter, but much had already been totally destroyed by the looters. The looting of the Spiro site is one of the greatest tragedies in the history of North American archaeology.

Many of the most remarkable artifacts were located within a small area known as the "Great Mortuary" beneath the tallest portion of the Craig Mound. Among these was the resting warrior figure known as "Big Boy," which may be the most famous example of prehistoric Native American art from North America. From the same location were numerous large, engraved conch shells, large ceremonial stone maces and celts, a variety of embossed copper plates, thousands of shell and freshwater pearl beads, as well as well-preserved textiles and basketry. The excavators made little effort to preserve the latter, as these perishables were viewed as being less valuable to buyers.

THE COLLECTIONS

As stories of the finds at Spiro began to circulate, several archaeologists visited the site. Among these was Samuel Dellinger, who was present in the summer of 1935 during the looting of the "Great Mortuary" in the largest mound. Dellinger actually witnessed some of the objects and human remains being carried out of a tunnel cut into the mound, and he later provided the most authoritative account of some of the findings.[45] He also purchased artifacts and human remains for the University of Arkansas Museum from the looters on several occasions. Many years later, Dellinger recounted to James Brown (now professor of anthropology, Northwestern University) that the diggers were a suspicious lot who were very arbitrary about what they would sell to him; hence, Dellinger could not get all that he was willing to buy.[46] A number of the museum's Spiro artifacts were purchased from or donated by Colonel T. H. Barton of El Dorado,[47] who also donated money for analysis, drawing, and photography of this material.[48] Dellinger obtained other Spiro artifacts, including the sculptural pipe known as "Big Boy," for the museum as part of a large purchase from Fain W. and Blanche B. King.[49]

Most of the funerary objects from the Spiro site date between about A.D. 1000 and 1450. Such objects were reserved for the use of persons with elite social status, such as political and religious leaders. These individuals received special burial treatment that included placement in a special mortuary, sometimes on litters fashioned from sacred cedar poles. The objects buried with these individuals, and all of the Spiro artifacts, are some of the most exquisitely decorated examples of prehistoric Native American art in North America.[50]

Included in the exhibit are several large, engraved conch shells. These are of the species *Busycon sinistrum* (formerly *B. perversum*), which occurs along the Gulf Coast "from the Florida Keys to the Straits of Yucatan."[51] Averaging about 11 inches in length, these shells were transported to Spiro, where they were decorated. The engraved lines were produced using sharp chert or flint implements, though no tools designed specifically for engraving shell have been identified at Spiro. These decorated shells provide a fascinating window on pre-Columbian Native American iconography.

The University of Arkansas Museum collections also contain examples of basketry and fabric, in which Dellinger probably had an interest because of his experience with the Ozark bluff shelter material. Though fragmentary, this material has great research potential.

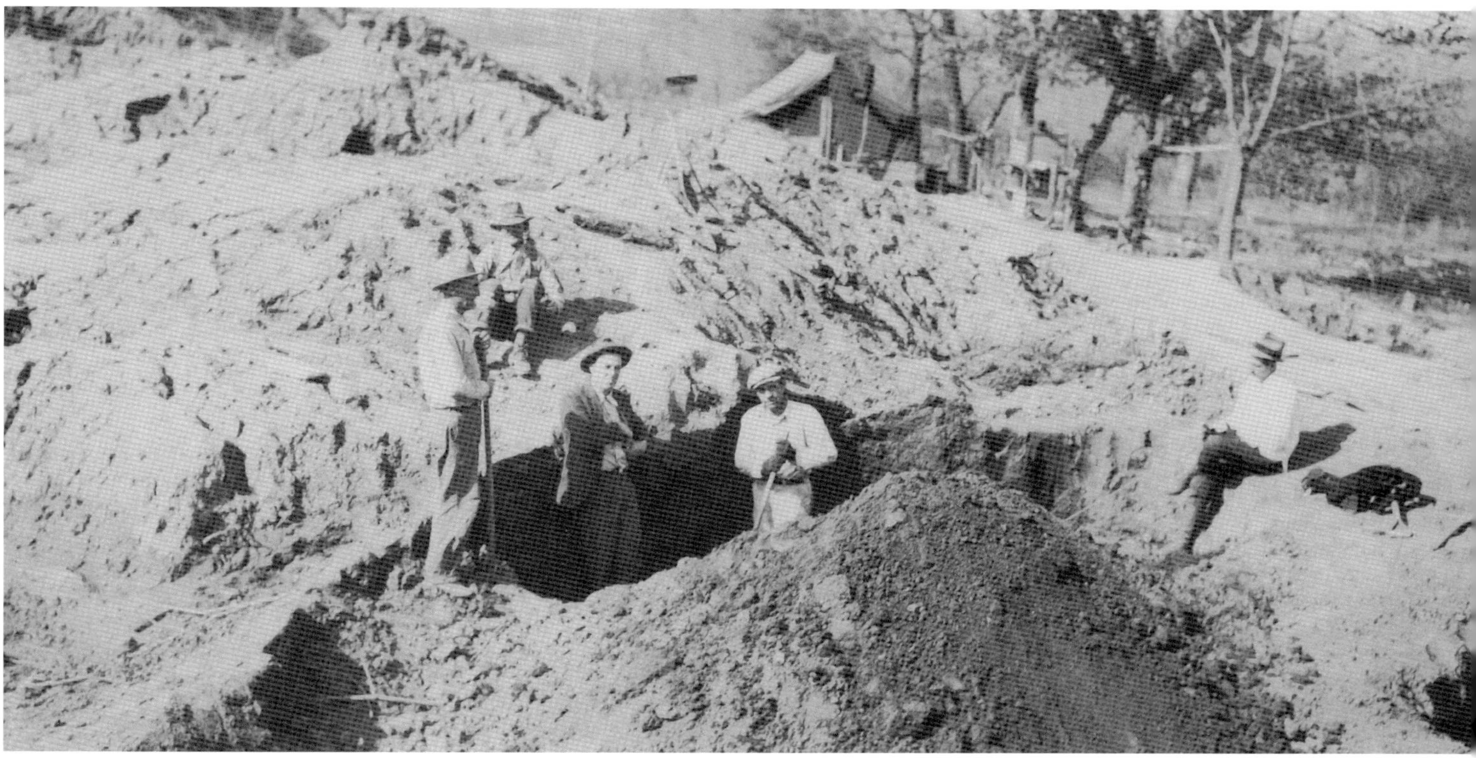

Figure 188. Members of the "Pocola Mining Company" at the Spiro site.

Figure 189. Some of the looter's excavations, including tunnels, at Spiro.

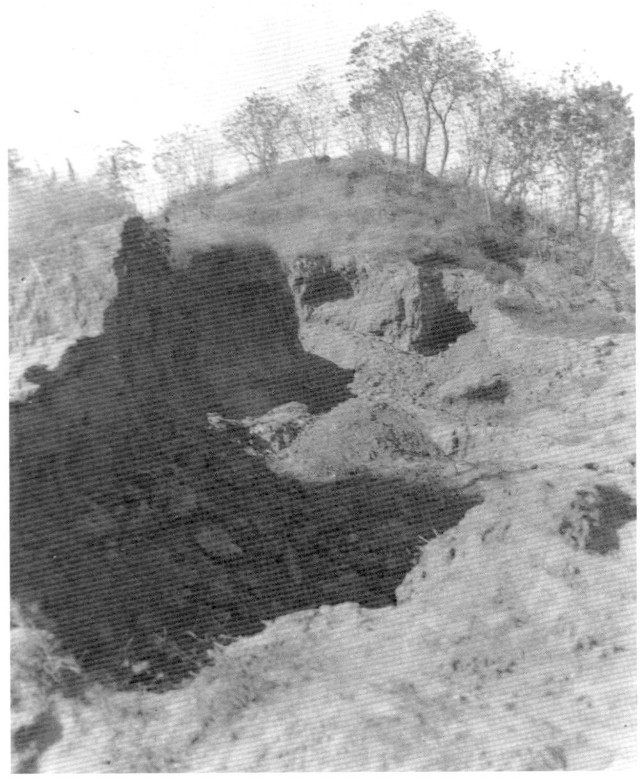

Figure 190. Joe Balloun, a prominent Arkansas River valley relic dealer. The pottery vessels probably are from the vicinity of Dardanelle, Arkansas; the beads and other objects are from Spiro, Oklahoma.

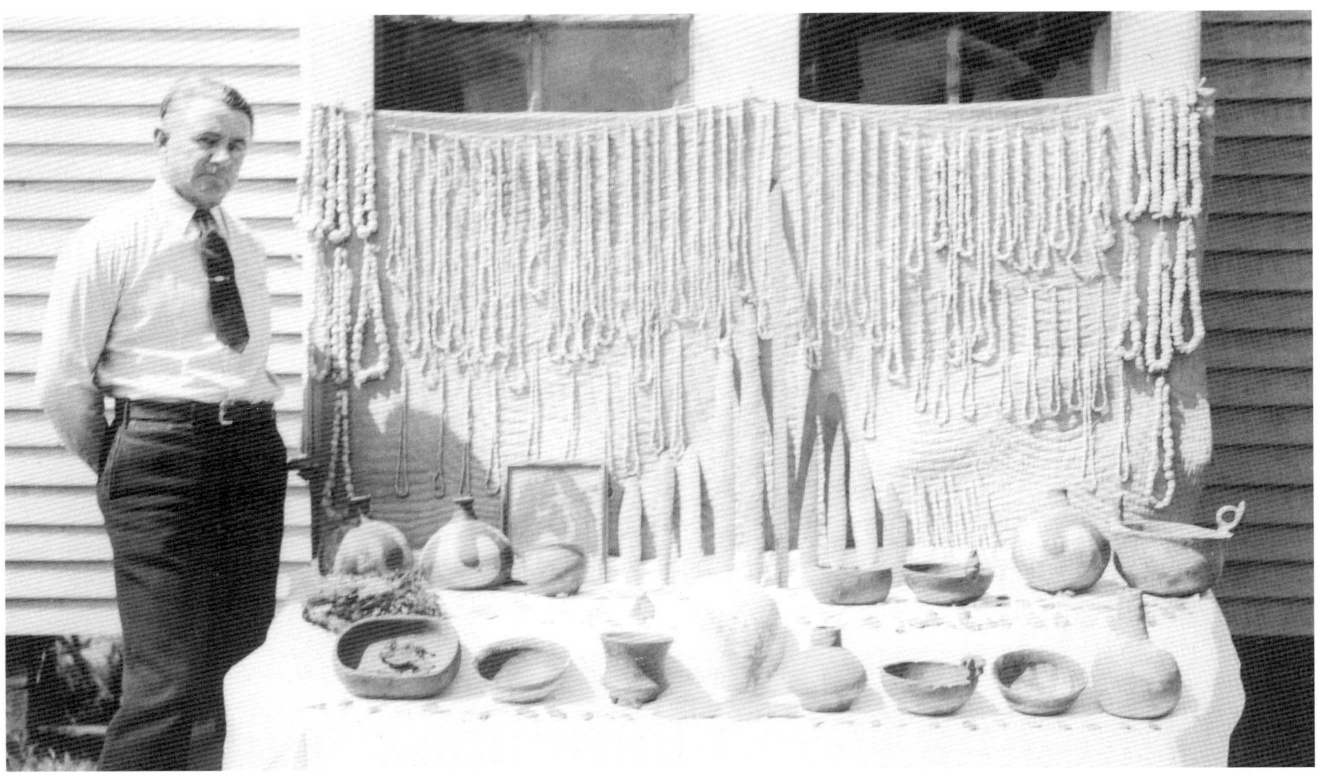

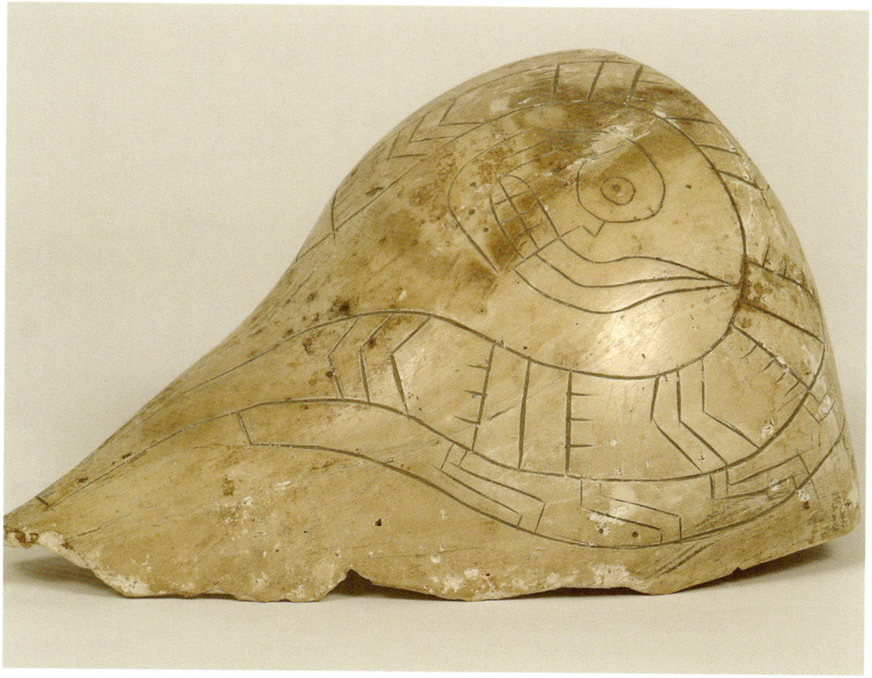

Figure 191. Engraved Shell Cup Showing Horned Serpent, Skull, and Hand (OSHTL2006.003.01)
Marine shell; 25.0 x 17.2 cm
Craig Mound, Spiro site, LeFlore County, Oklahoma
Spiro phase, Caddoan culture, A.D. 1200–1350

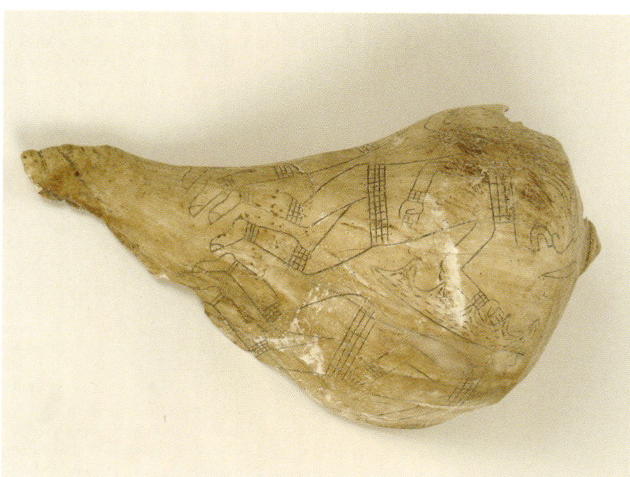

Figure 192a. Engraved Shell Cup Showing Empty-Handed Human Figures
(OSHTL2006.003.02)
Marine shell; 27.0 x 17.2 cm
Craig Mound, Spiro site, LeFlore County, Oklahoma
Spiro phase, Caddoan culture, A.D. 1200–1350

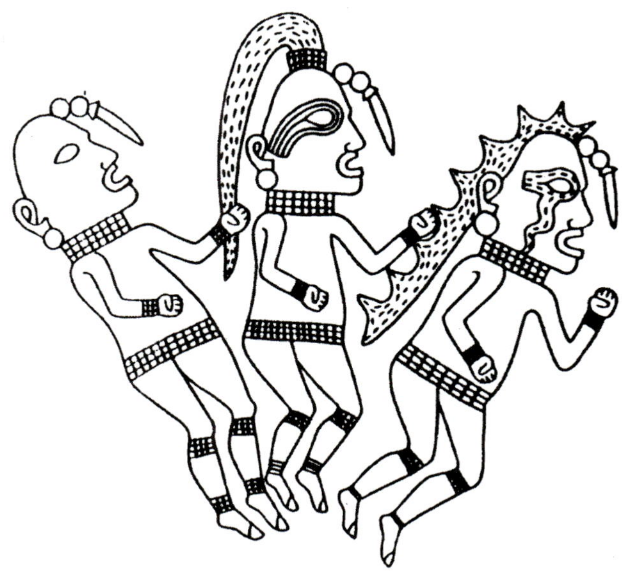

Figure 192b. Imagery on OSHTL2006.003.02

Figure 193. Engraved Shell Cup Showing Janus-Headed Rattlesnake with Antlers (OSHTL2006.003.03)
Marine shell; 32.6 x 17.8 cm
Craig Mound, Spiro site, LeFlore County, Oklahoma
Spiro phase, Caddoan culture, A.D. 1200–1350

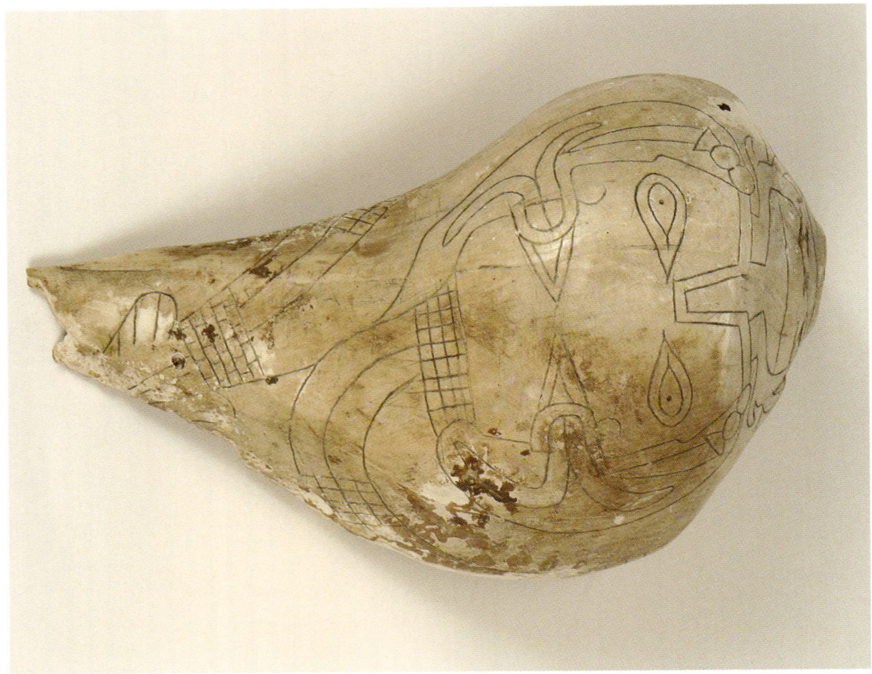

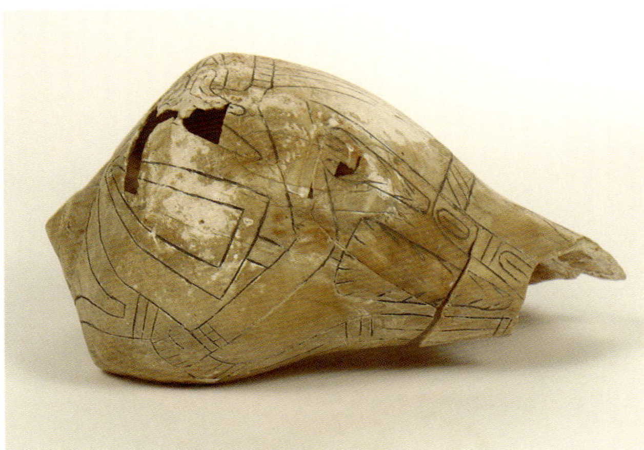

Figure 194a. Partial Engraved Shell Cup Showing Janus-Headed Figure Holding Serpent Staffs (OSHTL2006.003.04)
Marine shell; 26.2 x 18.3 cm
Craig Mound, Spiro site, LeFlore County, Oklahoma
Spiro phase, Caddoan culture, A.D. 1200–1350

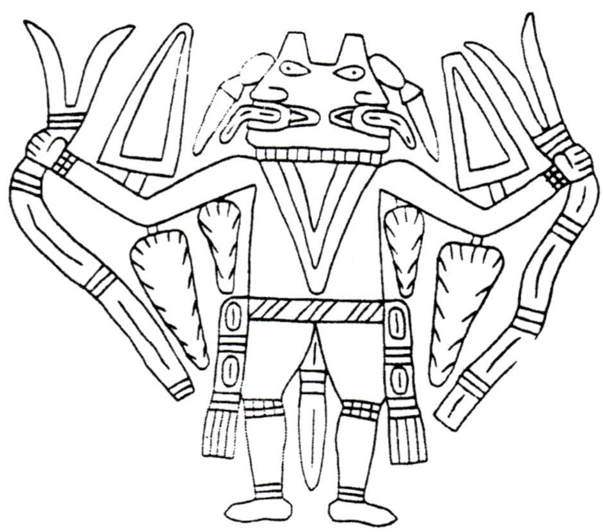

Figure 194b. Imagery on OSHTL2006.003.04

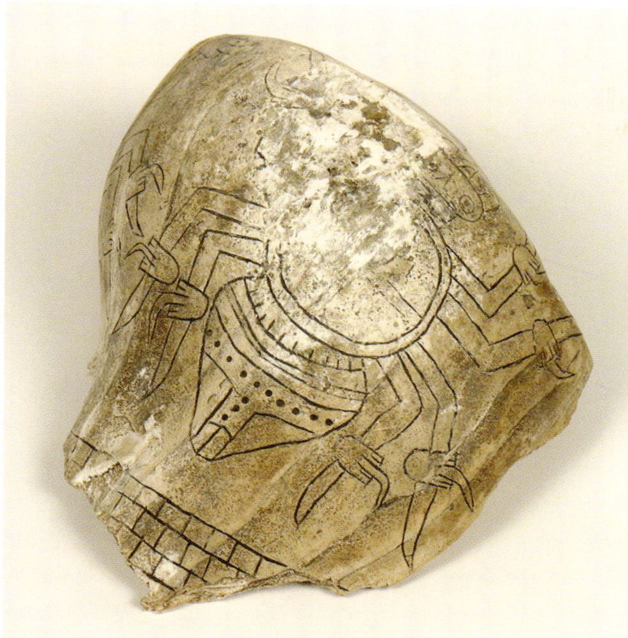

Figure 195a. Engraved Shell Cup Showing Spiders with Raccoon Hindquarters Motifs (OSHTL2006.003.05)
Marine shell; 16.7 x 16.2 cm
Craig Mound, Spiro site, LeFlore County, Oklahoma
Spiro phase, Caddoan culture, A.D. 1200–1350

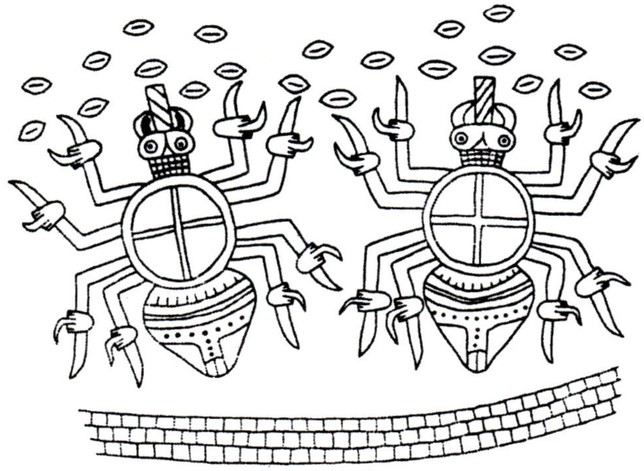

Figure 195b. Imagery on OSHTL2006.003.05

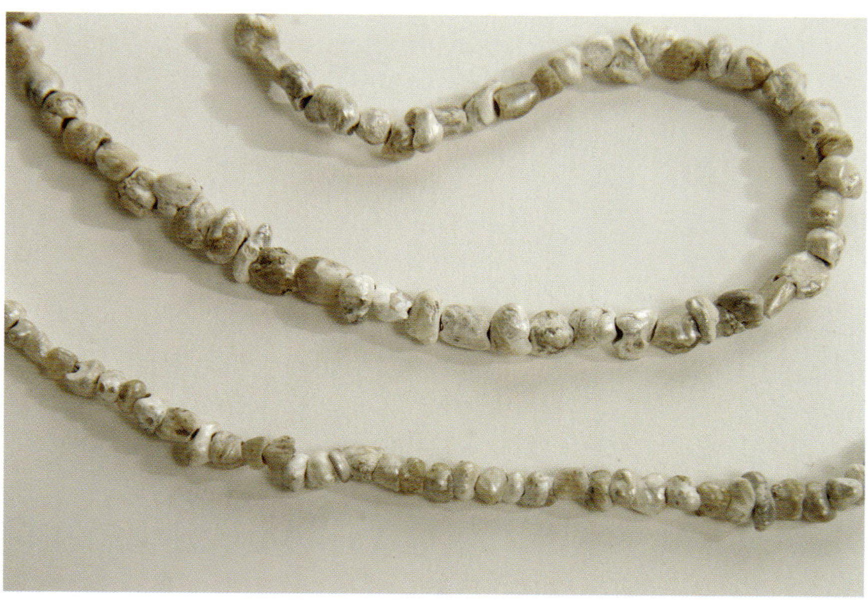

Figure 196. Beads (OSHTL2006.003.06)
Freshwater pearls; length, 28.0 cm
Probably Craig Mound, Spiro site, LeFlore County, Oklahoma
Spiro phase, Caddoan culture, A.D. 1200–1350

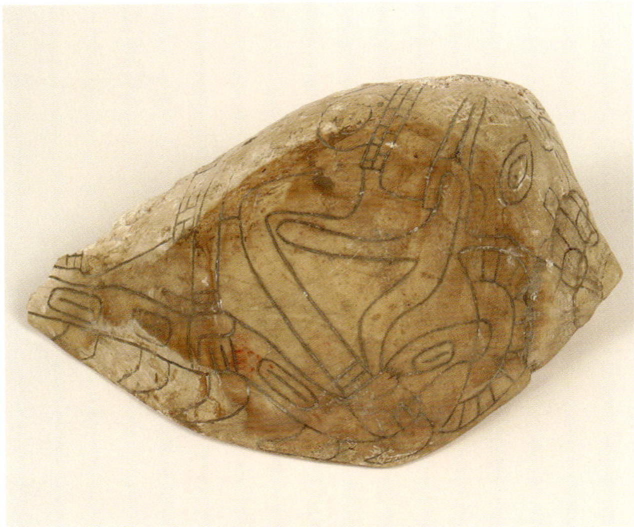

Figure 197a. Partial Engraved Shell Cup Showing Horned Figure Holding Serpent Staff (OSHTL2006.003.07)
Marine shell; 25.0 x 18.5 cm
Craig Mound, Spiro site, LeFlore County, Oklahoma
Spiro phase, Caddoan culture, A.D. 1200–1350

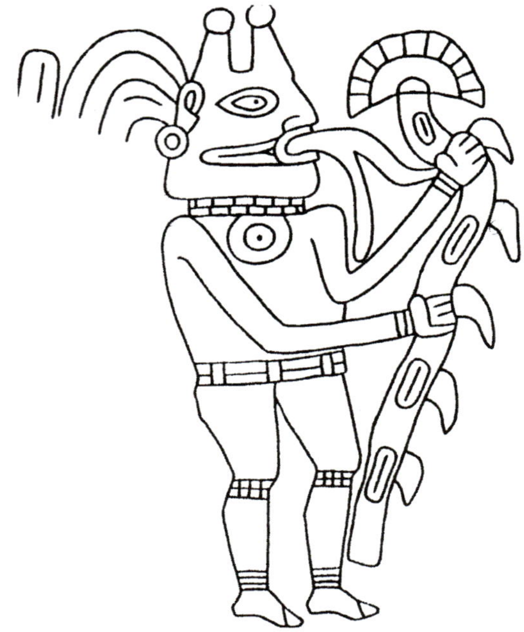

Figure 197b. Imagery on OSHTL2006.003.07

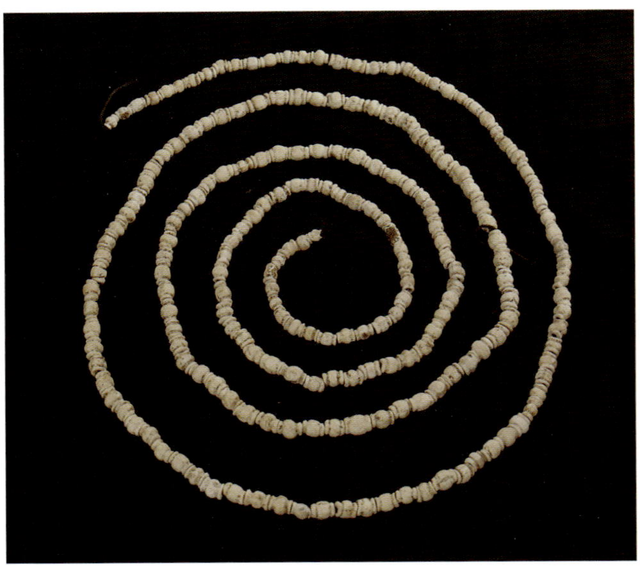

Figure 198. Beads, Some with Copper Stains (OSHTL2006.003.08)
Marine shell; apx. 1.0 x 0.9 cm each
Craig Mound, Spiro site, LeFlore County, Oklahoma
Spiro phase, Caddoan culture, A.D. 1200–1350

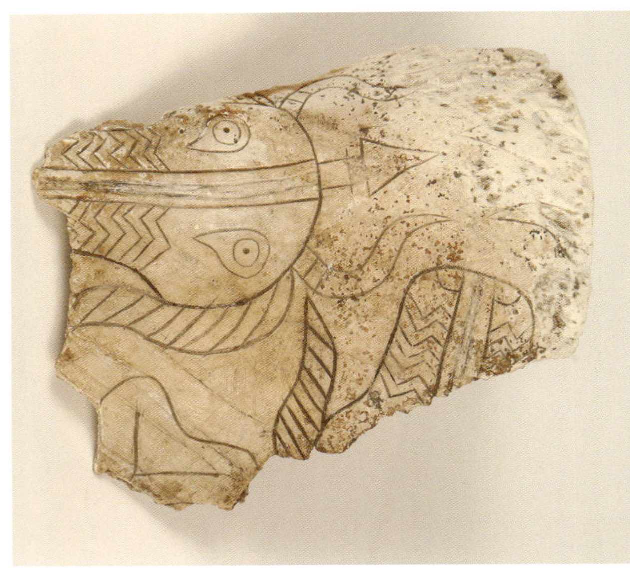

Figure 199. Engraved Shell Cup Fragment with Horned Heads (OSHTL2006.003.09)
Marine shell; 15.9 x 11.0 cm
Craig Mound, Spiro site, LeFlore County, Oklahoma
Spiro phase, Caddoan culture, A.D. 1200–1350

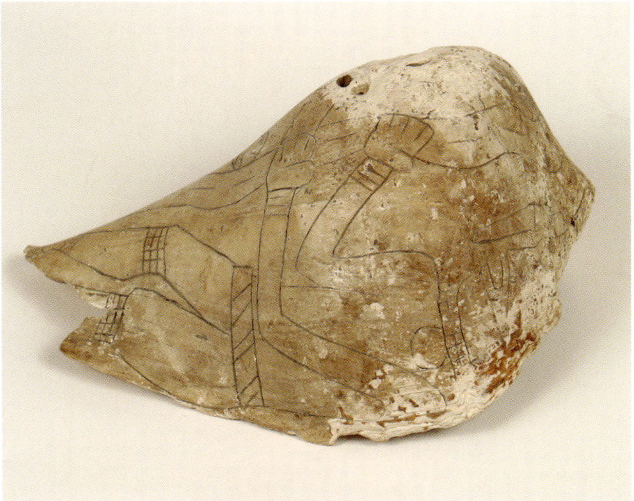

Figure 200a. Engraved Shell Cup Showing Bellows-Shaped Apron and Figure Holding Serpent Staff (OSHTL2006.003.10)
Marine shell; 28.0 x 18.5 cm
Craig Mound, Spiro site, LeFlore County, Oklahoma
Spiro phase, Caddoan culture, A.D. 1200–1350

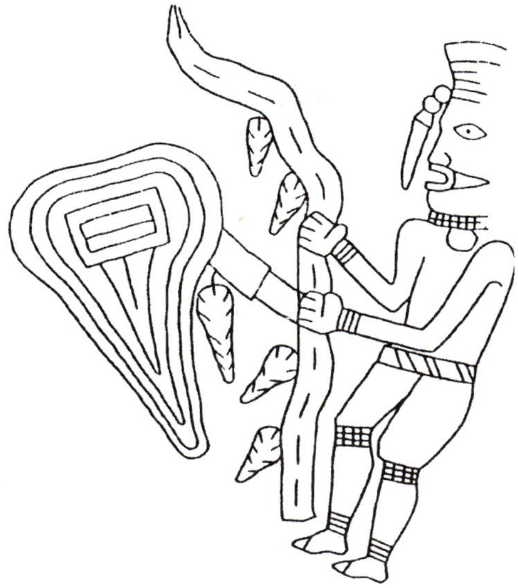

Figure 200b. Imagery on OSHTL2006.003.10

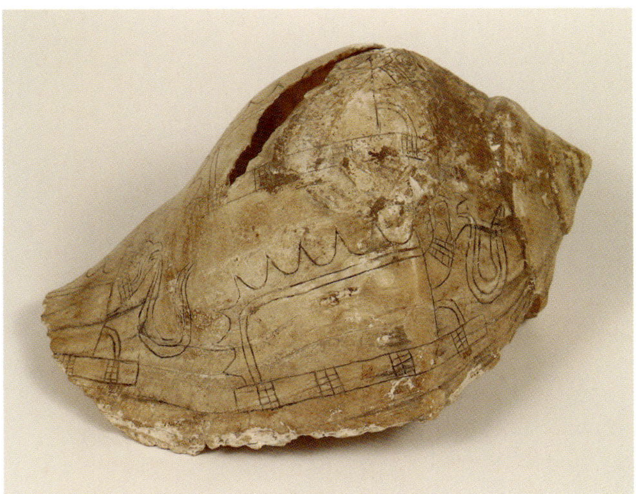

Figure 201a. Engraved Shell Cup Showing Birdlike Heads Emerging from Rectangular Structures (OSHTL2006.003.12)
Marine shell; 20.7 x 15.2 cm
Craig Mound, Spiro site, LeFlore County, Oklahoma
Spiro phase, Caddoan culture, A.D. 1200–1350

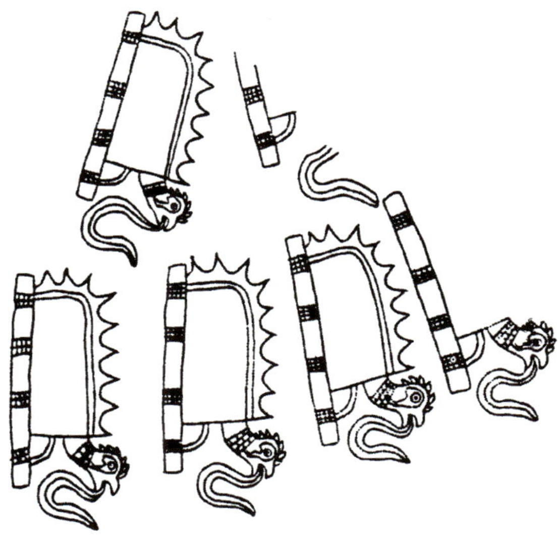

Figure 201b. Imagery on OSHTL2006.003.12

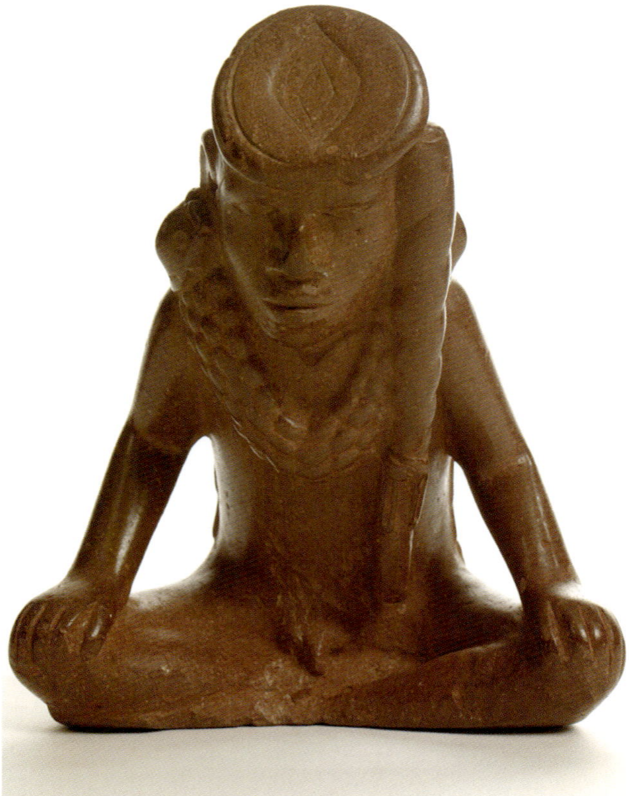

Figure 202a, b. Male Figurine Converted to Pipe ("Big Boy") (OSHTL2006.003.105)
Missouri Flint Clay; 24.0 x 27.0 cm
Craig Mound, Spiro site, LeFlore County, Oklahoma
Spiro phase, Caddoan Culture, A.D. 1200–1350

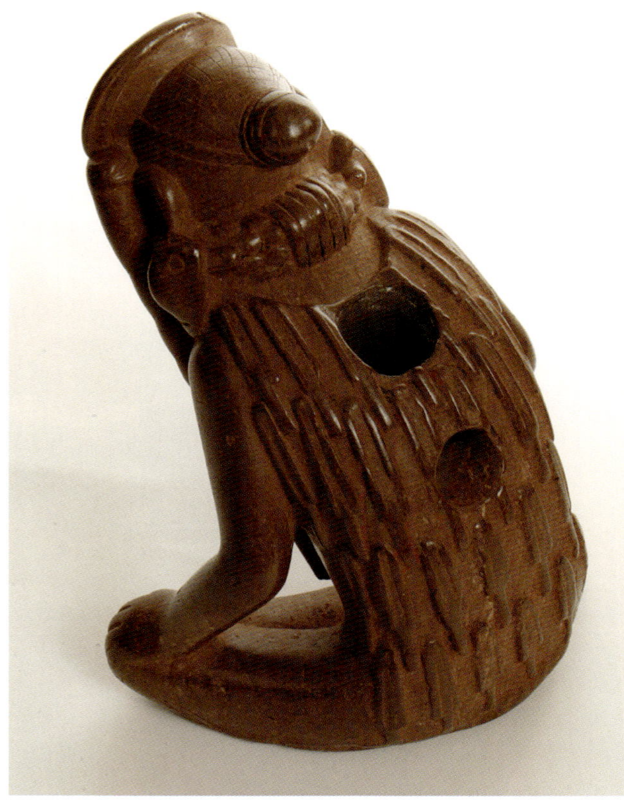

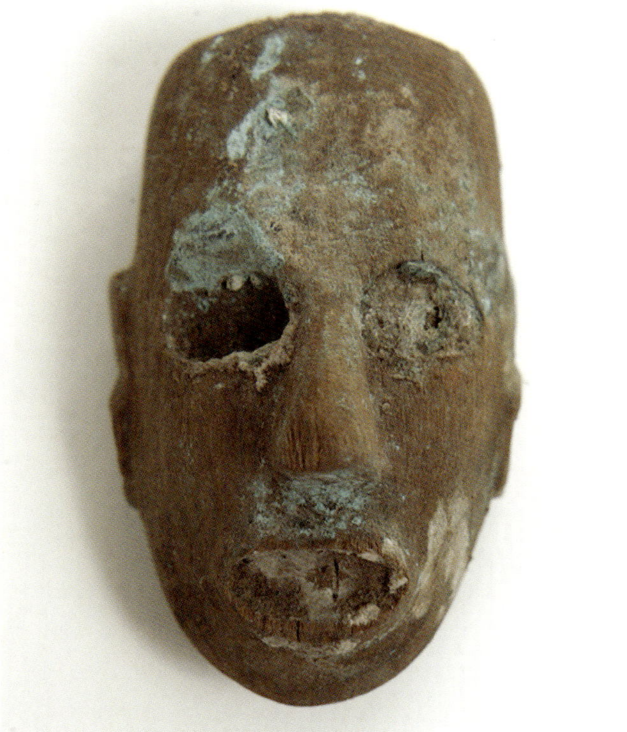

Figure 203. Human Face Maskette (OSHTL2006.003.156)
Wood (originally sheathed in copper); 5.8 x 3.5 cm
Craig Mound, Spiro site, LeFlore County, Oklahoma
Spiro phase, Caddoan culture, A.D. 1200–1350

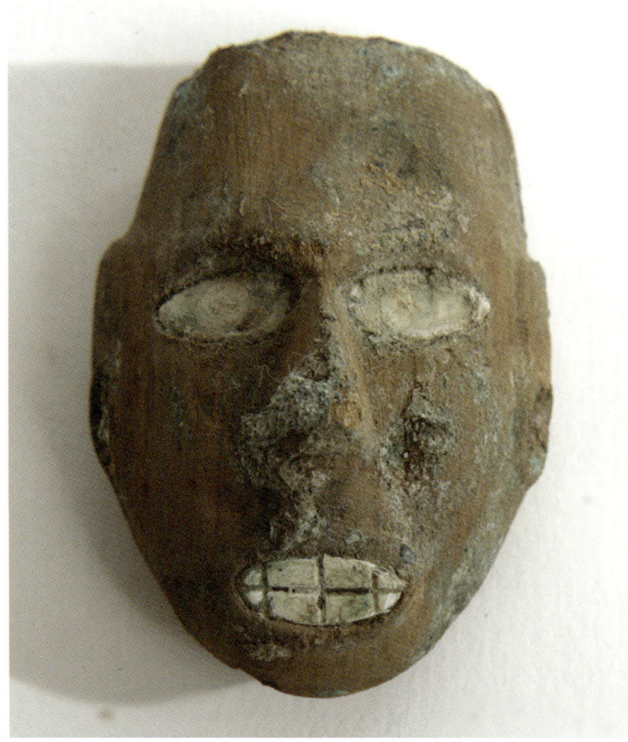

Figure 204. Human Face Maskette (OSHTL2006.003.157)
Wood with shell inserts (originally sheathed in copper); 5.8 x 4.1 cm
Craig Mound, Spiro site, LeFlore County, Oklahoma
Spiro phase, Caddoan culture, A.D. 1200–1350

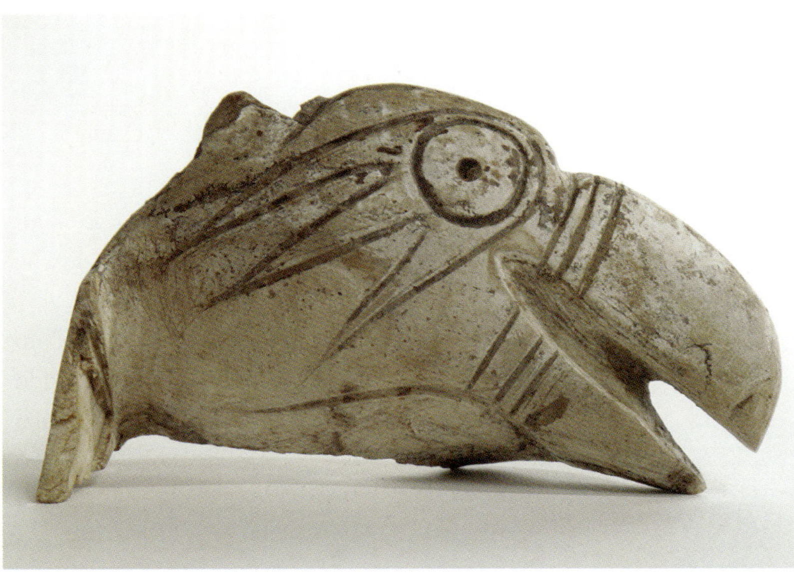

Figure 205. Bird Head Effigy with Forked Eye Motif (OSHTL2006.003.158)
Marine shell; 10.2 x 6.4 cm
Craig Mound, Spiro site, LeFlore County, Oklahoma
Spiro phase, Caddoan culture, A.D. 1200–1350

Ouachita River Valley

In the eighteenth century, several culturally related groups known collectively as the Caddo inhabited southwest Arkansas, including the middle and upper Ouachita River valley, and adjacent portions of Louisiana, Texas, and Oklahoma. Archaeological evidence indicates that the ancestors of modern Caddo occupied this region since at least A.D. 900 Mark R. Harrington, who spent roughly 20 months excavating in southwest Arkansas during 1916 and 1917, observed that prehistoric ceramics and stone tools from the region were antecedents of those made by the historic Caddo.[52]

The Caddo were corn agriculturalists that also grew squash, sunflower, beans, and tobacco. Unlike the Native American inhabitants of northeast Arkansas, the prehistoric and historic Caddo lived in small, unfortified hamlets. Their houses were tall, circular structures with a beehive shape that housed from two to as many as 10 families. They were constructed by initially setting a number of upright tree trunks in the ground, with the tops tapering inward to form a smoke hole. Smaller branches were then woven horizontally through the upright posts, and the entire exterior was covered with grass thatch.[53]

Among the Caddo, some members of the society were accorded burial in earthen mounds—another contrast with peoples in northeast Arkansas—but like their counterparts in northeast Arkansas, the late-prehistoric Caddo frequently buried pottery vessels with their dead. The Caddo also built flat-topped mounds, which likely supported civic-ceremonial buildings and the residences of headmen.

The Spanish expedition led by Hernando de Soto entered Caddoan territory in 1541 and met a powerful group named the Tula, who lived in the Ouachita mountain region. Survivors of the *entrada* visited Caddo settlements along the Red River the following year. The next significant encounter between the Caddo and Europeans did not occur until over 140 years later, when a party under Rene-Robert, sieur de La Salle, trekked northward from the Texas Gulf coast in search of provisions and directions to the Mississippi River.

As mentioned earlier, Dellinger conducted some of his first archaeological excavations in 1929 in the vicinity of Buckville, near the upper Ouachita River in Garland County. These excavations, funded by Harvey Couch, president of Arkansas Power and Light, were conducted over a period of four weeks in advance of completion of the Carpenter Dam.[54] The resulting impoundment would inundate several important archaeological sites. Unfortunately, there are no field records or photographs of the excavations, and the museum's pottery collections dating to this time consist primarily of vessels acquired from private individuals.

From mid-1939 into 1940, Dellinger supervised archaeological excavations at several mound and village sites in the middle and upper Ouachita River valley. Although Dellinger and his associates did not produce final site reports, there are good records of this work, some of which have been fruitfully used by modern researchers.[55]

THE COLLECTIONS

As in the Arkansas River valley and northeast Arkansas, it was the quality and quantity of pottery vessels placed with the dead that attracted early investigators to the Caddo area. Not surprisingly, such funerary objects are well represented in the museum's collections, and most probably date between about A.D. 1200 and 1700.

Thanks to Dellinger's excavations on behalf of the Works Progress Administration in 1939 and 1940, the museum's collections from southwest Arkansas also include large collections of pottery and chipped stone tools from "pre-Caddoan" Fourche Maline (circa 500 B.C. to A.D. 900) and Middle/Late Archaic (circa 3000 to 500 B.C.) occupations. This material lacks the aesthetic qualities of later products of Caddoan ceramic artisans, but it provides important data about the development of Caddo culture.[56]

As illustrated by the images in this volume, Caddo pottery is very distinctive with respect to vessel forms and decoration.[57] Although late prehistoric pottery from the Arkansas River valley, seen in the preceding section, shares some general commonalities with contemporary pottery from northeast Arkansas, Caddoan pottery from southwest Arkansas could not be more different. The same basic vessel shapes—bottles, bowls, and jars—are present, but the specific forms typically are distinctively Caddo. Among bottles, many Caddo examples have a flat base and a tapering or spool-shaped neck. The cazuela bowl, which is carinated (having a sharp corner) and has a base that tapers to an oval bottom, is a typical Caddo form that has no counterpart in northeast Arkansas.[58] Jars often have rims that are outflared and proportionately very tall relative to the body.

The Caddo decorated a number of their vessels with complex geometric designs created by engraving the surface; this technique is quite rare in northeast Arkansas. The quality of the designs and workmanship prompted pioneering archaeologist to comment: "The treatment is refined and even elegant, and the application of the designs to the diversified forms of the vessels is masterly."[59] Painting, seen commonly on Late Mississippian vessels from northeast Arkansas, is quite rare on Caddo vessels. Interestingly, not a single Caddoan pottery vessel has been found in northeast Arkansas, nor have any vessels from northeast Arkansas been documented at Caddo sites in southwest Arkansas.

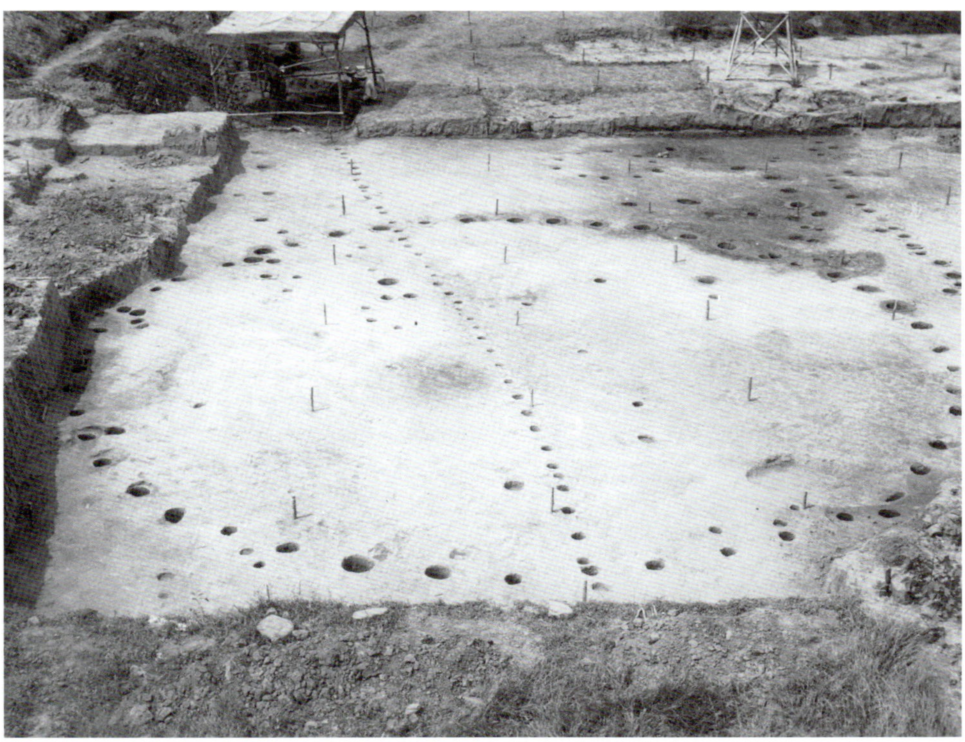

Figure 206. 1939 excavation of mound at Adair Place. Note the circular pattern of postmolds that represent the remains of a building.

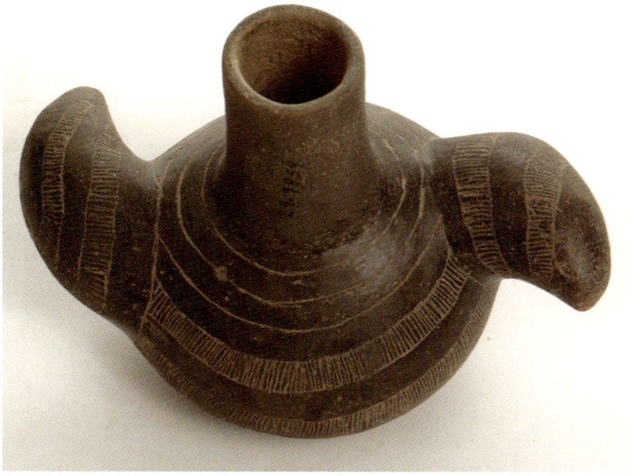

Figure 207. Engraved Bottle with Horns (OSHTL2006.003.111)
Ceramic; 15.2 x 52.1 cm
Housley site, Garland County, Arkansas
Middle Caddo period, A.D. 1300–1500

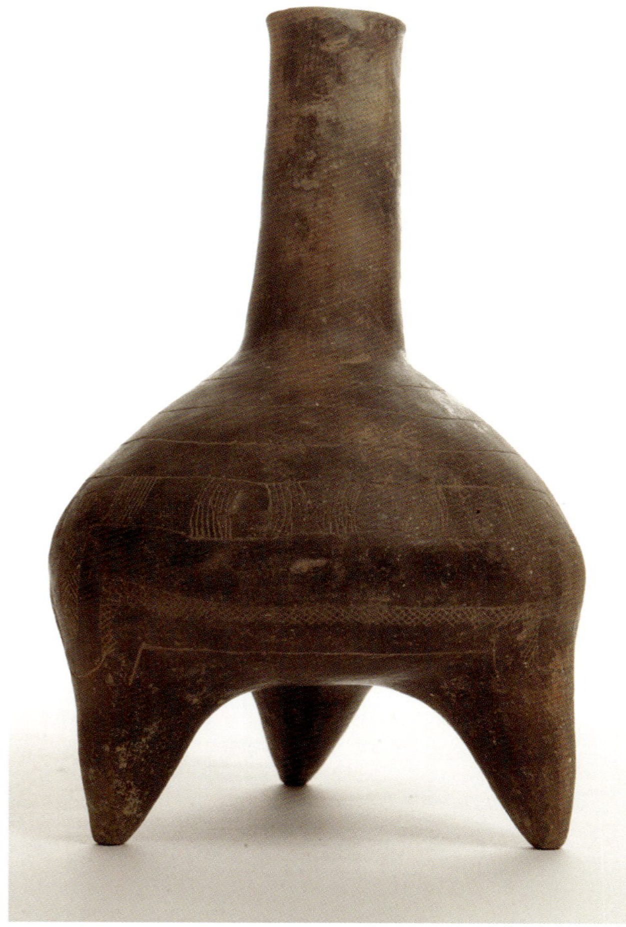

Figure 208. Engraved Tripod Bottle (OSHTL2006.003.112)
Ceramic; 22.9 x 45.7 cm
Housley site, Garland County, Arkansas
Middle Caddo period, A.D. 1300–1500

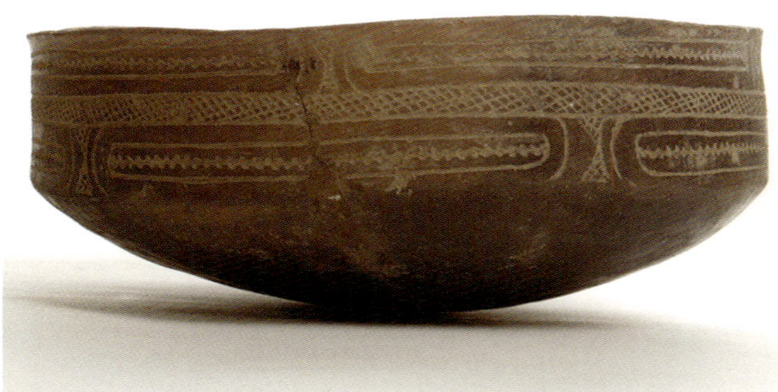

Figure 209. Engraved Carinated Bowl (Friendship Engraved) (OSHTL2006.003.113)
Ceramic; 21.6 x 68.6 cm
Adair Place, Garland County, Arkansas
Middle Caddo period, A.D. 1300–1500

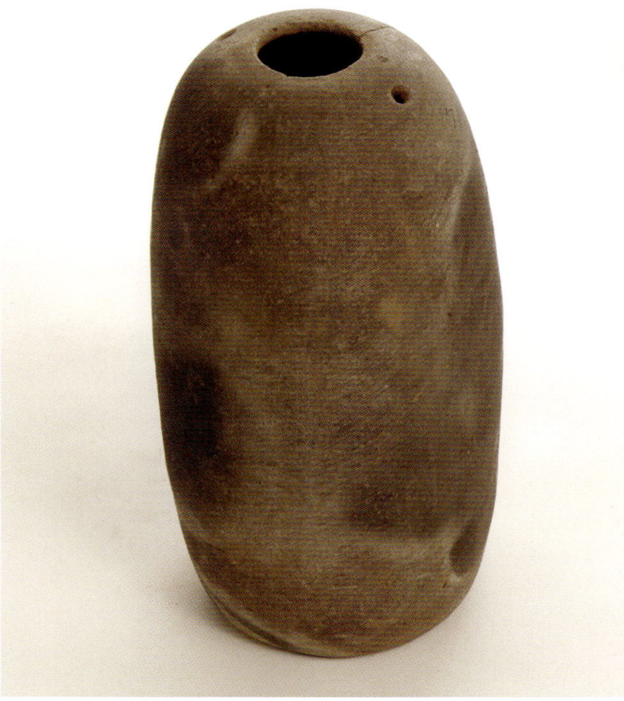

Figure 210. Watermelon Island Seed Jar (OSHTL2006.003.114)
Ceramic; 22.9 x 40.6 cm
Adair Place, Garland County, Arkansas
Middle Caddo period, A.D. 1300–1500

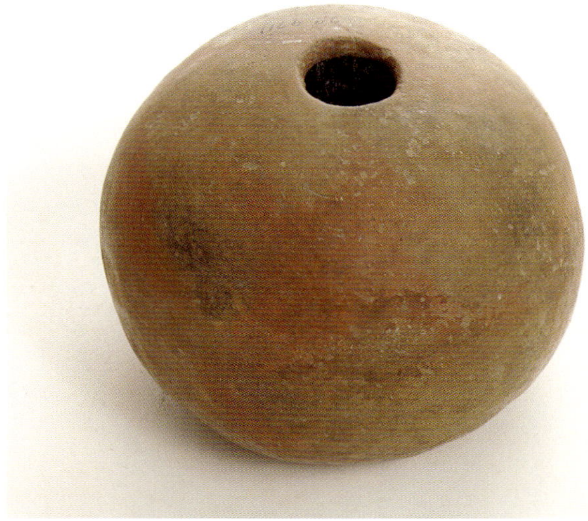

Figure 211. Seed Jar (OSHTL2006.003.115)
Ceramic; 12.7 x 33 cm
Near the Red River, Lafayette County, Arkansas
Late Caddo period, A.D. 1500–1700

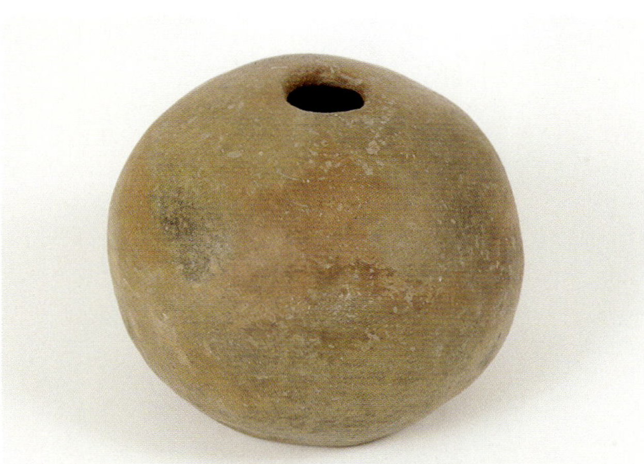

Figure 212. Seed Jar (OSHTL2006.003.116)
Ceramic; 10.2 x 36.8 cm
Bill Howell Place, Garland County, Arkansas
Late Caddo period, A.D. 1500–1700

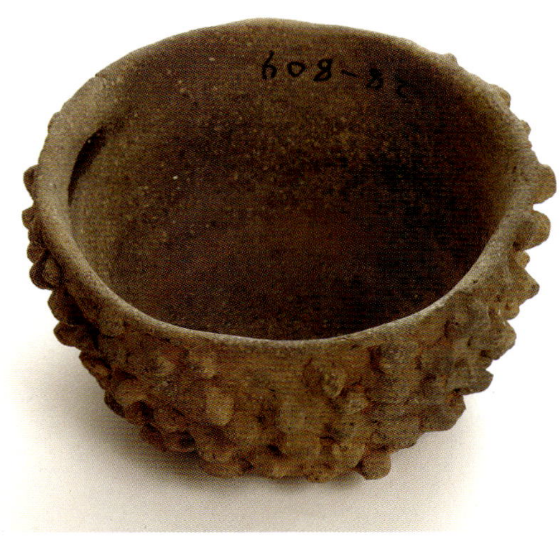

Figure 213. Noded Bowl (Moore Noded) (OSHTL2006.003.118)
Ceramic; 6.4 x 11.4 cm
Battle Place, Lafayette County, Arkansas
Middle to Late Caddo period, A.D. 1300–1700

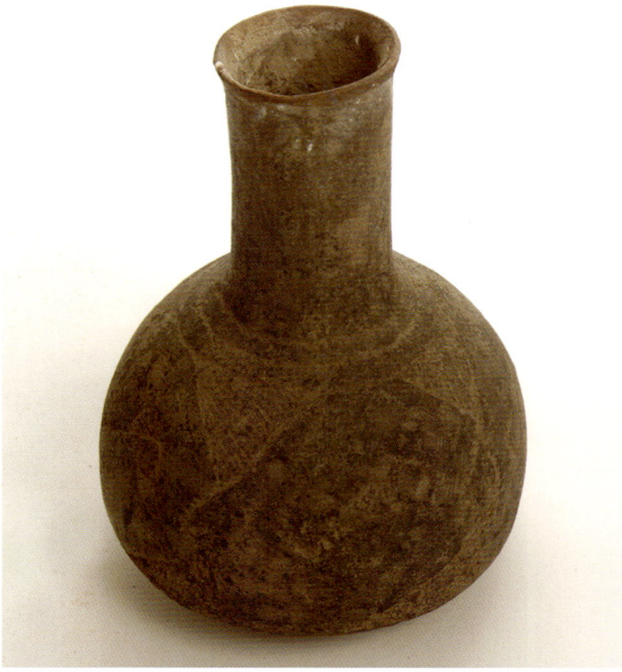

Figure 214. Engraved Bottle (OSHTL2006.003.119)
Ceramic; 20.3 x 44.5 cm
Friendship Place, Hot Spring County, Arkansas
Middle to Late Caddo period, A.D. 1300–1700

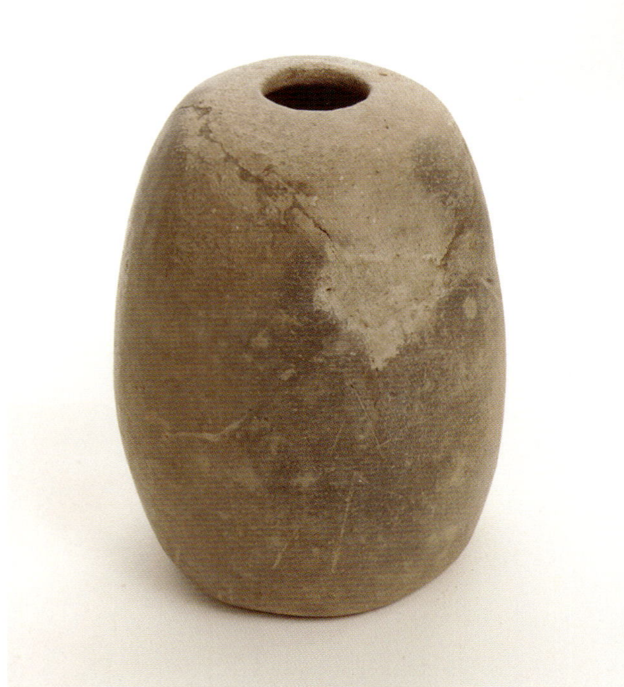

Figure 215. Watermelon Island Seed Jar (OSHTL2006.003.120)
Ceramic; 16.4 x 12.8 cm
J. E. Stanley Place, Hot Spring County, Arkansas
Middle Caddo period, A.D. 1300–1500

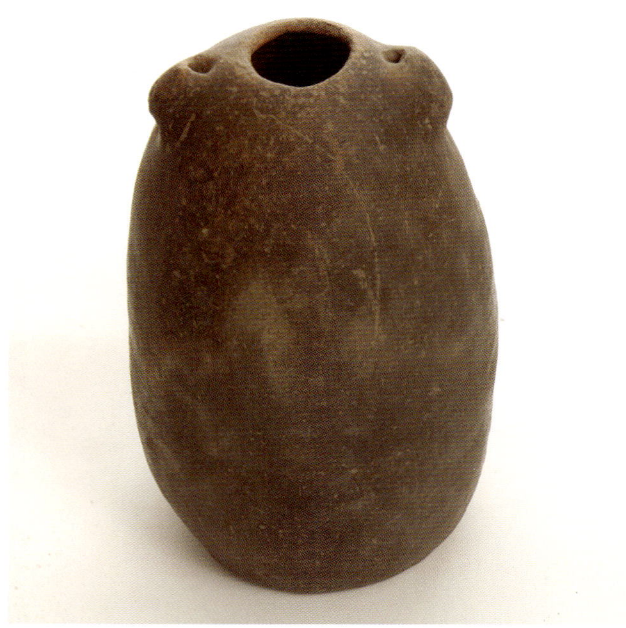

Figure 216. Watermelon Island Seed Jar (OSHTL2006.003.121)
Ceramic; 17.8 x 35.6 cm
Adair Place, Hot Spring County, Arkansas
Middle Caddo period, A.D. 1300–1500

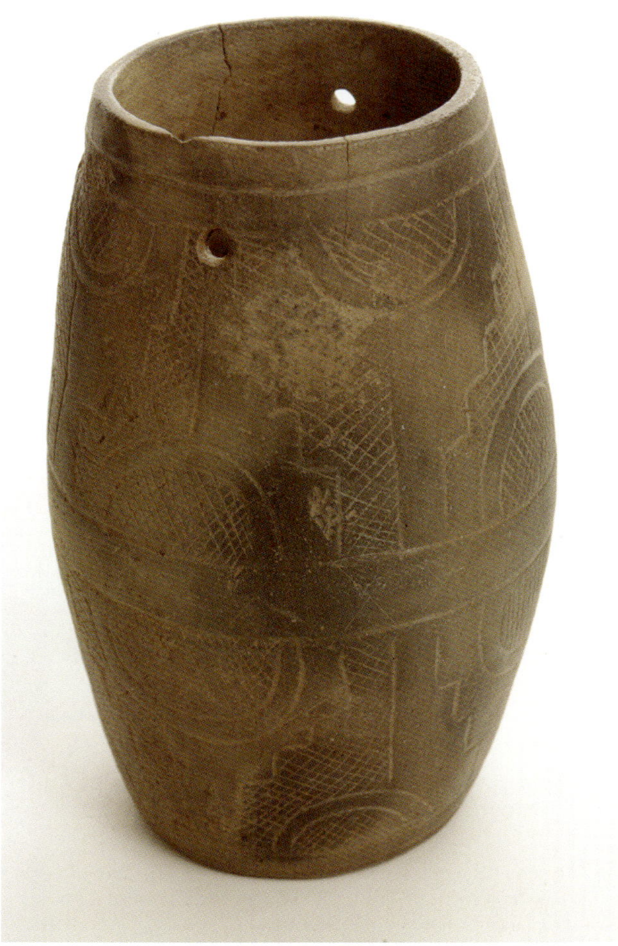

Figure 217. Engraved Beaker (OSHTL2006.003.122)
Ceramic; 20.3 x 52.1 cm
Emerson Place, Hot Spring County, Arkansas
Early to Middle Caddo period, A.D. 1000–1500

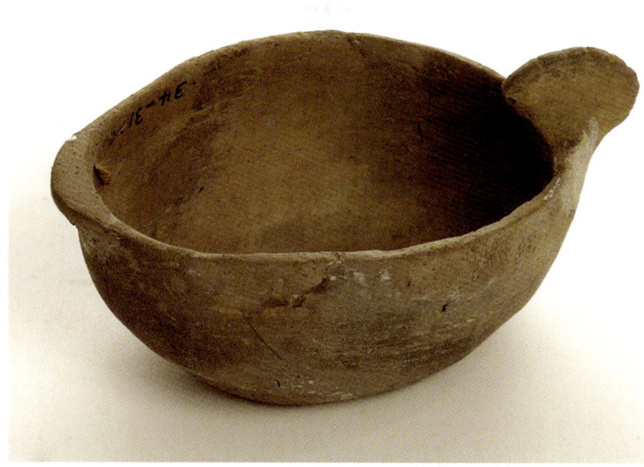

Figure 218. Plain Bowl with Notched Rim Rider (OSHTL2006.003.124)
Ceramic; 12.7 x 7.6 cm
Friendship Place, Hot Spring County, Arkansas
Middle to Late Caddo period, A.D. 1300–1700

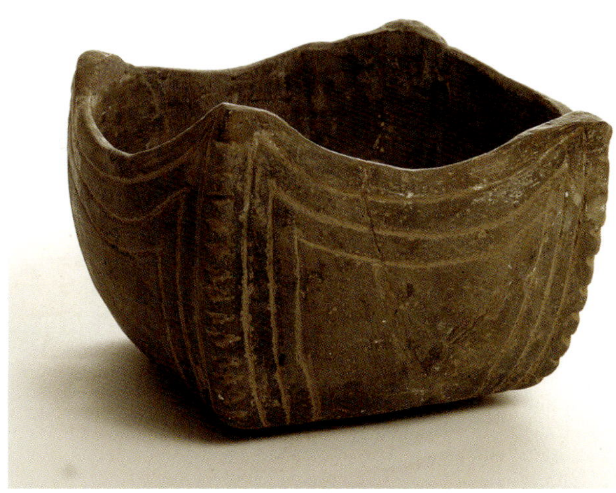

Figure 219. Engraved Castellated Bowl (OSHTL2006.003.127)
Ceramic; 12.7 x 40.6 cm
Adair Place, Garland County, Arkansas
Middle Caddo period, A.D. 1300–1500

NOTES

1. William H. Holmes, "Illustrated Catalogue of a Portion of the Collections Made by the Bureau of Ethnology during the Field Season of 1881," *Bureau of American Ethnology, Third Annual Report for 1881–1882* (Washington, 1884), 427–510; Robert C. Mainfort Jr. and Sarah R. Demb, "Edwin Curtiss' Archaeological Explorations along the St. Francis River, Northeast Arkansas," *Arkansas Archeologist* 41 (2001): 1–28; Clarence B. Moore, "Antiquities of the St. Francis, White, and Black Rivers, Arkansas," *Journal of the Academy of Natural Sciences of Philadelphia* 14 (1910): 255–364; Philip Phillips, *Archaeological Survey in the Lower Yazoo Basin, Mississippi, 1949–1955,* Papers of the Peabody Museum of American Archaeology and Ethnology, Volume 60 (Cambridge, 1970); Philip Phillips, James A. Ford, and James B. Griffin, *Archaeological Survey in the Lower Mississippi Alluvial Valley, 1940–1947.* Papers of the Peabody Museum of American Archaeology and Ethnology, Volume 25 (Cambridge, 1951).

2. Dan F. Morse, "On the Possible Origin of the Quapaws in Northeast Arkansas," *Arkansas before the Americans,* ed. H. A. Davis, Research Series No. 40 (Fayetteville: Arkansas Archeological Survey, 1991), 40–54; Dan F. Morse and Phyllis A. Morse, "Changes in Interpretation in the Archaeology of the Central Mississippi Valley Since 1983," *North American Archaeologist* 17(1) (1996): 1–35.

3. Dan F. Morse and Phyllis A. Morse, *Archaeology of the Central Mississippi Valley* (San Diego, 1983), 305–315.

4. John G. Shea, trans., "Voyages and Discoveries of Father James Marquette in the Mississippi Valley," *Collections of the Illinois State Historical Library,* Vol. 1 (Springfield, 1903), 8–40.

5. Rita Fisher-Carroll, "Environmental Dynamics of Drought and Its Impact on Sixteenth-Century Indigenous Populations in the Central Mississippi Valley," PhD dissertation, Environmental Dynamics Program, University of Arkansas, Fayetteville (2001), 34–36.

6. For a discussion of field methods, see Rita L. Fisher Carroll, *Mortuary Behavior at Upper Nodena,* Research Series No. 59 (Fayetteville: Arkansas Archeological Survey, 2001).

7. Jamie C. Brandon, "Death and the Parkin Phase: Mortuary Patterning in the Archeological Data Recovered in the Durham Excavations in Northeastern Arkansas, 1932–1933," MA thesis, Department of Anthropology, University of Arkansas, Fayetteville (1999); Rita Fisher-Carroll, "Sociopolitical Organization at Upper Nodena (3MS4) from a Mortuary Perspective," MA thesis, Department of Anthropology, University of Arkansas, Fayetteville (1997); Thomas N. Gannon, "A Mortuary Analysis of the Vernon Paul Site (3CS25): Sociopolitical Organization at a Late Mississippian Site in Cross County, Arkansas," MA thesis, Department of Anthropology, University of Arkansas, Fayetteville (1999); Fisher-Carroll, "Environmental Dynamics."

8. Teresa L. Brown, "Ceramic Variability within the Parkin Phase: A Whole Vessel Metric Analysis," MA thesis, Department of Anthropology, University of Arkansas, Fayetteville (2002); Maria M. Tavaszi, "Stylistic Variation in Ceramic Mortuary Vessels from Upper Nodena (3MS4) and Middle Nodena (3MS3)," MA thesis, Department of Anthropology, University of Arkansas, Fayetteville (2004); Marjorie L. Zinke, "An Analysis of Mississippian Burial Components from the Hazel Site, Poinsett County, Arkansas," MA thesis, Department of Anthropology, University of Arkansas, Fayetteville (1975).

9. Fisher-Carroll, "Environmental Dynamics," 41.

10. Morse and Morse, *Archaeology of the Central Mississippi Valley,* 271–281.

11. Fisher-Carroll, "Environmental Dynamics," 38–56.

12. D. I. Bushnell Jr., "Archeology of the Ozark Region of Missouri," *American Anthropologist* 6(2) (1904): 294–298; Charles Peabody, "Cave-deposits in the Ozark Mountains," *American Anthropologist* 5(2) (1903): 579–580; Charles Peabody, "Explorations in the Ozark Mountains of Missouri and Arkansas," *Anthropology* 1 (1917): 185–186; Charles Peabody and Warren K. Moorehead, *The Exploration of Jacobs Cavern, McDonald County, Missouri,* Phillips Academy Bulletin No. 1 (Norwood, MA, 1904).

13. Mark R. Harrington, "The Ozark Bluff-Dwellers," *American Anthropologist* 26(1) (1924): 1–21; Mark R. Harrington, *The Ozark Bluff-Dwellers,* Museum of the American Indian Notes and Monographs No. 12 (New York: Heye Foundation, 1960).

14. "Discovery in Arkansas," *Baxter Bulletin,* 3 April 1903. Warren K. Moorehead, a well-known "archaeologist" in his day, was the source of the quote, and his opinion was widely shared.

15. "UA Zoologist May Have 'Retired,' But . . .," *Arkansas Gazette,* 9 June 1968, 5E.

16. "Indian Remains in Arkansas Should Be Preserved in State Museum," *Arkansas Alumnus* 7(5) (1930): 5–6.

17. "Geology Students Find Old Relics," *Arkansas Traveler,* 8 January 1925, 1; (untitled), *Fayetteville Daily Democrat,* 8 April 1925, 8.

18. "Boone County Caves Yield Relics of Bluff Dwellers: Expedition Sent by Historical Society of Oklahoma Carrying on Extensive Study in Habitat of Ancient Race," *Arkansas Gazette,* 3 March 1926 (page number missing).

19. "Indian Remains in Arkansas."

20. Winslow M. Walker, "The Cave Cultures of Arkansas," in *Explorations and Field-Work of the Smithsonian Institution in 1932* (Washington, D.C.: Smithsonian Institution, 1932), 159–168.

21. "Dellinger Continues Archaeological Survey," *Arkansas Alumnus* 9(2) (1931): 9–10.

22. "Dellinger Continues."

23. "Millard to Tell of Adventures on Archeology Trip," *Arkansas Traveler,* 10 December 1931, 1; S. C. Dellinger, "Baby Cradles of the Ozark Bluff Dwellers," *American Antiquity* 1(3) (1936): 197–214.

24. Report Book No. 20, University of Arkansas Museum Collections Facility.

25. Harrington, *Ozark Bluff-Dwellers.*

26. Hester A. Davis, "Being some notes from memory and from the museum records on Sam Dellinger, the university museum, and Arkansas archeology," *Field Notes* 108, Arkansas Archeological Society (1973): 2–6, 8, 11–13.

27. Sandra Clements Scholtz, *Prehistoric Plies,* Research Series No. 9 (Fayetteville: Arkansas Archeological Survey, 1975).

28. Gayle J. Fritz, "A Three-Thousand-Year-Old Cache of Crop Seeds from Marble Bluff, Arkansas," in *People, Plants, and Landscapes,* ed. Kristen J. Gremillion (Tuscaloosa: University of Alabama Press, 1997), 42–62.

29. Scholtz, *Prehistoric Plies.*

30. "Indian Remains in Arkansas Should Be Preserved in State Museum," *Arkansas Alumnus* 7(5) (1930): 5–6.

31. Mark R. Harrington, "A Pot-Hunter's Paradise," *Indian Notes and Monographs* I (April 1924): 85.

32. "The Local Field," *Dardanelle Post-Dispatch,* 24 January 1924, 5.

33. Leslie Walker, "Carden Bottom Revisited: An Analytical Comparison of Archeological Ceramics in Museum Collections and Ceramic Data Excavated from Sites 3YE347 & 3YE25," unpublished senior honors thesis, Honors College, University of Central Arkansas (2001), 22.

34. "The Local Field—Carden Bottom," *Dardanelle Post-Dispatch,* 24 January 1924, 7.

35. Walker, "Carden Bottom Revisited."

36. "River Damaging Crops," *Dardanelle Post-Dispatch,* 24 May 1923; "Floods in Oklahoma Cause Big River Here," *Dardanelle Post-Dispatch,* 18 October 1923.

37. Phyllis A. Clancy, "The Carden's Bottom Puzzle Elucidated," unpublished MA thesis, Department of Anthropology, University of Arkansas (1985).

38. "Carden Bottoms, Near Dardanelle, along the Arkansas River, One of the Most Fruitful Fields for Seekers of Relics Left by Indians," *Little Rock Arkansas Democrat,* 6 April 1933; Harrington, "A Pot-Hunter's Paradise," 86.

39. Walker, "Carden Bottom Revisited," 22.

40. "University Gets Bailey Relics," *Atkins Chronicle,* 26 November 1926, 1; Untitled, *Arkansas Alumnus* 4(4) (1926): 7.

41. Michael P. Hoffman, "The Kinkead-Mainard Site, 3PU2: A Late Prehistoric Quapaw Phase Site Near Little Rock, Arkansas," *Arkansas Archeologist* (16–17–18) (1977): 1–41. The Kinkead and Mainard families owned the property at "Natural Steps."

42. Walker, "Carden Bottom Revisited," 22–23.

43. James A. Brown, *The Spiro Ceremonial Center.* Memoirs of the Museum of Anthropology, University of Michigan, Number 29 (Ann Arbor, 1996). This definitive two-volume set covers all aspects of the site, including a history of the looting.

44. "A 'King Tut' Tomb in the Arkansas Valley," *Kansas City Star,* 15 December 1935, 1C–2C. (The story was republished by Brown, *Spiro,* 43–45.)

45. Henry W. Hamilton, "The Spiro Mound," *Missouri Archaeologist* 14 (1952): 32–34. Neither Dellinger, nor any professional archaeologist, was permitted to view the actual excavations.

46. James A. Brown, personal communication, October 2007.

47. Accession Records, 1933–1939, University of Arkansas Museum Collections Facility; "University to Study Famed Indian Mound," *Arkansas Gazette,* 1 January 1937, 2.

48. Haun to Dellinger, 21 July 1937, and Haun to Dellinger, 20 October 1938, Walter R. Haun correspondence file, University of Arkansas Museum Collections Facility.

49. King 1947 file, University of Arkansas Museum Collections Facility. Fain and Blanche King were avid collectors of artifacts; the museum curates a large number of objects from their collection. For years they owned a Mississippi period mound site in Wickliffe, Kentucky, which they excavated extensively and operated as a roadside attraction.

50. An exhaustive discussion of the engraved shell is found in: Philip Phillips and James A. Brown, *Pre-Columbian Shell Engravings* (Cambridge: Peabody Museum Press, 1978). The entire artifact assemblage is treated in Brown, "*Spiro.*"

51. Phillips and Brown, *Engravings,* 26.

52. Mark R. Harrington, *Certain Caddo Sites in Arkansas,* Museum of the American Indian Notes and Monographs No. 10 (New York: Heye Foundation, 1920).

53. J. Daniel Roberts and George Sabo III, "Caddo," in *Handbook of North American Indians—Southeast,* ed. Raymond D. Ferguson (Washington, D.C.: Smithsonian Institution Press, 2004), 616–631.

54. "Dellinger's Efforts to Preserve Indian Remains in Arkansas Recognized," *Arkansas Alumnus* 7(4) (1930): 12; "Arkansas Caveman Relics Dug Up by Prof. Dellinger for Museum," *Arkansas Traveler,* 31 January 1930, 1, 3.

55. Frank F. Schambach, *Pre-Caddoan Cultures in the Trans-Mississippi South,* Research Series 53 (Fayetteville: Arkansas Archeological Survey, 1998).

56. Frank Schambach, "Fourche Maline: A Woodland Period Culture of the Trans-Mississippi South," *The Woodland Southeast,* ed. David G. Anderson and Robert C. Mainfort Jr. (Tuscaloosa: University of Alabama Press, 2002), 91–112.

57. See Dee Ann Suhm and Edward B. Jelks, *Handbook of Texas Archeology: Type Descriptions* (Austin: Texas Archeological Society and Texas Memorial Museum, 1962).

58. Harrington, *Certain Caddo Sites,* 177.

59. William H. Holmes quoted in Clarence B. Moore, "Antiquities of the Ouachita Valley," *Journal of the Academy of Natural Sciences of Philadelphia* 14 (1909): 7–170; quote on 15.

Detailed List of Figures and Exhibit Catalog

Frontispiece. Formal photograph of Samuel Dellinger, circa 1957.

Picture Collection, number 226. Special Collections, University of Arkansas Libraries, Fayetteville.

Figure 1. Formal photograph of Samuel Dellinger, 1916.

Hendrix College, *The Troubadour* (Conway, Ark., 1916), 12.

Figure 2. Formal photograph of Samuel Dellinger, 1918.

Hendrix College, *The Troubadour* (Conway, Ark., 1918), 20.

Figure 3. Party for A. H. Sturtevant (*front, center, leaning back in chair*) at Columbia University, 1919.

Dellinger is in back row, second from left; Professor T. H. Morgan is in back row, far right.

University of Arkansas Museum Collections Facility photograph number 000456.

Figure 4. Dellinger and Harvey Couch examining pottery vessels from excavations along the Ouachita River prior to the impoundment of Lake Hamilton.

University of Arkansas Museum Collections Facility photograph number 000421.

Figure 5. Pottery vessels from Dellinger's excavations exhibited at Harvey Couch's home ("Couchwood").

Photograph courtesy of Old State House Museum and the family of Harvey Couch.

Figure 6. Remmel Dam, by Adrian Brewer.

The myth of the "vanished" Indian is the theme of this painting, which was commissioned by Harvey C. Couch to accompany his collection of artifacts gathered by Dellinger from what would become Lake Catherine. Note that the historic Native Americans of Arkansas did not wear large headdresses. Photograph courtesy of Old State House Museum (Jon Kennedy, photographer).

Figure 7. Outside Cob Cave, 1931.

Left to right: Walter J. Lemke (for whom the University of Arkansas Department of Journalism is named), Mr. Slate, Thomas Millard (field assistant), Dellinger.

University of Arkansas Museum Collections Facility photograph number 310028.

Figure 8. Dellinger in the museum with a case of pottery vessels (most from the Arkansas River valley) and ground stone artifacts, circa 1930.

University of Arkansas Museum Collections Facility photograph number 000418.

Figure 9. *Official Highway Service Map* [1939].

State Highway Commission, Little Rock.

This graphic reflects Dellinger's success in making the public aware of the importance of Arkansas archaeology.

Figure 10. Dellinger giving a museum tour, circa 1960.

University of Arkansas Museum Collections Facility photograph number 001149.

Figure 11. Dellinger with some of his ornamental gourds in the backyard of his home, May 1968.

University of Arkansas Museum Collections Facility photograph number 680075.

Figure 12. Formal photograph of Samuel Dellinger, circa 1970.

Samuel C. Dellinger papers (MC 204), box 27, folder 14. Special Collections, University of Arkansas Libraries, Fayetteville.

Figure 13. The "Moundbuilders room" at the Peabody Museum, Harvard University, circa 1890.

Many of the objects displayed, as well as the human remains, were collected by Edwin Curtiss in Cross County, Arkansas.

©2007 Peabody Museum, Harvard University, Photo 2004.24.1113.

Figure 14. Another view of the "Moundbuilders room" at the Peabody Museum, Harvard University, circa 1890.

Many of the objects displayed, as well as the human remains, were collected by Edwin Curtiss in Cross County, Arkansas.

©2007 Peabody Museum, Harvard University, Photo 2004.24.1788.

Figure 15. Ladle (OSHTL2006.004.01).

Ceramic; 13.0 x 6.2 cm

Rose Mound, Cross County, Arkansas

Late Mississippi period, A.D. 1350–1600

Collected by Edwin Curtiss

©2007 Peabody Museum, Harvard University, Photo 80–20–10/22093.

Figure 16. Opossum Effigy (OSHTL2006.004.02).

Ceramic; 11.0 x 8.8 cm

Fortune Mound, Cross County, Arkansas

Late Mississippi period, A.D. 1350–1600

Collected by Edwin Curtiss

©2007 Peabody Museum, Harvard University, Photo 80–20–10/21436.

Figure 17. Red and Buff Headpot (OSHTL2006.004.03).

Ceramic; 16.4 x 19.0 cm

Fortune Mound, Cross County, Arkansas

Late Mississippi period, A.D. 1350–1600

Collected by Edwin Curtiss

Collected in 1880, this is the first reported headpot.

©2007 Peabody Museum, Harvard University, Photo 80–20–10/21542.

Figure 18. Cat Serpent Bowl (OSHTL2006.004.04).

Ceramic; 17.0 x 25.0 cm

Cross County, Arkansas

Late Mississippi period, A.D. 1350–1600

The "cat serpent" is one of the more common ceramic effigy forms found in northeast Arkansas.

Collected by Edwin Curtiss

©2007 Peabody Museum, Harvard University, Photo 01–16–10/56987.

Figure 19. Ear Plugs (OSHTL2006.004.05).

Marine shell; 4.9 x 3.3 cm

Rose Mound, Cross County, Arkansas

Late Mississippi period, A.D. 1350–1600

Collected by Edwin Curtiss

©2007 Peabody Museum, Harvard University, Photo 80–20–10/22348.

Figure 20. Smoking Pipe (OSHTL2006.004.06).

Ceramic; 6.0 x 8.9 cm

Togo site, Cross County, Arkansas

Late Mississippi period, A.D. 1350–1600

Collected by Edwin Curtiss

©2007 Peabody Museum, Harvard University, Photo 01–16–10/21727.

Figure 21. Catfish Effigy Bowl (OSHTL2006.004.07).

Ceramic; 9.0 x 30.7 cm

Figure 32. Stylized version of engraving by H. J. Lewis showing some of the work done by Edward Palmer in eastern Arkansas; Lewis's original engraving has been lost.

As discussed by Jeter (1990), the *Leslie's* versions of Lewis's engravings often are sensationalized and inaccurate with regard to mounds and artifacts; in this case, the depictions of Lewis and Palmer do not closely resemble caricatures by Lewis himself.

Frank Leslie's Illustrated Newspaper, May 26, 1883.

Arkansas Archeological Survey Negative No. 872810.

Figure 33. C. B. (Clarence Bloomfield) Moore and his steamboat.

Courtesy, Dan and Phyllis Morse.

Figure 34. Feline Effigy Jar with Incised Spirals (OSHTL2006.008.31).

Ceramic; 6.2 x 11.0 cm

Rose Mound, Cross County, Arkansas

Late Mississippi period, A.D. 1350–1600

Courtesy, National Museum of the American Indian, Smithsonian Institution (173260.000). Photo by NMAI Photo Services Staff.

Figure 35. Celts (OSHTL2006.008.32).

Unidentified stone; various sizes

Rose Mound, Cross County, Arkansas

Late Mississippi period, A.D. 1350–1600

Collected by C. B. Moore

Courtesy, National Museum of the American Indian, Smithsonian Institution (171584.000). Photo by NMAI Photo Services Staff.

Figure 36. Discoidals (OSHTL2006.008.33).

Unidentified stone; diameter, apx. 8.0 cm

Rose Mound, Cross County, Arkansas

Late Mississippi period, A.D. 1350–1600

Collected by C. B. Moore

Courtesy, National Museum of the American Indian, Smithsonian Institution (171586.000). Photo by NMAI Photo Services Staff.

Figure 37. Zoomorphic Effigy Jar with Incising (OSHTL2006.008.37).

Ceramic; 6.4 x 14.0 cm

Rose Mound, Cross County, Arkansas

Late Mississippi period, A.D. 1350–1600

Collected by C. B. Moore

Courtesy, National Museum of the American Indian, Smithsonian Institution (173430.000). Photo by NMAI Photo Services Staff.

Ceramic portrayals of the same creature are shown in Figures 72 and 95.

Figure 38. Mark R. Harrington at a mound near Ozan, Hempstead County, Arkansas, in 1916.

Courtesy, National Museum of the American Indian, Smithsonian Institution (NO3045).

Figure 39. Net (OSHTL2006.008.01).

Vegetal fiber; 19.5 x 16.0 cm

Allred Bluff, Benton County, Arkansas

Probably Woodland period, 200 B.C.–A.D. 900

Courtesy, National Museum of the American Indian, Smithsonian Institution (117356.000). Photo by NMAI Photo Services Staff.

Figure 40. Twined Fabric Bag Containing Acorns (OSHTL2006.008.02).

Vegetal fiber; 32.5 x 20.0 cm

Bushwhack Shelter, Benton County, Arkansas

Probably Woodland or Mississippi period, 200 B.C.–A.D. 1600

Courtesy, National Museum of the American Indian, Smithsonian Institution (116123.000). Photo by NMAI Photo Services Staff.

Figure 41. Twined Fiber Bag (OSHTL2006.008.03).

Vegetal fiber; 26.0 x 8.0 cm

Judian Bluff, Benton County, Arkansas

Probably Woodland or Mississippi period, 200 B.C.–A.D. 1600

Courtesy, National Museum of the American Indian, Smithsonian Institution (116588.000). Photo by NMAI Photo Services Staff.

Figure 42. Small Plain Weave Basket (OSHTL2006.008.04).

Cane; 11.5 x 11.5 cm

Judian Bluff, Benton County, Arkansas

Probably Woodland or Mississippi period, 200 B.C.–A.D. 1600

Courtesy, National Museum of the American Indian, Smithsonian Institution (116584.000). Photo by NMAI Photo Services Staff.

Figure 43. Hafted Celt (OSHTL2006.008.05).

Unidentified ground stone and wood; 42.2 x 11.0 cm

Buffalo River near Yellville, Marion County, Arkansas

Age unknown

Courtesy, National Museum of the American Indian, Smithsonian Institution (104996.000). Photo by NMAI Photo Services Staff.

Figure 44. Hafted Axe (OSHTL2006.008.06).

Unidentified chipped stone and wood; 31.4 x 6.5 cm

Allred Bluff, Benton County, Arkansas

Probably Woodland or Mississippi period, 200 B.C.–A.D. 1600

Courtesy, National Museum of the American Indian, Smithsonian Institution (117235.000). Photo by NMAI Photo Services Staff.

Figure 45. Atlatl (Throwing Stick) (OSHTL2006.008.07).

Unidentified wood; 49.3 x 3.0 cm

Allred Bluff, Benton County, Arkansas

Probably Woodland period, 200 B.C.–A.D. 1600

Courtesy, National Museum of the American Indian, Smithsonian Institution (117236.000). Photo by NMAI Photo Services Staff.

Figure 46. Arrow Shafts (OSHTL2006.008.14).

Unidentified wood; 11 to 57 cm long

Bushwhack Shelter, Benton County, Arkansas

Late Woodland or Mississippi period, A.D. 700–1600

Courtesy, National Museum of the American Indian, Smithsonian Institution (194671.000). Photo by NMAI Photo Services Staff.

Figure 47. Stick (OSHTL2006.008.15).

Unidentified wood; 19.0 x 1.5 cm

Bushwhack Shelter, Benton County, Arkansas

Age unknown

Courtesy, National Museum of the American Indian, Smithsonian Institution (116308.000). Photo by NMAI Photo Services Staff.

Figure 48. *Left to right:* John Dodd, David DeJarnette, Jimmy Hays, and Walter B. Jones during the Alabama Museum of Natural History excavations at Walnut Mound (Floodway), Mississippi County, Arkansas, August 25, 1931.

University of Alabama Museums (AMNH negative no. 1453).

Figure 49. Alabama Museum of Natural History excavations at Upper Nodena, 1932.

University of Arkansas Museum Collections Facility photograph number 713552 (from an original photograph in the scrapbook of Dr. James Hampson).

Figure 50. Spatulate Celt (OSHTL2006.006.01).

Concretionary siderite; 14.0 x 12.2 cm

Upper Nodena, Mississippi County, Arkansas

Late Mississippi period, A.D. 1350–1600

Alabama Museum of Natural History 1932.002.663 (NOD 591).

Courtesy of University of Alabama Museums.

Figure 51. Spatulate Celt (OSHTL2006.006.02).

Concretionary siderite; 14.5 x 12.0 cm

Upper Nodena, Mississippi County, Arkansas

Late Mississippi period, A.D. 1350–1600

Alabama Museum of Natural History 1932.002.662 (NOD 583).

Courtesy of University of Alabama Museums.

Figure 52. Spatulate Celt (OSHTL2006.006.03).

Greenstone (Hillabee metabasite); 17.5 x 12.8 cm

Upper Nodena, Mississippi County, Arkansas

Late Mississippi period, A.D. 1350–1600

Hillabee metabasite outcrops in the Hatchet Creek valley in eastern-central Alabama. This spatulate celt probably was fashioned in Alabama, perhaps at Moundville.

Alabama Museum of Natural History 1932.002.692 (NOD 711).

Courtesy of University of Alabama Museums.

Figure 53. Disk Pipe with Incised Figure (OSHTL2006.006.04).

Catlinite; 9.8 x 6.2 cm

Upper Nodena, Mississippi County, Arkansas

Late Mississippi period, A.D. 1350–1600

Alabama Museum of Natural History 1932.002.663 (NOD 591).

Courtesy of University of Alabama Museums.

Figure 54. Bear(?) Effigy Jar (OSHTL2006.006.05).

Ceramic; 14.0 x 12.4 cm

Upper Nodena, Mississippi County, Arkansas

Late Mississippi period, A.D. 1350–1600

Alabama Museum of Natural History 1932.002.337 (NOD 409a).

Courtesy of University of Alabama Museums.

Figure 55. Cat Serpent Bottle with Legs (OSHTL2006.006.06).

Ceramic; 21.6 x 14.3 cm

Upper Nodena, Mississippi County, Arkansas

Late Mississippi period, A.D. 1350–1600

Alabama Museum of Natural History 1932.002.300 (NOD 570a).

Courtesy of University of Alabama Museums.

Figure 56. Triune Bottle (OSHTL2006.006.07).

Ceramic; 16.8 x 15.9 cm

Upper Nodena, Mississippi County, Arkansas

Late Mississippi period, A.D. 1350–1600

Several bottles with three human faces (hence the term "triune," which typically refers to a being with three aspects) have been reported from northeast Arkansas and southeast Missouri.

Alabama Museum of Natural History 1932.002.232 (NOD 435).

Courtesy of University of Alabama Museums.

Figure 57. Kneeling Human Effigy Bottle (OSHTL2006.006.08).

Ceramic; 15.2 x 20.3 cm

Middle Nodena, Mississippi County, Arkansas

Late Mississippi period, A.D. 1350–1600

Alabama Museum of Natural History 1932.002.62 (NOD 76).

Courtesy of University of Alabama Museums.

Figure 58. Bird Effigy Bowl (OSHTL2006.006.09).

Ceramic; 12.7 x 20.3 cm

Middle Nodena County, Arkansas

Late Mississippi period, A.D. 1350–1600

Alabama Museum of Natural History 1932.002.124 (NOD 232).

Courtesy of University of Alabama Museums.

Figure 59. Francis Leroy Harvey, the founder of the University of Arkansas Museum.

Reproduced from: John H. Reynolds and David Y. Thomas, *History of the University of Arkansas* (Fayetteville, 1910), 468.

Figure 60. The University of Arkansas Museum, circa 1894.

Reproduced from: University of Arkansas, *Twenty-second Catalogue of the Arkansas Industrial University* (Little Rock, 1894), 19.

Figure 61. "Corner of the museum" in 1902.

Reproduced from: University of Arkansas, *Catalogue of the University of Arkansas, Thirteenth Edition, 1902–1903* (Fayetteville, 1902).

Figure 62. Photographs of the museum in 1922. Junior Class, University of Arkansas, *The "Golden" Razorback* (Jefferson City, Mo.: 1922), 37.

Figure 63. University of Arkansas Museum exhibits in the basement of Vol Walker Hall, circa 1950.

University of Arkansas Museum Collections Facility photograph number 000503.

Figure 64. University of Arkansas Museum exhibits in the old Men's Gymnasium, circa 1988.

University of Arkansas Museum Collections Facility photograph number 881128.

Figure 65. Map showing regions from which most of the museum's archaeological collections were obtained.

Figure 66. Museum field camp at the Vernon Paul site, 1933.

University of Arkansas Museum Collections Facility photograph number 330053.

Figure 67. Museum excavations at the Vernon Paul site (Cross County, Arkansas), 1933. Note the plane table to the right of the excavator.

University of Arkansas Museum Collections Facility photograph number 330045.

Figure 68. Mound A at Upper Nodena, circa 1932, prior to excavations at the site by the University of Arkansas Museum and the Alabama Museum of Natural History. View is to the east.

University of Arkansas Museum Collections 713544 (from an original photograph in the scrapbook of Dr. James Hampson).

Figure 69. Engraved Bottle with Crosshatched Spirals (Walls Engraved) (OSHTL2006.003.37).

Ceramic; 20.3 x 69.9 cm

Beck Place, Crittenden County, Arkansas

Late Mississippi period, A.D. 1350–1600

University of Arkansas Museum Collections 30–2–473.

Figure 70. Engraved Bottle with Swastikas and Crosshatched Designs (Walls Engraved) (OSHTL2006.003.38).

Ceramic; 17.8 x 58.4 cm

Beck Place, Crittenden County, Arkansas

Late Mississippi period, A.D. 1350–1600

University of Arkansas Museum Collections 30–2–472.

Figure 71. Engraved Bottled with Winged Rattlesnake (Walls Engraved) OSHTL2006.003.39).

Ceramic; 17.5 x 20.5 cm

Beck Place, Crittenden County, Arkansas

Late Mississippi period, A.D. 1350–1600

University of Arkansas Museum Collections 30–2–471.

Figure 72. Incised Animal Effigy Jar (Kent Incised) (OSHTL2006.003.40).

Ceramic; 17.8 x 61.0 cm

Beck Place, Crittenden County, Arkansas

Late Mississippi period, A.D. 1350–1600

University of Arkansas Museum Collections 30–2–487.

Ceramic portrayals of the same creature are shown in Figures 37 and 95.

Figure 73. Incised Bottle with Swirls and Swastikas (Rhodes Incised) (OSHTL2006.003.41).

Ceramic; 14.0 x 40.6 cm

Beck Place, Crittenden County, Arkansas

Late Mississippi period, A.D. 1350–1600

University of Arkansas Museum Collections 30–2–489.

Figure 74. Red and White Slipped Bottle (Nodena Red and White) (OSHTL2006.003.42).

Ceramic; 22.9 x 63.5 cm

Beck Place, Crittenden County, Arkansas

Late Mississippi period, A.D. 1350–1600

University of Arkansas Museum Collections 30–2–467.

Figure 75. High Shouldered Jar with Incised Spirals (Rhodes Incised) (OSHTL2006.003.43).

Ceramic; 19.1 x 25.4 cm

Beck Place, Crittenden County, Arkansas

Late Mississippi period, A.D. 1350–1600

University of Arkansas Museum Collections 30–2–491.

Figure 76. Jar with Incised Spirals (Rhodes Incised) (OSHTL2006.003.44).

Ceramic; 17.8 x 66.7 cm

Beck Place, Crittenden County, Arkansas

Late Mississippi period, A.D. 1350–1600

University of Arkansas Museum Collections 30–2–417.

Figure 77. Incised Jar with Applied Effigy Handles (Barton Incised/Kent Incised) OSHTL2006.003.45).

Ceramic; 19.1 x 62.2 cm

Beck Place, Crittenden County, Arkansas

Late Mississippi period, A.D. 1350–1600

University of Arkansas Museum Collections 30–2–423.

Figure 78. Swamp Rabbit Effigy Jar (Bell Plain) (OSHTL2006.003.48).

Ceramic; 14.0 x 50.8 cm

Upper Nodena, Mississippi County, Arkansas

Late Mississippi period, A.D. 1350–1600

The swamp rabbit (*Sylvilagus aquaticus*) is larger than the common cottontail and inhabits wetland areas in the Southeast.

University of Arkansas Museum Collections 32–5–27a.

Image reproduced courtesy of the Quapaw Tribe of Oklahoma.

Figure 79. Flared Rim Bowl with Appliqué Hands (Bell Plain) (OSHTL2006.003.50).

Ceramic; 8.5 x 28.3 cm (restored)

Middle Nodena, Mississippi County, Arkansas

Late Mississippi period, A.D. 1350–1600

University of Arkansas Museum Collections 32–103–77.

Figure 80. Red and White Owl Effigy Bottle (Nodena Red and White) (OSHTL2006.003.51).

Ceramic; 18.4 x 45.7 cm

Liddon Place, Pecan Point Bend, Mississippi County, Arkansas

Late Mississippi period, A.D. 1350–1600

University of Arkansas Museum Collections 34–77–1.

Figure 81. Red and White Bottle with Stairstep Designs (Nodena Red and White) (OSHTL2006.003.52).

Ceramic; 17.1 x 19.7 cm

Neeley's Ferry, Cross County, Arkansas

Late Mississippi period, A.D. 1350–1600

University of Arkansas Museum Collections 47–6–277.

Ex. King collection.

Figure 82. Incised Jar (Leland Incised, *var. Leflore*) (OSHTL2006.003.54).

Ceramic; 11.5 x 17.2 cm

Upper Nodena, Mississippi County, Arkansas

Late Mississippi period, A.D. 1350–1600

University of Arkansas Museum Collections 32–103–69.

Figure 83. Compound ("Jar-Necked") Bottle (Bell Plain with punctations on neck) (OSHTL2006.003.55).

Ceramic; 16.7 x 20.4 cm

Middle Nodena, Mississippi County, Arkansas

Late Mississippi period, A.D. 1350–1600

University of Arkansas Museum Collections 32–103–52a.

Figure 84. Fish (Bowfin) Effigy Bowl (Bell Plain) (OSHTL2006.003.56).

Ceramic; 10.0 x 24.0 cm

Hazel site, Poinsett County, Arkansas

Late Mississippi period, A.D. 1350–1600

University of Arkansas Museum Collections 33–3–262b.

Image reproduced courtesy of the Quapaw Tribe of Oklahoma.

Figure 85a. Red on Buff Bottle with Four Appliqué Faces (Carson Red on Buff) (OSHTL2006.003.57).

Ceramic; 18.4 x 25.4 cm

Hazel site, Poinsett County, Arkansas

Late Mississippi period, A.D. 1350–1600

University of Arkansas Museum Collections 33–3–217a.

Image reproduced courtesy of the Quapaw Tribe of Oklahoma.

Figure 85b. Detail of Appliqué Head (OSHTL2006.003.57).

Figure 86. Red Slipped Bottle with Flared Mouth (Old Town Red) (OSHTL2006.003.58).

Ceramic; 16.5 x 16.5 cm

Cross County, Arkansas

Late Mississippi period, A.D. 1350–1600

University of Arkansas Museum Collections 47–6–147.

Ex. King collection.

Figure 87. Bird Effigy Bowl (Bell Plain) (OSHTL2006.003.59).

Ceramic; 14.0 x 23.2 cm

Middle Nodena, Mississippi County, Arkansas

Late Mississippi period, A.D. 1350–1600

University of Arkansas Museum Collections 32–103–71.

Figure 88. Red and White Turtle Effigy Bottle (Nodena Red and White) (OSHTL2006.003.60).

Ceramic; 16.8 x 22.8 cm (neck removed prehistorically)

Near Marked Tree (probably Hazel site), Poinsett County, Arkansas

Late Mississippi period, A.D. 1350–1600

University of Arkansas Museum Collections 47–36–40.

Ex. King collection.

Figure 89. Bottle with Appliqué Ogee Design (Bell Plain) (OSHTL2006.003.61).

Ceramic; 15.8 x 20.5 cm

Middle Nodena, Mississippi County, Arkansas

Late Mississippi period, A.D. 1350–1600

University of Arkansas Museum Collections 32–103–63a.

Image reproduced courtesy of the Quapaw Tribe of Oklahoma.

Figure 90. Animal Effigy Bowl (Bell Plain) (OSHTL2006.003.62).

Ceramic; 16.5 x 52.1 cm (restored)

Upper Nodena, Mississippi County, Arkansas

Late Mississippi period, A.D. 1350–1600

University of Arkansas Museum Collections 32–5–246b.

Image reproduced courtesy of the Quapaw Tribe of Oklahoma.

Figure 91. Bear Effigy Bottle (Bell Plain) (OSHTL2006.003.63).

Ceramic; 20.3 x 50.8 cm

Beck Place, Crittenden County, Arkansas

Late Mississippi period, A.D. 1350–1600

University of Arkansas Museum Collections 30–2–474.

Figure 92. Negative Painted Bottle with Human Hand Motifs (OSHTL2006.003.64).

Ceramic; 15.2 x 30.5 cm

Barton Ranch, Crittenden County, Arkansas

Late Mississippi period, A.D. 1350–1600

University of Arkansas Museum Collections 32–65–14a.

Image reproduced courtesy of the Quapaw Tribe of Oklahoma.

Figure 93. Bat Effigy Bowl (Bell Plain) (OSHTL2006.003.65).

Ceramic; 15.9 x 68.6 cm

Upper Nodena, Mississippi County, Arkansas

Late Mississippi period, A.D. 1350–1600

University of Arkansas Museum Collections 32–5–127a.

Image reproduced courtesy of the Quapaw Tribe of Oklahoma.

Figure 94. Goose or Swan Effigy Bowl (Bell Plain) (OSHTL2006.003.66).

Ceramic; 13.3 x 60.3 cm

Banks-Danner site, Crittenden County, Arkansas

Late Mississippi period, A.D. 1350–1600

University of Arkansas Museum Collections 32–62–18.

Figure 95a. Red Slipped (Old Town Red) Effigy Bowl (mythological beast?) (OSHTL2006.003.67).

Ceramic; 15.9 x 56.5 cm

Marked Tree (probably Hazel site), Poinsett County, Arkansas

Late Mississippi period, A.D. 1350–1600

University of Arkansas Museum Collections 39–6–3.

Ceramic portrayals of the same creature are shown in Figures 37 and 72.

Figure 95b. Detail of face (OSHTL2006.003.67).

Figure 96. Bigmouth Buffalo Fish Effigy Bowl (Bell Plain) (OSHTL2006.003.68).

Ceramic; 17.8 x 27.8 cm

Upper Nodena, Mississippi County, Arkansas

Late Mississippi period, A.D. 1350–1600

University of Arkansas Museum Collections 32–5–342.

Figure 97. Bowl with Mace(?) Effigy Rim Rider (Bell Plain) (OSHTL2006.003.69).

Ceramic; 24.1 x 71.1 cm

Bradley Place, Crittenden County, Arkansas

Late Mississippi period, A.D. 1350–1600

University of Arkansas Museum Collections 32–74–72b.

Image reproduced courtesy of the Quapaw Tribe of Oklahoma.

Figure 98. Red Slipped Bottle with Excised Spiral and Stairstep Designs (OSHTL2006.003.70).

Ceramic; 22.2 x 55.9 cm

Hazel site, Poinsett County, Arkansas

Late Mississippi period, A.D. 1350–1600

University of Arkansas Museum Collections 33–3–12a.

Image reproduced courtesy of the Quapaw Tribe of Oklahoma.

Figure 99. Zoomorphic Effigy Jar with Incised Spirals (Rhodes Incised) (OSHTL2006.003.71).

Ceramic; 22.9 x 71.1 cm

Beck Place, Crittenden County, Arkansas

Late Mississippi period, A.D. 1350–1600

University of Arkansas Museum Collections 30–2–494.

Figure 100. Bottle with Crudely Incised Hands (Bell Plain) (OSHTL2006.003.72).

Ceramic; 19.1 x 68.6 cm

Bob Rhodes Place, Crittenden County, Arkansas

Late Mississippi period, A.D. 1350–1600

University of Arkansas Museum Collections 32–115–3.

Figure 101. Red Slipped Bottle with Wide Neck (Old Town Red) (OSHTL2006.003.73).

Ceramic; 16.3 x 15.9 cm

Vernon Paul site, Cross County, Arkansas

Late Mississippi period, A.D. 1350–1600

University of Arkansas Museum Collections 33–4–26a.

Figure 102. Carinated Bottle (Bell Plain) (OSHTL2006.003.74).

Ceramic; 27.3 x 53.3 cm

Hazel site, Poinsett County, Arkansas

Late Mississippi period, A.D. 1350–1600

University of Arkansas Museum Collections 33–3–504c.

Figure 103. Effigy Bowl with Brook Lamprey Head and Fish Tail (Bell Plain) (OSHTL2006.003.75).

Ceramic; 16.5 x 54.6 cm

Bell Place, Mississippi County, Arkansas

Late Mississippi period, A.D. 1350–1600

University of Arkansas Museum Collections 32–70–34.

Figure 104. Red on Buff Tripod Bottle (Carson Red on Buff) (OSHTL2006.003.76).

Ceramic; 19.0 x 26.0 cm

Vernon Paul site, Cross County, Arkansas

Late Mississippi period, A.D. 1350–1600

University of Arkansas Museum Collections 33–4–24a.

Image reproduced courtesy of the Quapaw Tribe of Oklahoma.

Figure 105. Red and Buff Slipped Bottle with Chevron Designs (OSHTL2006.003.77).

Ceramic; 20.3 x 38.7 cm

Hazel site, Poinsett County, Arkansas

Late Mississippi period, A.D. 1350–1600

University of Arkansas Museum Collections 33–3–389a.

Image reproduced courtesy of the Quapaw Tribe of Oklahoma.

Figure 106. Red and White Slipped Bottle with Spirals and Hands (Nodena Red and White) (OSHTL2006.003.78).

Ceramic; 22.9 x 55.9 cm

Rhodes Place, Crittenden County, Arkansas

Late Mississippi period, A.D. 1350–1600

University of Arkansas Museum Collections 32–115–2.

Figure 107. Red on Buff Bottle with Swastikas within Sun Bursts (Carson Red on Buff) (OSHTL2006.003.79).

Ceramic; 25.4 x 53.3 cm

Hazel site, Poinsett County, Arkansas

Late Mississippi period, A.D. 1350–1600

University of Arkansas Museum Collections 33–3–165a.

Image reproduced courtesy of the Quapaw Tribe of Oklahoma.

Figure 108. Incised Bottle with Curvilinear Scrolls (Mississippi Plain) (OSHTL2006.003.80).

Ceramic; 17.8 x 58.4 cm

Hazel site, Poinsett County, Arkansas

Late Mississippi period, A.D. 1350–1600

University of Arkansas Museum Collections 33–3–180a.

Image reproduced courtesy of the Quapaw Tribe of Oklahoma.

Figure 109. Engraved Bottle with Four Dimples (Walls Engraved) (OSHTL2006.003.81).

Ceramic; 17.8 x 50.8 cm

Rhodes Place, Crittenden County, Arkansas

Late Mississippi period, A.D. 1350–1600

University of Arkansas Museum Collections 32–15–1.

Figure 110. Red on Buff Bowl with Spirals (Carson Red on Buff) (OSHTL2006.003.82).

Ceramic; 28.6 x 88.9 cm

Hazel site, Poinsett County, Arkansas

Late Mississippi period, A.D. 1350–1600

University of Arkansas Museum Collections 33–3–164e.

Image reproduced courtesy of the Quapaw Tribe of Oklahoma.

Figure 111. Red on Buff Bottle with Spirals on Stairstep Design (Carson Red on Buff) (OSHTL2006.003.83).

Ceramic; 30.5 x 63.5 cm

Hazel site, Poinsett County, Arkansas

Late Mississippi period, A.D. 1350–1600

University of Arkansas Museum Collections 33–3–469a.

Image reproduced courtesy of the Quapaw Tribe of Oklahoma.

Figure 112. Incised Jar with Excised Symbolic Handles (Leland Incised, *var. Leflore*) (OSHTL2006.003.84).

Ceramic; 17.1 x 43.2 cm

Upper Nodena, Mississippi County, Arkansas

Late Mississippi period, A.D. 1350–1600

University of Arkansas Museum Collections 32–5–257b.

Image reproduced courtesy of the Quapaw Tribe of Oklahoma.

Figure 113. Compound ("Jar-Necked") Bottle (Bell Plain with Kent Incised on neck) (OSHTL2006.003.85).

Ceramic; 14.0 x 59.1 cm

Hazel site, Poinsett County, Arkansas

Late Mississippi period, A.D. 1350–1600

University of Arkansas Museum Collections 32–5–166a.

Image reproduced courtesy of the Quapaw Tribe of Oklahoma.

Figure 114. Red on Buff Bottle with Vertical Stripes (Carson Red on Buff) (OSHTL2006.003.86).

Ceramic; 22.9 x 63.5 cm

Upper Nodena, Mississippi County, Arkansas

Late Mississippi period, A.D. 1350–1600

University of Arkansas Museum Collections 32–5–99a.

Image reproduced courtesy of the Quapaw Tribe of Oklahoma.

Figure 115. Bottle with Engraved Curvilinear Scroll and Four Dimples (Walls Engraved) (OSHTL2006.003.89).

Ceramic; 22.6 x 66.0 cm

Bell Place, Mississippi County, Arkansas

Late Mississippi period, A.D. 1350–1600

University of Arkansas Museum Collections 32–70–97.

Figure 116. Red Slipped Head Pot with Incising (tattooing?) (Old Town Red) (OSHTL2006.003.91).

Ceramic; 13.3 x 50.8 cm

Lower Friend Place, Mississippi County, Arkansas

Late Mississippi period, A.D. 1350–1600

University of Arkansas Museum Collections 34–79–1a.

Image reproduced courtesy of the Quapaw Tribe of Oklahoma.

Figure 117. Red and Buff Head Pot (Carson Red and Buff) (OSHTL2006.003.92).

Ceramic; 15.0 x 38.1 cm

Bradley Place, Mississippi County, Arkansas

Late Mississippi period, A.D. 1350–1600

Partially restored.

University of Arkansas Museum Collections 32–74–36a.

Image reproduced courtesy of the Quapaw Tribe of Oklahoma.

Figure 118. Frog Effigy Jar (Bell Plain) (OSHTL2006.003.93).

Ceramic; 22.9 x 73.7 cm

Near Earle, Crittenden County, Arkansas

Late Mississippi period, A.D. 1350–1600

University of Arkansas Museum Collections 32–88–17.

Figure 119. Horn or Boat Effigy Bottle (Bell Plain) (OSHTL2006.003.95).

Ceramic; 8.9 x 20.3 cm (neck removed prehistorically)

Bradley Place, Crittenden County, Arkansas

Late Mississippi period, A.D. 1350–1600

University of Arkansas Museum Collections 32–74–47a.

Image reproduced courtesy of the Quapaw Tribe of Oklahoma.

Figure 120. Red Slipped Mussel Shell Effigy Bowl (Old Town Red) (OSHTL2006.003.96).

Ceramic; 21.6 x 16.5 x 7.5 cm

Bradley Place, Crittenden County, Arkansas

Late Mississippi period, A.D. 1350–1600

University of Arkansas Museum Collections 32–74–69a.

Image reproduced courtesy of the Quapaw Tribe of Oklahoma.

Figure 121. Human Effigy Bottle (Bell Plain) (OSHTL2006.003.98).

Ceramic; 17.8 x 44.5 cm

Near Earle, Crittenden County, Arkansas

Late Mississippi period, A.D. 1350–1600

University of Arkansas Museum Collections 32–88–18.

Figure 122. Bird Effigy Bowl (Mississippi Plain) (OSHTL2006.003.99).

Ceramic; 24.1 x 16.5 x 53.3 cm

Hazel site, Poinsett County, Arkansas

Late Mississippi period, A.D. 1350–1600

University of Arkansas Museum Collections 33–3–371b.

Image reproduced courtesy of the Quapaw Tribe of Oklahoma.

Figure 123. Red on Buff Head Pot with Incising (tattooing?) (Carson Red on Buff) (OSHTL2006.003.101).

Ceramic; 16.0 x 19.5 cm

Bradley Place, Crittenden County, Arkansas

Late Mississippi period, A.D. 1350–1600

University of Arkansas Museum Collections 32–74–129.

Image reproduced courtesy of the Quapaw Tribe of Oklahoma.

Figure 124. Owl Effigy Carinated Bottle (Mississippi Plain) (OSHTL2006.003.102).

Ceramic; 17.8 x 45.7 cm

Hazel site, Poinsett County, Arkansas

Late Mississippi period, A.D. 1350–1600

University of Arkansas Museum Collections 33–3–500a.

Image reproduced courtesy of the Quapaw Tribe of Oklahoma.

Figure 125. Red and White Head Pot with Incising (tattooing?) (Nodena Red and White) (OSHTL2006.003.104).

Ceramic; 15.1 x 18.1 cm

Shawnee Village site, Mississippi County, Arkansas

Late Mississippi period, A.D. 1350–1600

University of Arkansas Museum Collections 31–35–3.

Figure 126. Minnow Effigy Bowl (Bell Plain) (OSHTL2006.003.106).

Ceramic; 17.8 x 55.9 cm

Chapman Dewey farm, Mississippi County, Arkansas

Late Mississippi period, A.D. 1350–1600

University of Arkansas Museum Collections 31–14–1.

Figure 127. Sturgeon Effigy Bowl (Mississippi Plain) (OSHTL2006.003.107).

Ceramic; 6.6 x 11.4 cm

Neeley's Ferry or Togo site, Cross County, Arkansas

Late Mississippi period, A.D. 1350–1600

The modeled nodes on this vessel probably represent the rows of bony plates characteristic of freshwater sturgeon, which were common historically in the Mississippi River.

University of Arkansas Museum Collections 59–46–47.

Ex. McPherson collection.

Figure 128. Red Slipped Sunfish Effigy Bottle (Old Town Red) (OSHTL2006.003.108).

Ceramic; 12.7 x 58.4 cm

Little Warner (near Shawnee Village), Mississippi County, Arkansas

Late Mississippi period, A.D. 1350–1600

University of Arkansas Museum Collections 31–33–2.

Figure 129. Fish Effigy (Drum) Bowl (Bell Plain) (OSHTL2006.003.110).

Ceramic; 3.8 x 6.0 cm

Near Osceola, Mississippi County, Arkansas

Late Mississippi period, A.D. 1350–1600

University of Arkansas Museum Collections 47–39–1.

Ex. King collection.

Figure 130. Jar with Outflaring Incised Rim (Mississippi Plain) (OSHTL2006.003.117).

Ceramic; 26.7 x 40.6 cm

Big Piney Creek, Poinsett County, Arkansas

Late Mississippi period, A.D. 1350–1600

University of Arkansas Museum Collections 27–8–1.

Figure 131. Kneeling Female Effigy Bottle (Bell Plain) (OSHTL2006.003.125).

Ceramic; 21.6 x 58.4 cm

Bradley Place, Crittenden County, Arkansas

Late Mississippi period, A.D. 1350–1600

University of Arkansas Museum Collections 32–74–61a.

Image reproduced courtesy of the Quapaw Tribe of Oklahoma.

Figure 132. Miniature Bottle (Mississippi Plain) (OSHTL2006.003.131).

Ceramic; 9.4 x 9.4 cm

Vernon Paul site, Cross County, Arkansas

Late Mississippi period, A.D. 1350–1600

University of Arkansas Museum Collections 33–4–32b.

Image reproduced courtesy of the Quapaw Tribe of Oklahoma.

Figure 133. Incised Jar with Excised Symbolic Handles (Kent Incised and Ranch Incised) (OSHTL2006.003.135).

Ceramic; 7.6 x 8.3 cm

Higginbottom Place at Shawnee Village, Mississippi County, Arkansas

Late Mississippi period, A.D. 1350–1600

University of Arkansas Museum Collections 34–71–1.

Figure 134. Bone Awl (OSHTL2006.003.148).

Animal bone; 12.7 x 2.5 cm

Hazel site, Poinsett County, Arkansas

Late Mississippi period, A.D. 1350–1600

University of Arkansas Museum Collections 33–3–282c.

Figure 135. Piercing Tool (OSHTL2006.003.149).

Deer horn; 27.3 x 2.5 cm

Hazel site, Poinsett County, Arkansas

Late Mississippi period, A.D. 1350–1600

University of Arkansas Museum Collections 33–3–262d.

Image reproduced courtesy of the Quapaw Tribe of Oklahoma.

Figure 136. Astragalus Die Replica (OSHTL2006.003.150).

Ceramic; 3.2 x 3.2 cm

Bradley Place, Crittenden County, Arkansas

Late Mississippi period, A.D. 1350–1600

University of Arkansas Museum Collections 32–74–42.

Image reproduced courtesy of the Quapaw Tribe of Oklahoma.

Figure 137. Ground Astragali "Dice" (*left to right:* OSHTL2006.003.154, 151, 152, 153).

Astragali (ankle bone) of deer, elk, and bison; 5.1 x 5.1 cm (largest example)

Bradley Place, Crittenden County, Arkansas

Late Mississippi period, A.D. 1350–1600

University of Arkansas Museum Collections 32–74–36e, 97d, 97c, 69d.

Image reproduced courtesy of the Quapaw Tribe of Oklahoma.

Figure 138. Discoidal (OSHTL2006.003.155).

Unidentified stone; 7.9 x 7.6 cm

Bradley Place, Crittenden County, Arkansas

Late Mississippi period, A.D. 1350–1600

University of Arkansas Museum Collections 32–74–90b.

Image reproduced courtesy of the Quapaw Tribe of Oklahoma.

Figure 139. Dellinger with four of his field assistants at Cob Cave, 1931.

Left to right: James Durham, James Gore, Dellinger, Thomas Millard, Eugene Cypert Jr.

University of Arkansas Museum Collections Facility photograph number 310075.

Figure 140. Dellinger at Edgemont Cave, circa 1931. *Left to right:* Dellinger, Thomas Millard, and two unknown individuals.

Walter J. Lemke Papers (MSL 541), series 4, box 2, folder 14, photograph number 523. Special Collections, University of Arkansas Libraries, Fayetteville.

Figure 141. Rock art at Edgemont Cave.

University of Arkansas Museum Collections Facility photograph number 310054.

Figure 142. Detail of Edgemont Cave rock art.

"Chalking" is no longer considered to be an appropriate aid to photographing rock art. Note the more recent markings above the prehistoric rock art panel. University of Arkansas Museum Collections Facility photograph number 310065.

Figure 143. One of the field notebooks used during the museum's excavations at bluff shelters.

University of Arkansas Museum Collections Facility.

Figure 144. Page from Marble Bluff field notebook with Wayne Henbest's sketch of a "cache" of woven fiber bags that contained native cultigens (goosefoot, marshelder, sunflower, squash/gourd).

University of Arkansas Museum Collections Facility.

Figure 145. Patterned Float Weave Basket (OSHTL2006.003.11).

Split cane; 54.0 x 52.0 x 6.0 cm

Cob Cave, Newton County, Arkansas

Probably Mississippi period, circa A.D. 900–1600

University of Arkansas Museum Collections 31–15–2d.

Figure 146. Fragment of Twined Fabric (OSHTL2006.003.13).

Hard plant fibers (species unidentified); 56.5 x 37.0 cm

Eden Bluff site, Benton County, Arkansas

Probably Woodland or Mississippi period, circa A.D. 1–1600

University of Arkansas Museum Collections 32–3–688.

Figure 147. Fragment of Even Regular Twill Basket (OSHTL2006.003.14).

Bark (species unidentified); 38.0 x 40.5 cm

Eden Bluff site, Benton County, Arkansas

Probably Woodland or Mississippi period, circa A.D. 1–1600

University of Arkansas Museum Collections 32–3–523.

Figure 148. Twined Fabric Bag (OSHTL2006.003.15).
Plant fibers (species unidentified); 25.5 x 9.0 cm
Arch Vaughn Shelter, Madison County, Arkansas
Probably Late Woodland or Mississippi period, circa A.D. 400–1600
University of Arkansas Museum Collections 32–129.

Figure 149. Grass Ornament (OSHTL2006.003.16).
Grass woven around a curved stick; 10.0 x 2.0 cm
Cob Cave, Newton County, Arkansas
Probably Mississippi period, circa A.D. 900–1600
University of Arkansas Museum Collections 31–15–17.

Figure 150. Grass Ornament (OSHTL2006.003.17).
Grass on rectangular stick frame; 10.5 x 3.2 cm
Cob Cave, Newton County, Arkansas
Probably Mississippi period, circa A.D. 900–1600
University of Arkansas Museum Collections 31–15–17.

Figure 151. Baby's Moccasin (OSHTL2006.003.18).
Buckskin lined with fibers of Indian hemp (*Apocynum cannabinum*); 9.5 x 6.5 cm
Cob Cave, Newton County, Arkansas
Probably Mississippi period, circa A.D. 900–1600
University of Arkansas Museum Collections 31–15–27.

Figure 152. Buckskin Moccasin (OSHTL2006.003.19).
Buckskin lined with twined fibers; 21.5 x 11.5 cm
Eden Bluff, Benton County, Arkansas
Probably Woodland or Mississippi period, circa A.D. 1–1600
University of Arkansas Museum Collections 32–3–66.

Figure 153. Plied Cordage (OSHTL2006.003.20).
Bark fibers (species unidentified); length, 18.3 cm
Eden Bluff, Benton County, Arkansas
Probably Woodland or Mississippi period, circa A.D. 1–1600
University of Arkansas Museum Collections 32–3–6.

Figure 154. Fragment of Basketry (OSHTL2006.003.22).
Material unidentified; 19.1 x 8.9 cm
Eden Bluff, Benton County, Arkansas
Probably Woodland or Mississippi period, circa A.D. 1–1600
University of Arkansas Museum Collections 32–3–83.

Figure 155. Basket with Complicated Float Weave in Base (OSHTL2006.003.49).
Cane strips; 8.8 x 12.1 cm
Montgomery Farm Shelter, Barry County, Missouri
Probably Mississippi period, A.D. 900–1600
University of Arkansas Museum Collections 32–33–13.

Figure 156. Interlaced and Twined Fiber Sandal Fragment (OSHTL2006.003.136).
Unidentified fiber; 17.8 x 17.8 cm
Cob Cave, Newton County, Arkansas
Probably Late Mississippi period, A.D. 1350–1600
University of Arkansas Museum Collections 31–15–16.

Figure 157. Twined Fabric (OSHTL2006.003.137).
Indian hemp; 20.0 x 6.4 cm
Cob Cave, Newton County, Arkansas
Probably Late Mississippi period, A.D. 1350–1600
University of Arkansas Museum Collections 31–15–18.

Figure 158. Two Pieces of Cordage (OSHTL2006.003.138).
Bark (species unidentified); apx. 40 cm long
Cob Cave, Newton County, Arkansas
Probably Late Mississippi period, A.D. 1350–1600
University of Arkansas Museum Collections 31–15–24.

Figure 159. Float Weave Basketry Fragment (OSHTL2006.003.139).
Probably cane splints; 10.5 x 4.5 cm
Cob Cave, Newton County, Arkansas
Probably Late Mississippi period, A.D. 1350–1600
University of Arkansas Museum Collections 31–15–35.

Figure 160. Plied Cordage (OSHTL2006.003.140).

Feathers wrapped over bast fibers; apx. 173 cm long

Cob Cave, Newton County, Arkansas

Probably Late Mississippi period, A.D. 1350–1600

University of Arkansas Museum Collections 31–15–39.

Figure 161. 3-element Braided Rope (OSHTL2006.003.141).

Unidentified hard fibers (grass?); 35.6 cm long

Cob Cave, Newton County, Arkansas

Probably Late Mississippi period, A.D. 1350–1600

University of Arkansas Museum Collections 31–15–44.

Figure 162. Twined Fabric Fragment (OSHTL2006.003.146).

Indian hemp; 33.0 x 7.6 cm

Cob Cave, Newton County, Arkansas

Probably Mississippi period, A.D. 900–1600

University of Arkansas Museum Collections 31–15–14.

Figure 163. Float Weave Basketry Fragment (OSHTL2006.003.147).

Switch cane (*Arundinaria tecta*); 17.8 x 17.8 cm

Cob Cave, Newton County, Arkansas

Probably Mississippi period, A.D. 900–1600

University of Arkansas Museum Collections 31–15–15.

Figure 164. Handbill for H. T. Daniels, a well-known dealer in prehistoric Native American artifacts. Circa 1925. The town of Dardanelle, mentioned as Daniels's address, is located south of Russellville in the Arkansas River valley. Courtesy, Arkansas Archeological Survey.

Figure 165. Dellinger in the museum circa 1928 with a number of pottery vessels and other objects from the central Arkansas River valley (some from the Fields Chapel site).

University of Arkansas Museum Collections Facility photograph number 000425a.

Figure 166. Incised Bowl (Hodges Engraved) (OSHTL2006.003.23).

Ceramic; 12.7 x 25.4 cm

Carden Bottom, Yell County, Arkansas

Late Caddo period, A.D. 1500–1700

This vessel was produced in the middle Ouachita River basin.

University of Arkansas Museum Collections 27–11–190.

Figure 167. Red on Buff Bowl (OSHTL2006.003.24).

Ceramic; 10.2 x 24.1 cm

Carden Bottom, Yell County, Arkansas

Late Mississippi period, A.D. 1350–1600

University of Arkansas Museum Collections 27–11–111.

Figure 168. Red on Buff Bowl (OSHTL2006.003.25).

Ceramic; 7.6 x 24.8 cm

Carden Bottom, Yell County, Arkansas

Late Mississippi period, A.D. 1350–1600

University of Arkansas Museum Collections 27–11–162.

Figure 169. Red Slipped Bottle (OSHTL2006.003.26).

Ceramic (restored); 17.5 x 19.3 cm

Carden Bottom, Yell County, Arkansas

Late Mississippi period, A.D. 1350–1600

University of Arkansas Museum Collections 27–11–108.

Figure 170. Incised Bottle (OSHTL2006.003.27).

Ceramic; 23.0 x 25.6 cm

Near Dardanelle, Yell County, Arkansas

Late Mississippi period, A.D. 1350–1600

University of Arkansas Museum Collections 30–8–1.

Figure 171. Incised Bottle (Hudson Engraved) (OSHTL2006.003.28).

Ceramic; 19.1 x 49.5 cm

Carden Bottom, Yell County, Arkansas

Late Caddo period, A.D. 1500–1700

This vessel was produced in the Arkansas River valley.

University of Arkansas Museum Collections 27–11–203.

Figure 172. Bottle with Red and White Spiral Design (OSHTL2006.003.29).

Ceramic; 20.3 x 63.5 cm

Carden Bottom, Yell County, Arkansas
Late Mississippi period, A.D. 1350–1600
University of Arkansas Museum Collections 27–11–146.

Figure 173. Frog Effigy Bowl (OSHTL2006.003.30).
Ceramic; 16.5 x 55.9 cm
Carden Bottom, Yell County, Arkansas
Late Mississippi period, A.D. 1350–1600
University of Arkansas Museum Collections 27–11–152.

Figure 174. Engraved Bowl (cf. Natchitoches Engraved) (OSHTL2006.003.31).
Ceramic; 18.4 x 58.4 cm
Carden Bottom, Yell County, Arkansas
Late Caddo period, A.D. 1500–1700
The vessel shape and decorative modes suggest a southwest Arkansas origin.
University of Arkansas Museum Collections 27–11–84.

Figure 175. Red on Buff Bowl (OSHTL2006.003.32).
Ceramic; 22.9 x 63.5 cm
Carden Bottom, Yell County, Arkansas
Late Mississippi period, A.D. 1350–1600
University of Arkansas Museum Collections 27–11–165.

Figure 176a. Red Slipped "Corn God" Effigy Bowl (OSHTL2006.003.33).
Ceramic; 17.8 x 55.9 cm (some restoration)
Carden Bottom, Yell County, Arkansas
Late Mississippi period, A.D. 1350–1600
University of Arkansas Museum Collections 27–11–100.

Figure 176b. Detail of head (OSHTL2006.003.33).

Figure 177. Incised Jar with Flared Rim (Foster Trailed Incised) (OSHTL2006.003.35).
Ceramic; 12.7 x 33.0 cm (reconstructed)
Carden Bottom, Yell County, Arkansas
Late Caddo period, A.D. 1500–1700
University of Arkansas Museum Collections 27–11–210.

Figure 178. Red Slipped Incised Bowl (OSHTL2006.003.36).
Ceramic; 17.8 x 48.3 cm (a portion of a second bowl rests within)
Carden Bottom, Yell County, Arkansas
Late Mississippi period, A.D. 1350–1600
University of Arkansas Museum Collections 27–11–184.

Figure 179. Red Slipped Stirrup Neck Bottle (OSHTL2006.003.46).
Ceramic; 25.4 x 53.3 cm (restored)
Owen Place, Perry County, Arkansas
Late Mississippi period, A.D. 1350–1600
University of Arkansas Museum Collections 31–42–2.

Figure 180. Engraved Bottle (Hodges Engraved, *var. Hodges*) (OSHTL2006.003.47).
Ceramic (red pigment in engraved decoration); 7.0 x 19.9 cm
Field's Chapel, Yell County, Arkansas
Late Caddo period, A.D. 1400–1700
This vessel was produced in the middle Ouachita River basin.
University of Arkansas Museum Collections 27–5–53.

Figure 181. Red Slipped Head Pot (OSHTL2006.003.100).
Ceramic; 24.1 x 58.4 cm
Kinkead-Mainard site, Pulaski County, Arkansas
Late Mississippi period, A.D. 1350–1600
University of Arkansas Museum Collections 32–101–13a.
Image reproduced courtesy of the Quapaw Tribe of Oklahoma.

Figure 182. Trailed and Incised Jar (Foster Trailed Incised, *var. Foster*) (OSHTL2006.003.123).
Ceramic; 17.8 x 35.6 cm
Carden Bottom, Yell County, Arkansas
Late Caddo period, A.D. 1500–1700
This vessel was made in southwest Arkansas.
University of Arkansas Museum Collections 31–3–2.

Figure 183. Red on Buff Bowl (OSHTL2006.003.126).
Ceramic; 36.3 x 19.0 cm
Carden Bottom, Yell County, Arkansas
Late Mississippi period, A.D. 1350–1600
University of Arkansas Museum Collections 31–12–14.

Figure 184. Engraved Four-legged Animal Effigy Bottle (OSHTL2006.003.128).
Ceramic; 21.0 x 13.0 cm
Near Shoal Creek, Logan County, Arkansas
Late Mississippi period, A.D. 1350–1600
University of Arkansas Museum Collections 31–54–9.

Figure 185. Incised Bottle with Swirls (OSHTL2006.003.142).
Ceramic; 15.8 x 14.9 cm
Carden Bottom, Yell County, Arkansas
Late Mississippi period, A.D. 1350–1600
This vessel was produced in the Arkansas River valley.
University of Arkansas Museum Collections 27–5–36.

Figure 186. Red Slipped "Teapot" (OSHTL2006.003.143).
Ceramic; 14.5 x 16.1 cm
Carden Bottom, Yell County, Arkansas
Late Mississippi period, A.D. 1350–1600
University of Arkansas Museum Collections 27–5–37.

Figure 187. Incised Tripod Bottle (OSHTL2006.003.144).
Ceramic; 27.9 x 48.3 cm
Field's Chapel, Yell County, Arkansas
Middle to Late Caddo period, A.D. 1300–1700
This vessel was produced in the Ouachita River basin.
University of Arkansas Museum Collections 31–19–9.

Figure 188. Members of the "Pocola Mining Company" at the Spiro site. Photograph by Robert E. Bell. Sam Noble Oklahoma Museum of Natural History, University of Oklahoma.

Figure 189. Some of the looter's excavations, including tunnels, at Spiro. Photograph by Robert E. Bell. Sam Noble Oklahoma Museum of Natural History, University of Oklahoma.

Figure 190. Joe Balloun, a prominent Arkansas River valley relic dealer. The pottery vessels probably are from the vicinity of Dardanelle, Arkansas; the beads and other objects are from Spiro, Oklahoma. Photograph by Robert E. Bell. Sam Noble Oklahoma Museum of Natural History, University of Oklahoma.

Figure 191. Engraved Shell Cup Showing Horned Serpent, Skull, and Hand (OSHTL2006.003.01).
Marine shell; 25.0 x 17.2 cm
Craig Mound, Spiro site, LeFlore County, Oklahoma
Spiro phase, Caddoan culture, A.D. 1200–1350
University of Arkansas Museum Collections 37–1–19.

Figure 192a. Engraved Shell Cup Showing Empty-Handed Human Figures (OSHTL2006.003.02).
Marine shell; 27.0 x 17.2 cm
Craig Mound, Spiro site, LeFlore County, Oklahoma
Spiro phase, Caddoan culture, A.D. 1200–1350
University of Arkansas Museum Collections 37–1–41.

Figure 192b. Imagery on OSHTL2006.003.02.

Figure 193. Engraved Shell Cup Showing Janus-Headed Rattlesnake with Antlers (OSHTL2006.003.03).
Marine shell; 32.6 x 17.8 cm
Craig Mound, Spiro site, LeFlore County, Oklahoma
Spiro phase, Caddoan culture, A.D. 1200–1350
University of Arkansas Museum Collections 37–1–32.

Figure 194a. Partial Engraved Shell Cup Showing Janus-Headed Figure Holding Serpent Staffs (OSHTL2006.003.04).
Marine shell; 26.2 x 18.3 cm
Craig Mound, Spiro site, LeFlore County, Oklahoma
Spiro phase, Caddoan culture, A.D. 1200–1350
University of Arkansas Museum Collections 37–1–42.

Note: Another portion of this cup is curated by Houston Museum of Fine Arts (Phillips and Brown 1978, vol. 2: 289a).

Figure 194b. Imagery on OSHTL2006.003.04.

Figure 195a. Engraved Shell Cup Spiders with Raccoon Hindquarters Motifs (OSHTL2006.003.05).

Marine shell; 16.7 x 16.2 cm

Craig Mound, Spiro site, LeFlore County, Oklahoma

Spiro phase, Caddoan culture, A.D. 1200–1350

University of Arkansas Museum Collections 37–1–37.

Figure 195b. Imagery on OSHTL2006.003.05.

Figure 196. Beads (OSHTL2006.003.06).

Freshwater pearls; length, 28.0 cm

Probably Craig Mound, Spiro site, LeFlore County, Oklahoma

Spiro phase, Caddoan culture, A.D. 1200–1350

University of Arkansas Museum Collections 37–1–115.

Figure 197a. Partial Engraved Shell Cup Showing Horned Figure Holding Serpent Staff (OSHTL2006.003.07).

Marine shell; 25.0 x 18.5 cm

Craig Mound, Spiro site, LeFlore County, Oklahoma

Spiro phase, Caddoan culture, A.D. 1200–1350

University of Arkansas Museum Collections 37–1–35.

Figure 197b. Imagery on OSHTL2006.003.07.

Figure 198. Beads, Some with Copper Stains (OSHTL2006.003.08).

Marine shell; apx. 1.0 x 0.9 cm each

Craig Mound, Spiro site, LeFlore County, Oklahoma

Spiro phase, Caddoan culture, A.D. 1200–1350

University of Arkansas Museum Collections 37–1–113.

Figure 199. Engraved Shell Cup Fragment with Horned Heads (OSHTL2006.003.09).

Marine shell; 15.9 x 11.0 cm

Craig Mound, Spiro site, LeFlore County, Oklahoma

Spiro phase, Caddoan culture, A.D. 1200–1350

University of Arkansas Museum Collections 37–1–46.

Figure 200a. Engraved Shell Cup Showing Bellows-Shaped Apron and Figure Holding Serpent Staff (OSHTL2006.003.10).

Marine shell; 28.0 x 18.5 cm

Craig Mound, Spiro site, LeFlore County, Oklahoma

Spiro phase, Caddoan culture, A.D. 1200–1350

University of Arkansas Museum Collections 37–1–38.

Figure 200b. Imagery on OSHTL2006.003.10.

Figure 201a. Engraved Shell Cup Showing Birdlike Heads Emerging from Rectangular Structures (OSHTL2006.003.12).

Marine shell; 20.7 x 15.2 cm

Craig Mound, Spiro site, LeFlore County, Oklahoma

Spiro phase, Caddoan culture, A.D. 1200–1350

University of Arkansas Museum Collections 37–1–44.

Figure 201b. Imagery on OSHTL2006.003.12.

Figure 202a, b. Male Figurine Converted to Pipe ("Big Boy") (OSHTL2006.003.105).

Missouri Flint Clay; 24.0 x 27.0 cm

Craig Mound, Spiro site, LeFlore County, Oklahoma

Spiro phase, Caddoan Culture, A.D. 1200–1350

University of Arkansas Museum Collections 47–2–1.

Ex. King collection.

Figure 203. Human Face Maskette (OSHTL2006.003.156).

Wood (originally sheathed in copper); 5.8 x 3.5 cm

Craig Mound, Spiro site, LeFlore County, Oklahoma

Spiro phase, Caddoan culture, A.D. 1200–1350

University of Arkansas Museum Collections 37–1–150.

Figure 204. Human Face Maskette (OSHTL2006.003.157).

Wood with shell inserts (originally sheathed in copper); 5.8 x 4.1 cm

Craig Mound, Spiro site, LeFlore County, Oklahoma

Spiro phase, Caddoan culture, A.D. 1200–1350

University of Arkansas Museum Collections 37–1–145.

Figure 205. Bird Head Effigy with Forked Eye Motif (OSHTL2006.003.158).

Marine shell; 10.2 x 6.4 cm

Craig Mound, Spiro site, LeFlore County, Oklahoma

Spiro phase, Caddoan culture, A.D. 1200–1350

University of Arkansas Museum Collections 37–1–18.

Figure 206. 1939 excavation of mound at Adair Place. Note the circular pattern of postmolds that represent the remains of a building.

University of Arkansas Museum Collections Facility photograph number 390056.

Figure 207. Engraved Bottle with Horns (OSHTL2006.003.111).

Ceramic; 15.2 x 52.1 cm

Housley site, Garland County, Arkansas

Middle Caddo period, A.D. 1300–1500

University of Arkansas Museum Collections 29–30–49.

Figure 208. Engraved Tripod Bottle (OSHTL2006.003.112).

Ceramic; 22.9 x 45.7 cm

Housley site, Garland County, Arkansas

Middle Caddo period, A.D. 1300–1500

University of Arkansas Museum Collections 29–30–51.

Figure 209. Engraved Carinated Bowl (Friendship Engraved) (OSHTL2006.003.113).

Ceramic; 21.6 x 68.6 cm

Adair Place, Garland County, Arkansas

Middle Caddo period, A.D. 1300–1500

University of Arkansas Museum Collections 29–1–12.

Figure 210. Watermelon Island Seed Jar (OSHTL2006.003.114).

Ceramic; 22.9 x 40.6 cm

Adair Place, Garland County, Arkansas

Middle Caddo period, A.D. 1300–1500

University of Arkansas Museum Collections 31–2–131.

Figure 211. Seed Jar (OSHTL2006.003.115).

Ceramic; 12.7 x 33 cm

Near the Red River, Lafayette County, Arkansas

Late Caddo period, A.D. 1500–1700

University of Arkansas Museum Collections 29–92–1.

Figure 212. Seed Jar (OSHTL2006.003.116).

Ceramic; 10.2 x 36.8 cm

Bill Howell Place, Garland County, Arkansas

Late Caddo period, A.D. 1500–1700

University of Arkansas Museum Collections 29–32–29.

Figure 213. Noded Bowl (Moore Noded) (OSHTL2006.003.118).

Ceramic; 6.4 x 11.4 cm

Battle Place, Lafayette County, Arkansas

Middle to Late Caddo period, A.D. 1300–1700

University of Arkansas Museum Collections 28–2–4.

Figure 214. Engraved Bottle (OSHTL2006.003.119).

Ceramic; 20.3 x 44.5 cm

Friendship Place, Hot Spring County, Arkansas

Middle to Late Caddo period, A.D. 1300–1700

University of Arkansas Museum Collections 34–65–8.

Figure 215. Watermelon Island Seed Jar (OSHTL2006.003.120).

Ceramic; 16.4 x 12.8 cm

J. E. Stanley Place, Hot Spring County, Arkansas

Middle Caddo period, A.D. 1300–1500

University of Arkansas Museum Collections 27–58–1.

Figure 216. Watermelon Island Seed Jar (OSHTL2006.003.121).

Ceramic; 17.8 x 35.6 cm
Adair Place, Hot Spring County, Arkansas
Middle Caddo period, A.D. 1300–1500
University of Arkansas Museum Collections 31–2–130.

Figure 217. Engraved Beaker (OSHTL2006.003.122).
Ceramic; 20.3 x 52.1 cm
Emerson Place, Hot Spring County, Arkansas
Early to Middle Caddo period, A.D. 1000–1500
University of Arkansas Museum Collections 29–48–1.

Figure 218. Plain Bowl with Notched Rim Rider (OSHTL2006.003.124).
Ceramic; 12.7 x 7.6 cm
Friendship Place, Hot Spring County, Arkansas
Middle to Late Caddo period, A.D. 1300–1700
University of Arkansas Museum Collections 34–65–1.

Figure 219. Engraved Castellated Bowl (OSHTL2006.003.127).
Ceramic; 12.7 x 40.6 cm
Adair Place, Garland County, Arkansas
Middle Caddo period, A.D. 1300–1500
University of Arkansas Museum Collections 31–2–84.

The following objects were included in the exhibit but are not illustrated in the volume:

Kneeling Human Effigy Bottle (OSHTL2006.001.01).
Ceramic; 15.0 x 12.0 cm
Rose Mound, Cross County, Arkansas
Late Mississippi period, A.D. 1350–1600
American Museum of Natural History 1946–4 (20.2/5549).

Incised and Stamped Vessel (Marksville Stamped) (OSHTL2006.001.02).
Ceramic; 14.2 x 22.5 cm
Helena Crossing site, Phillips County, Arkansas
Middle Woodland period, 100 B.C.–A.D. 200
American Museum of Natural History 1963–50 (20.2/6696).

Incised Quadrapedal Effigy Bottle (OSHTL2006.003.145).
Ceramic; 19.1 x 43.2 cm
Bill Howell Place, Garland County, Arkansas
Late Caddoan, A.D. 1200–1600
University of Arkansas Museum Collections 31–29–5.

Beads (OSHTL2006.003.160).
Freshwater pearls; 27.9 cm long as strung
Craig Mound, Spiro site, LeFlore County, Oklahoma
Spiro phase, Caddoan culture, A.D. 1200–1350
University of Arkansas Museum Collections 37–1–114.

Pierced shell (OSHTL2006.005.01).
Shell; 8.0 x 8.3 cm
Baytown site, Monroe County, Arkansas
Probably Woodland period, A.D. 400–1000
University of Michigan Museum of Anthropology 55685.

Daub (OSHTL2006.005.02).
Burned clay, 14.0 x 13.5 cm
Huber site, St. Francis County, Arkansas
Woodland or Mississippi period, A.D. 1–1600
University of Michigan Museum of Anthropology 55635.

Chisel (OSHTL2006.005.03).
Chert; 7.0 x 3.0 cm
Notgrass Place, Mississippi County, Arkansas
Probably Mississippi period, A.D. 1000–1600
University of Michigan Museum of Anthropology 55531.

Petrified wood object (OSHTL2006.005.04).
Petrified wood; 9.0 x 4.5 cm
Castile Landing site, St. Francis County, Arkansas
Probably Mississippi period, A.D. 1000–1600
University of Michigan Museum of Anthropology 55632a.

Petrified wood object (OSHTL2006.005.05).
Petrified wood; 5.5 x 4.3 cm
Castile Landing site, St. Francis County, Arkansas
Probably Mississippi period, A.D. 1000–1600
University of Michigan Museum of Anthropology 55632b.

Petrified wood object (OSHTL2006.005.06).
Petrified wood; 9.0 x 4.5 cm
Castile Landing site, St. Francis County, Arkansas
Probably Mississippi period, A.D. 1000–1600
University of Michigan Museum of Anthropology 55632c.

Petrified wood object (OSHTL2006.005.07).
Petrified wood; 5.0 x 4.0 cm
Castile Landing site, St. Francis County, Arkansas
Probably Mississippi period, A.D. 1000–1600
University of Michigan Museum of Anthropology 55632d.

Beads (OSHTL2006.008.08).
Marine shell; diameter, apx. 1.25 cm
Rose Mound, Cross County, Arkansas
Late Mississippi period, A.D. 1350–1600
National Museum of the American Indian, Smithsonian Institution (172384.000).

Beads (OSHTL2006.008.09).
Marine shell; various sizes
Rose Mound, Cross County, Arkansas
Late Mississippi period, A.D. 1350–1600
National Museum of the American Indian, Smithsonian Institution (172385.000).

Beads (OSHTL2006.008.10).
Unidentified bird bones; various sizes
Rose Mound, Cross County, Arkansas
Late Mississippi period, A.D. 1350–1600
National Museum of the American Indian, Smithsonian Institution (117387.000).

Beads (OSHTL2006.008.11).
Unidentified bird bones; various sizes
Rose Mound, Cross County, Arkansas
Late Mississippi period, A.D. 1350–1600
National Museum of the American Indian, Smithsonian Institution (172386.000).

Contracting Stem Point and Cache Blades (OSHTL2006.008.16).
Chert; various sizes
Ozan, Site 7, Hempstead County, Arkansas
Probably Late Archaic or Woodland period, 3000 B.C.–A.D. 900
National Museum of the American Indian, Smithsonian Institution (054113.000).

Chert Cores (OSHTL2006.008.17).
Chert; various sizes
Bushwhack Shelter, Benton County, Arkansas
Age unknown
National Museum of the American Indian, Smithsonian Institution (116189.000).

Stone Hoes (OSHTL2006.008.18).
Unidentified stone; various sizes
Bushwhack Shelter, Benton County, Arkansas
Age unknown
National Museum of the American Indian, Smithsonian Institution (194694.000).

Grooved Axes (OSHTL2006.008.19).
Unidentified stone; apx. 11.0 x 5.0 cm
Bushwhack Shelter, Benton County, Arkansas
Middle to Late Archaic period, 6000–1000 B.C.
National Museum of the American Indian, Smithsonian Institution (194687.000).

Point, Drill, Hafted Scraper, Scraper (OSHTL2006.008.21).
Chert; various sizes
Prairie Creek, Benton County, Arkansas

Middle to Late Archaic period (point); other ages unknown

National Museum of the American Indian, Smithsonian Institution (115638.000).

Cobble (OSHTL2006.008.22).

Chert

Near Mundell, Carroll County, Arkansas

Age unknown

National Museum of the American Indian, Smithsonian Institution (117236.000).

Corner-Notched Points (OSHTL2006.008.23).

Chert; various sizes

Bouchet Hollow, Benton County, Arkansas

Early to Middle Archaic period, 8000–3000 B.C.

National Museum of the American Indian, Smithsonian Institution (115629.000).

Scraper, Point Base, and Drill (OSHTL2006.008.24).

Chert; various sizes.

Bullhead Bluff, Benton County, Arkansas

Ages unknown

National Museum of the American Indian, Smithsonian Institution (117458.000).

Nodena Arrowpoint (OSHTL2006.008.25).

Chert; 4.7 x 1.7 cm

Bentonville, Benton County, Arkansas

Late Mississippi period, A.D. 1350–1600

National Museum of the American Indian, Smithsonian Institution (062285.000).

Eccentric object (OSHTL2006.008.26).

Chert

Siloam Springs, Benton County, Arkansas

Age unknown

National Museum of the American Indian, Smithsonian Institution (026331.000).

Hammerstone (OSHTL2006.008.27).

Chert

Between LaRue and Rogers, Benton County, Arkansas

Age unknown

National Museum of the American Indian, Smithsonian Institution (117425.000).

Points/Knives (OSHTL2006.008.35).

Chert; various sizes

Howard Bluff, Benton County, Arkansas

Ages unknown

National Museum of the American Indian, Smithsonian Institution (120130.000).

Basket Fragment (OSHTL2006.008.36).

Cane

Fate Webb Shelter, Benton County, Arkansas

Age unknown

National Museum of the American Indian, Smithsonian Institution (115684.000).

Three Points (two Standlee, one Searcy) and Stemmed Scraper (OSHTL2006.008.38).

Chert; various sizes

Edward's Shelter, Benton County, Arkansas

Early (Searcy) and Middle (Standlee) Archaic periods, 8000–4000 B.C.

National Museum of the American Indian, Smithsonian Institution (115670.000).

The following accession numbers duplicate others in the exhibit catalog: OSHTL2006.003.11, 22, 34, 53, 87, 88, 90, 94, 97, 109, 129, 130, 132, and 133.

Bibliography of Samuel Claudius Dellinger

Compiled by James A. Scholtz
University of Arkansas Museum, 1973

1930 Archaeological Field Work in North America during 1929: Arkansas. *American Anthropologist* 32(2):348.

1931 Archaeological Field Work in North America during 1930: Arkansas. *American Anthropologist* 33(3):465.

1932 Archaeological Field Work in North America during 1931: Arkansas. *American Anthropologist* 34(3):485–486.

The Bluff Shelters of Arkansas. National Research Council, Birmingham Conference on Southern Prehistory, Committee on State Archaeological Surveys, 31–34. Washington (mimeographed).

1933 Archaeological Field Work in North America during 1932: Arkansas. *American Anthropologist* 35(3):490.

1936 Baby Cradles of the Ozark Bluff Dwellers. *American Antiquity* 1(3):197–214.

(with Elmer G. Wakefield) Obstetric Effigies of the Mound Builders of Eastern Arkansas. *American Journal of Obstetrics and Gynecology* 31(4):683–684.

(with Elmer G. Wakefield) A Report of Identical Albino Twins of Negro Parents. *Annals of Internal Medicine* 9(8):1149–1153.

(with Elmer G. Wakefield) The Probable Adaptation of Utilitarian Implements for Surgical Procedures by the "Mound Builders" of Eastern Arkansas. *Journal of Bone and Joint Surgery* 18(2):434–438.

(with Elmer G. Wakefield) Diet of the Bluff-Dwellers of the Ozark Mountains and Its Skeletal Effects. *Annals of Internal Medicine* 9(10):1412–1418.

1937 (with Elmer G. Wakefield and John D. Camp) Study of the Osseous Remains of a Primitive Race Who Once Inhabited the Shelters of the Bluffs of the Ozark Mountains. *American Journal of the Medical Sciences* 193(2):223–231.

(with Elmer G. Wakefield and John D. Camp) A Study of the Osseous Remains of the "Mound Builders" of Eastern Arkansas. *American Journal of the Medical Sciences* 193(4):488–496.

(with Elmer G. Wakefield) Artifacts Found among the Remains of the "Mound Builders." *Bulletin of the Institute of the History of Medicine* 5(5):452–460.

1938 (with J. D. Black) Herpetology of Arkansas, Part One: The Reptiles. *University of Arkansas Museum, Occasional Papers,* No. 1. Fayetteville.

Herpetology of Arkansas, Part Two: The Amphibians. Occasional Papers, No. 2, University of Arkansas Museum. Fayetteville.

1939 (with Elmer G. Wakefield) Possible Reasons for Trephining the Skull in the Past. *Ciba Symposia* 1(6):166–169.

(with Samuel D. Dickinson) Possible Antecedents of the Middle Mississippian Ceramic Complex in Northeastern Arkansas. *American Antiquity* 6(2):133–147.

A Survey of the Historic Earthenware of the Lower Arkansas Valley. *Texas Archeological and Paleontological Society Bulletin* 12:76–97.

(with J. D. Black) Notes on Arkansas Mammals. *Journal of Mammalogy* 21(2):187–191.

1942 Conservation of Wild Animal Life in Arkansas. In *Arkansas' Natural Resources— Their Conservation and Use,* ed. R. W. Roberts et al., 289–350. Source Book Committee, Fayetteville, Arkansas.

(with S. D. Dickinson) Pottery from the Ozark Bluff Shelters. *American Antiquity* 7(3):276–289, 311–318.

1948 A Cache of Batons from Northeast Arkansas. *Tennessee Archaeologist* 5(1):10.

The Museum. In *University of Arkansas, 1871–1949,* by Harrison Hale, 210–211. University of Arkansas Alumni Association, Fayetteville.

Publications, Theses, and Dissertations That Have Used the Dellinger Collections

(Dellinger's own publications are listed separately in the contribution by James Scholtz.)

Braly, Bobby R.

2005 An Examination of Non-Ceramic Grave Inclusions from Late Period Sites in Northeast Arkansas. Unpublished MA thesis, Department of Anthropology, University of Arkansas.

Brandon, Jamie C.

1999 Death and the Parkin Phase: Mortuary Patterning in the Archaeological Data Recovered from the Durham Excavations in Northeastern Arkansas, 1932–1933. Unpublished MA thesis, Department of Anthropology, University of Arkansas, Fayetteville.

Brown, James A.

1996 *The Spiro Ceremonial Center* (2 vols.). Memoirs of the Museum of Anthropology, University of Michigan, No. 29. Ann Arbor.

Brown, Teresa L.

2005 *Ceramic Variability within the Parkin Phase: A Whole Vessel Metric Analysis from Northeast Arkansas*. Research Report 32. Arkansas Archeological Survey, Fayetteville.

Clancy, Phyllis A.

1985 The Cardens Bottom Puzzle Elucidated. Unpublished MA thesis, Department of Anthropology, University of Arkansas.

Cleland, Charles E.

1960 Analysis of Animal Remains in the Prehistoric Ozark Bluff-dwellings of Northwest Arkansas. Unpublished MS thesis, Department of Zoology, University of Arkansas.

Fisher-Carroll, Rita

2001a *Mortuary Behavior at Upper Nodena*. Research Series No. 59, Arkansas Archeological Survey, Fayetteville.

2001b Environmental Dynamics of Drought and Its Impact on Sixteenth-Century Indigenous Populations in the Central Mississippi Valley. Unpublished PhD dissertation, Environmental Dynamics Program, University of Arkansas, Fayetteville.

Fisher-Carroll, Rita, and Robert C. Mainfort Jr.

2000 Late Prehistoric Mortuary Behavior at Upper Nodena. *Southeastern Archaeology* 19(2):105–119.

Fritz, Gayle J.

1984 Identification of Cultigen Amaranth and Chenopod from Rockshelter Sites in Northwest Arkansas. *American Antiquity* 49(3):558–572.

1986 Prehistoric Ozark Agriculture, the University of Arkansas Rockshelter Collections. Unpublished PhD dissertation, Department of Anthropology, University of North Carolina at Chapel Hill.

1997 A Three-Thousand-Year-Old Cache of Crop Seeds from Marble Bluff, Arkansas. In *People, Plants, and Landscapes*, ed. K. J. Gremillion, 42–62. University of Alabama Press, Tuscaloosa.

Gall, Daniel G., Robert C. Mainfort Jr., and Rita Fisher-Carroll

2002 The Occurrence of Greenstone at Late Period Sites in Northeast Arkansas. *Southeastern Archaeology* 21(2):235–244.

Gannon, Thomas N.

2002 *A Mortuary Analysis of the Vernon Paul Site.* Research Report 30. Arkansas Archeological Survey, Fayetteville.

Hilliard, Jerry E.

1980 Prehistoric Ozark Settlement-Subsistence and Nut Resource Utilization. Unpublished MA thesis, Department of Anthropology, University of Arkansas, Fayetteville.

Hoffman, Michael P.

1977 The Kinkead-Mainard Site, 3PU2: A Late Prehistoric Quapaw Phase Site Near Little Rock, Arkansas. *Arkansas Archeologist* 16, 17, 18:1–41.

Mainfort, Robert C., Jr., and Charles H. McNutt

2004 Dating the Hazel Site. *Arkansas Archaeologist* 43:63–69.

Mintz, John J.

1989 Prehistoric Ceramic Variability in the Arkansas Ozarks. Unpublished MA thesis, Department of Anthropology, University of Arkansas, Fayetteville.

Renfro, Bryan D.

1999 Standardized Analysis of Three Late-Mississippian Sites from Northeast Arkansas. Unpublished MA thesis, Department of Anthropology, University of Arkansas.

Schambach, Frank F.

1998 *Pre-Caddoan Cultures in the Trans-Mississippi South.* Research Series 53. Arkansas Archeological Survey, Fayetteville.

Tavaszi, Maria M.

2004 Stylistic Variation in Ceramic Mortuary Vessels from Upper Nodena (3MS4) and Middle Nodena (3MS3). Unpublished MA thesis, Department of Anthropology, University of Arkansas, Fayetteville.

Wilson, Hugh D.

1981 Domesticated *Chenopodium* of the Ozark Bluff Dwellers. *Economic Botany* 35:233–239.

Zinke, Marjorie L.

1975 An Analysis of Mississippian Burial Components from the Hazel Site, Poinsett County, Arkansas. Unpublished MA thesis, Department of Anthropology, University of Arkansas, Fayetteville.

INDEX

(Page numbers in italics refer to illustrations.)

Robert C. Mainfort Jr. is an archaeolgist with the Arkansas Archeological Survey and professor of anthropology at the University of Arkansas. He is coeditor of a number of books, including *Arkansas Archaeology, Ancient Earthern Enclosures of Eastern North America, Societies in Eclipse, The Woodland Southeast,* and *Woodland Period Systematics in the Middle Ohio Valley.* Mainfort is the past editor of *Southeastern Archaeology* and serves on the editorial board of the *Midcontinental Journal of Archaeology.*